"The virtues of the seed are revealed in the tree;
it puts forth branches, leaves, blossoms,
and produces fruits.
All these virtues
were hidden and potential in the seed.
Through the blessing and bounty of cultivation
these virtues became apparent.
Similarly the merciful God our creator
has deposited within human realities
certain virtues latent and potential.
Through education and culture,
these virtues deposited by the loving God
will become apparent in the human reality
even as the unfoldment of the tree
from within the germinating seed."

'Abdu'l-Bahá

COPYRIGHT NOTICE
Limited reproduction permission is granted to the purchaser of this book, to reproduce Black Line Masters, illustrations and letters to parents, as may be required for classroom use and / workshops.

© Written and Illustrated by Ruth Gordon-Smith
gsfamily19@yahoo.com
Printed – March 2008

CONTENTS PAGE

AUTHOR'S NOTES .... page 1
DISCUSSION PROMPTS .... page 3
HAPPY / SAD FACE .... page 5
TOOLBOX .... page 7

Term Starters
OUR PURPOSE .... page 19
THE SPIRIT WITHIN .... page 25
PRAYER .... page 33
DEEDS NOT WORDS .... page 39

Virtues
GENEROSITY .... page 49
HELPFULNESS .... page 57
FRIENDLINESS .... page 65
GENTLENESS .... page 73
REVERENCE .... page 81
ASSERTIVENESS .... page 87
EXCELLENCE .... page 95
PEACEFULNESS .... page 105
CREATIVITY .... page 113
FORGIVENESS .... page 121
TOLERANCE .... page 129
THANKFULNESS .... page 137
ENTHUSIASM .... page 145
CONSIDERATION .... page 153
SELFLESSNESS .... page 163
UNDERSTANDING .... page 171
CO-OPERATION .... page 179
MODERATION .... page 187
CARING .... page 195
COMPASSION .... page 203

Extra
SONGS .... page 213
BADGES .... page 221

AUTHOR'S NOTES

PURPOSE:

This program uses the Bahá'í writings to develop the virtues and noble qualities latent within all children. Children will familiarize themselves with quotations, explore the meaning of each virtue and understand the importance of their individual spiritual development and progress.

FORMAT:

Duration: A program for one year with a lesson each week.

Terms: Each term begins with two lessons on the topic of either Our Purpose, The Spirit Within, Prayer or Deeds not Words. This is then followed by lessons based on the virtues, each of which are covered over two weeks. The order of the virtues does not matter, however the topics that begin each term are best done in the order in which they are presented..

CONTENT:

Scenarios: The purpose of these scenarios is to introduce children to the virtue and the quotation. It is designed to encourage children to look at life situations and understand that we always have a choice as to how we deal with them. The virtues are described as the tools to fix the problems or difficulties we have when faced with these choices.

Quote Visualizations: These are used to help the children become familiar with and to try to memorize the quotation. It helps in the discussion of what the meaning is of the whole quote and also specific words. Ask the children to say each part of the quotation with you. Go over it several times. The children, by the end of the two weeks should be able to say the quotation using only the pictures or even better, they will have memorized it completely. The purpose is to internalize the quotation rather than memorize although it is wonderful if they can say it by themselves. In other words, they will become familiar with the words and understand the meaning.

To help memorization other activities can be implemented including:
- covering up one picture and then another until they can say the whole thing without any pictures or words.
- after they have cut the pictures out, see if the children can put them back into order from memory.

Discussions: The discussion prompt sheet provided allows the children to have a simple visual focus while learning what the virtue means. You can also compare and contrast the virtue with the opposite or lack of the virtue to make the meaning very clear to the children. For example, you could ask the question; What might we say if we are not being 'thoughtful' of others? Other books which describe the virtues in more detail may be beneficial for the development of your own understanding before the class starts.

Stories: Each story relates to the virtue or quotation being discussed and finishes with a moral which can either be read out or discussed informally with the class.

Songs: Children usually respond well when you teach them some actions to the words of the songs.

AUTHOR'S NOTES

Prayers: Always ask the children to be reverent and wait for them to be sitting reverently before starting the prayer. Once children are familiar with a prayer you could ask if any of them would like to say it on their own.

Games: The games are designed to give the children a more complete understanding of the virtue or quotation being discussed.

HINTS:

Materials: Double-sided sticky tape can be used instead of glue. It can be bought from most craft shops. It can be stuck on before the lesson, does not take drying time and is very strong. Otherwise use glue sticks, Clag glue or PVA.

Crayons are often preferable to textas for young children as they cover areas more quickly and easily. They also are less likely to cover up line work such as quotations.

Shops like Spotlight have craft material such as plastic eyes, magnets, etc... If specific materials like plastic eyes are not easily available they could be made out of paper, drawn on or the activity could be adapted to make it more practical.

Preparation: Depending on the size and age of the class, it may be beneficial to do some cutting and preparing of activities before class to help with lesson flow and assist those children who may take a long time to complete some tasks.

Before class make a sample of each activity so that children can see what they will be making.

It is advisable to always make an extra one or two spares for the activities in case of mistakes or extra students.

DISCUSSION PROMPTS

DISCUSSION FOCUS QUESTIONS - VIRTUES

INSTRUCTIONS:
- Fill in the virtue of the week in the space provided.
- Discuss how the virtue can be expressed through our actions, words and thoughts.
- The ideas can be written in and the picture coloured in (optional).
- Older children can do their own (optional).

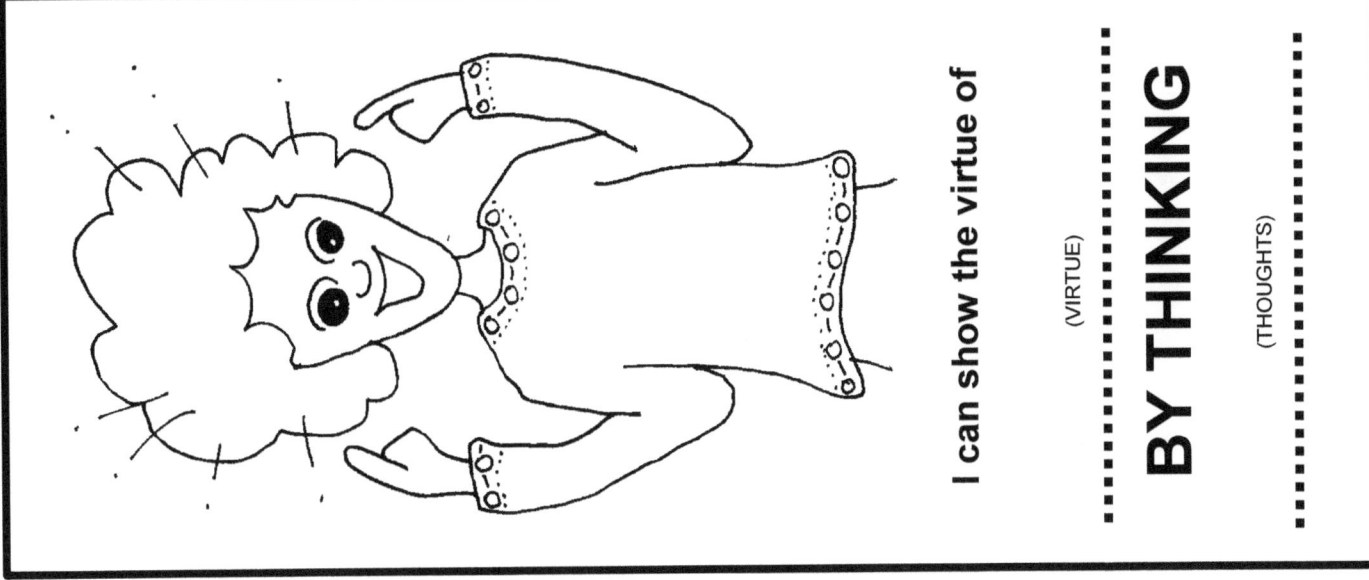

I can show the virtue of _____ (VIRTUE)

BY THINKING

_____ (THOUGHTS)

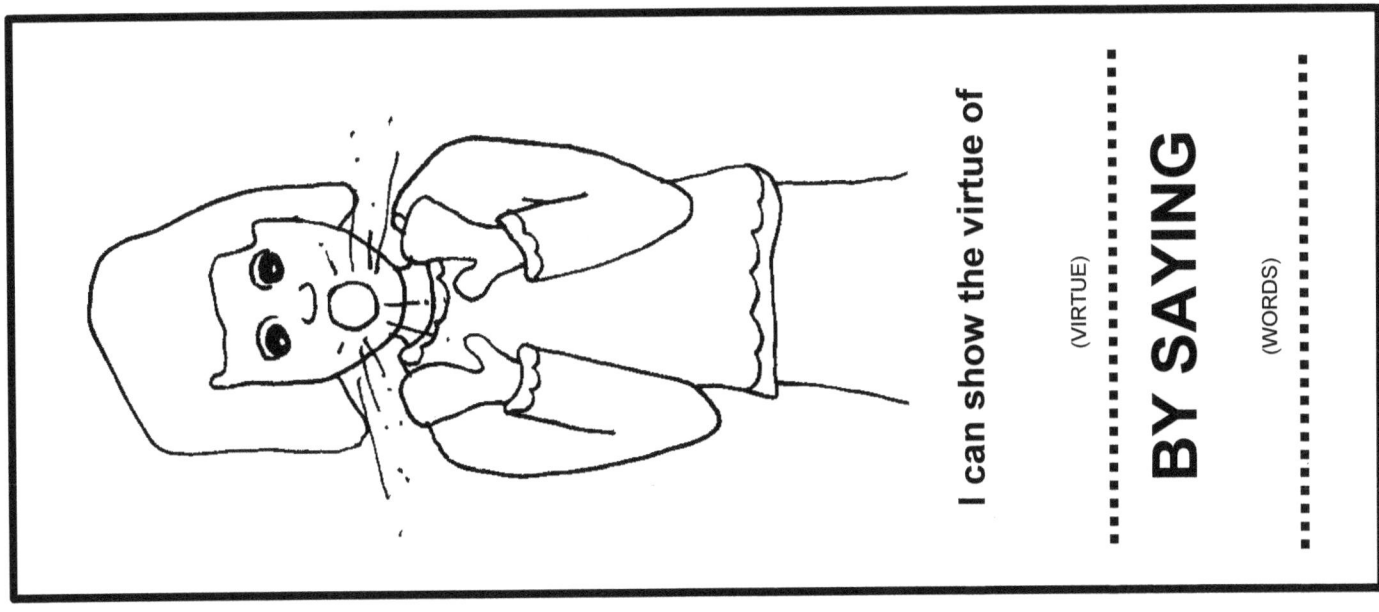

I can show the virtue of _____ (VIRTUE)

BY SAYING

_____ (WORDS)

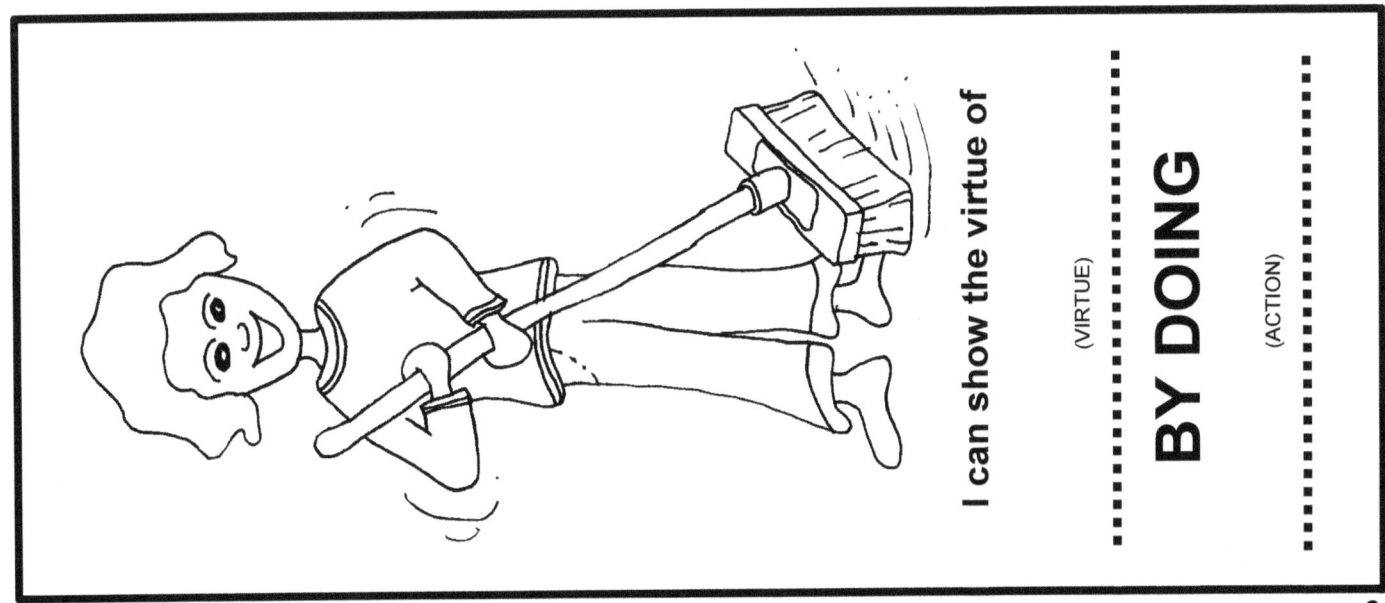

I can show the virtue of _____ (VIRTUE)

BY DOING

_____ (ACTION)

SCENARIO MATERIALS

HAPPY / SAD FACE

INSTRUCTIONS:
• Copy this page on to white card.
• Cut out the face and the mouth.
• Put a paper fastener through the middle of the mouth so that it can spin around from being sad to happy.
• Colour in (optional)

SCENARIO MATERIALS

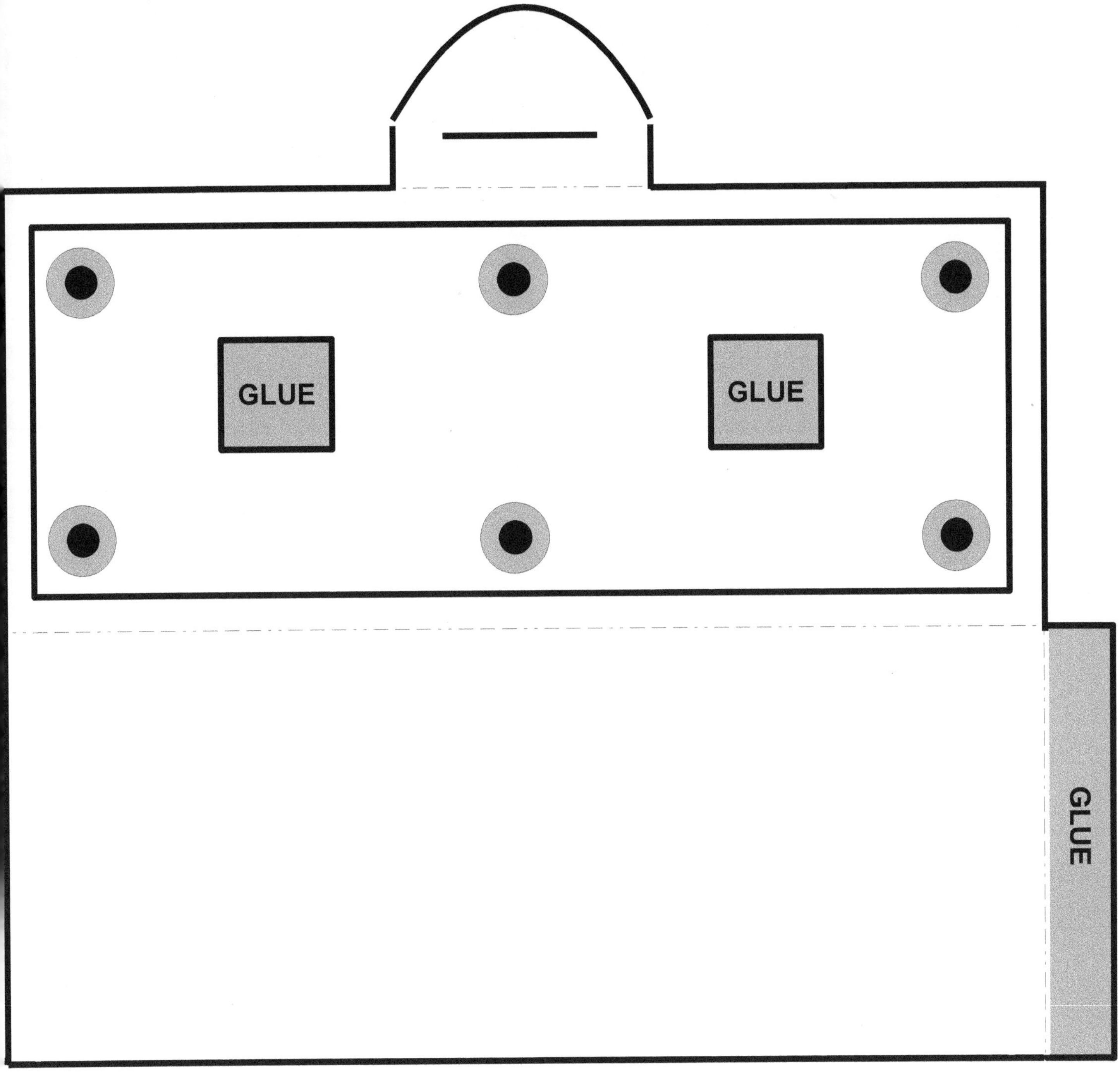

TOOLBOX

HANDLE

INSTRUCTIONS:
- Copy this page and the next page on to coloured card.
- Cut along all the dark lines and fold along all the dotted lines.
- Glue where marked.
- Glue handle on to marked areas.
- Photocopy the tools provided that matches the week's virtue and put it inside the toolbox.

SCENARIO MATERIALS

TOOLBOX

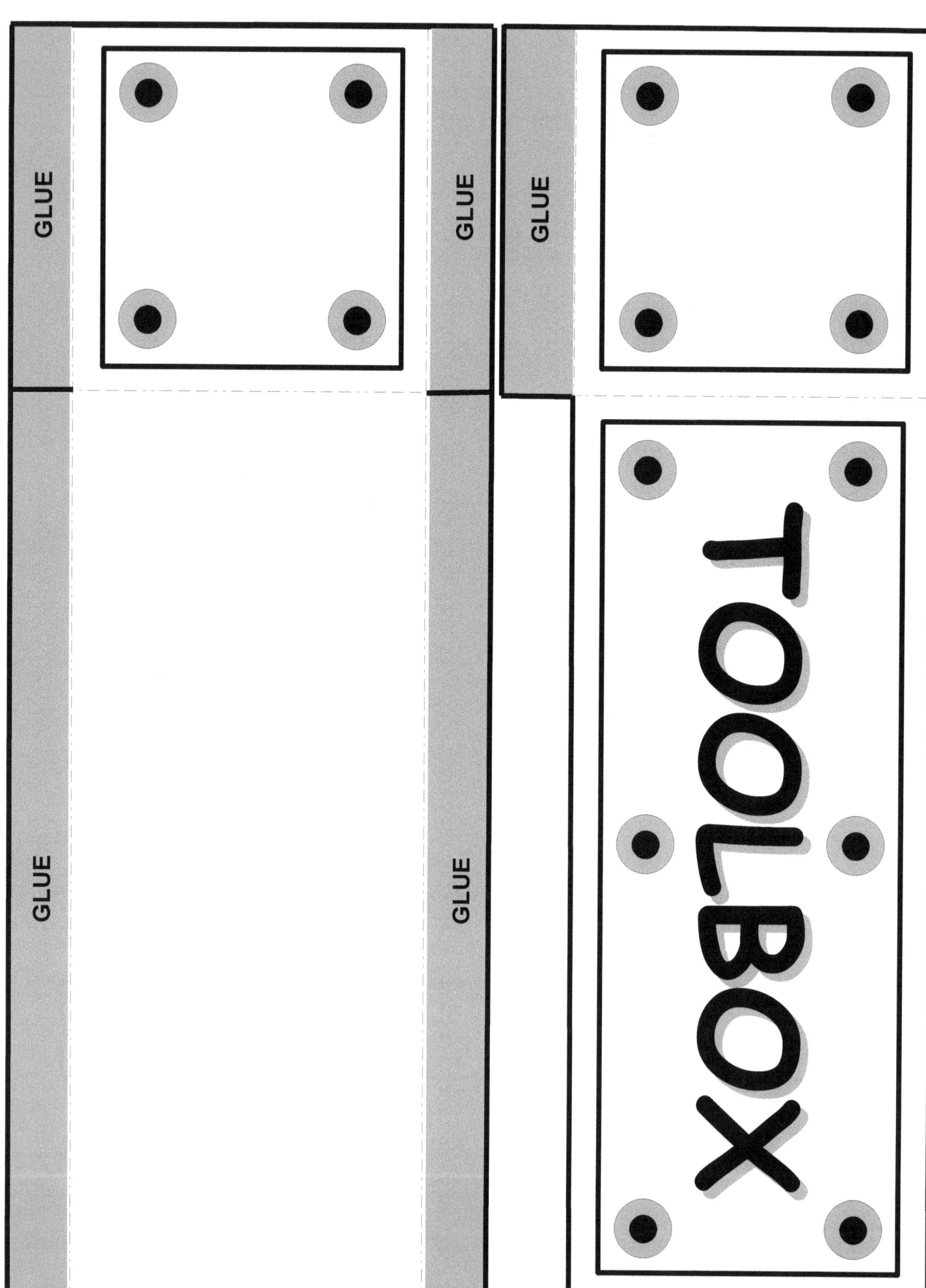

TOOLBOX

SCENARIO MATERIALS

INSTRUCTIONS:
- Copy relevant tool on to white card.
- Colour in.
- Cut around the outside.
- Place in toolbox ready for class.

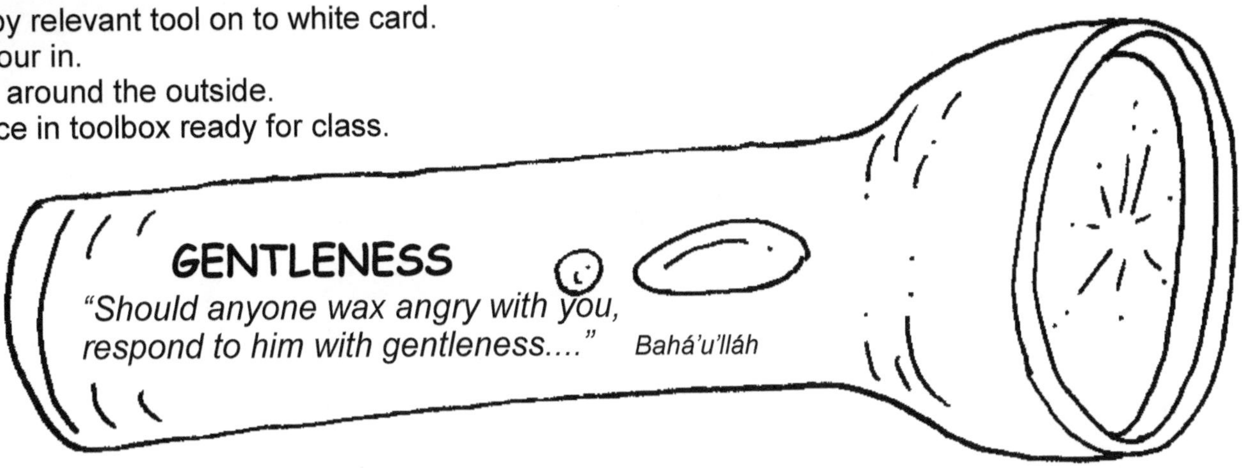

GENTLENESS
"Should anyone wax angry with you, respond to him with gentleness...." *Bahá'u'lláh*

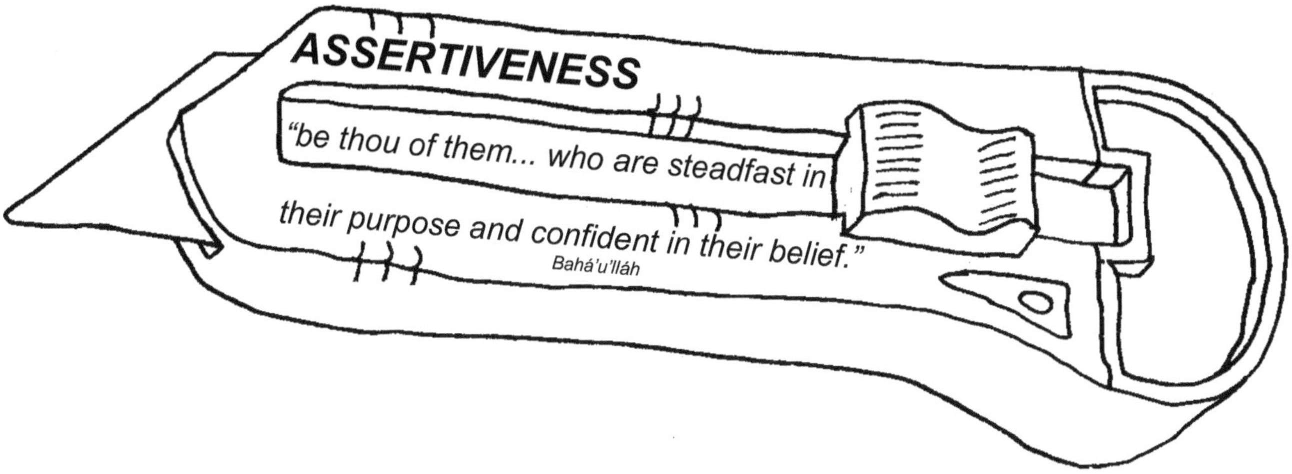

ASSERTIVENESS
"be thou of them... who are steadfast in their purpose and confident in their belief." *Bahá'u'lláh*

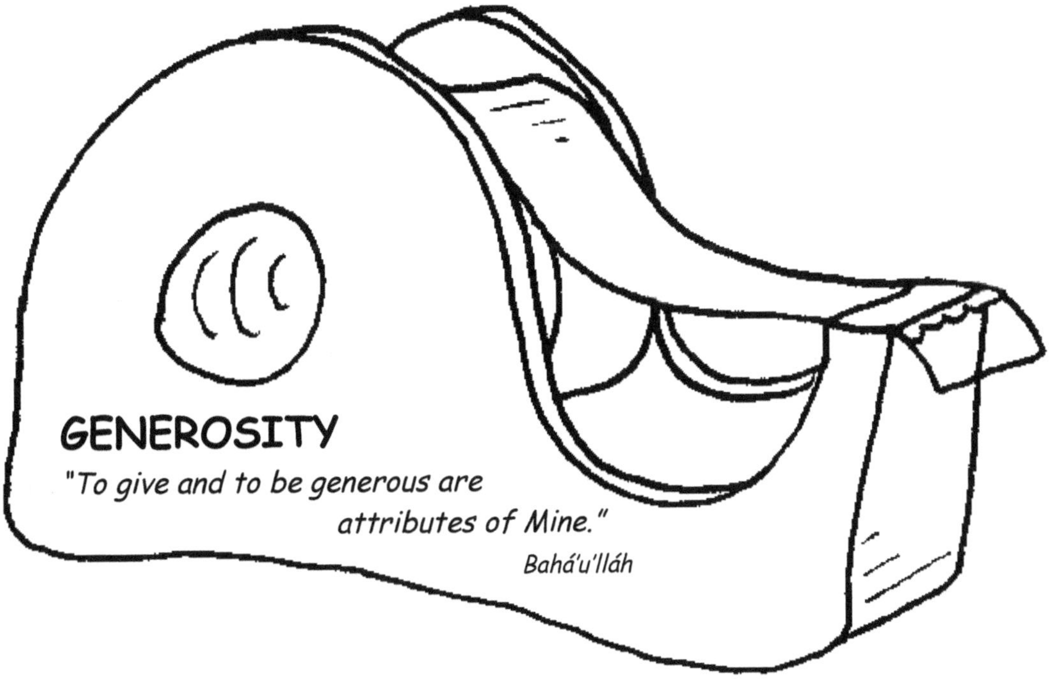

GENEROSITY
"To give and to be generous are attributes of Mine." *Bahá'u'lláh*

SCENARIO MATERIALS — **TOOLBOX**

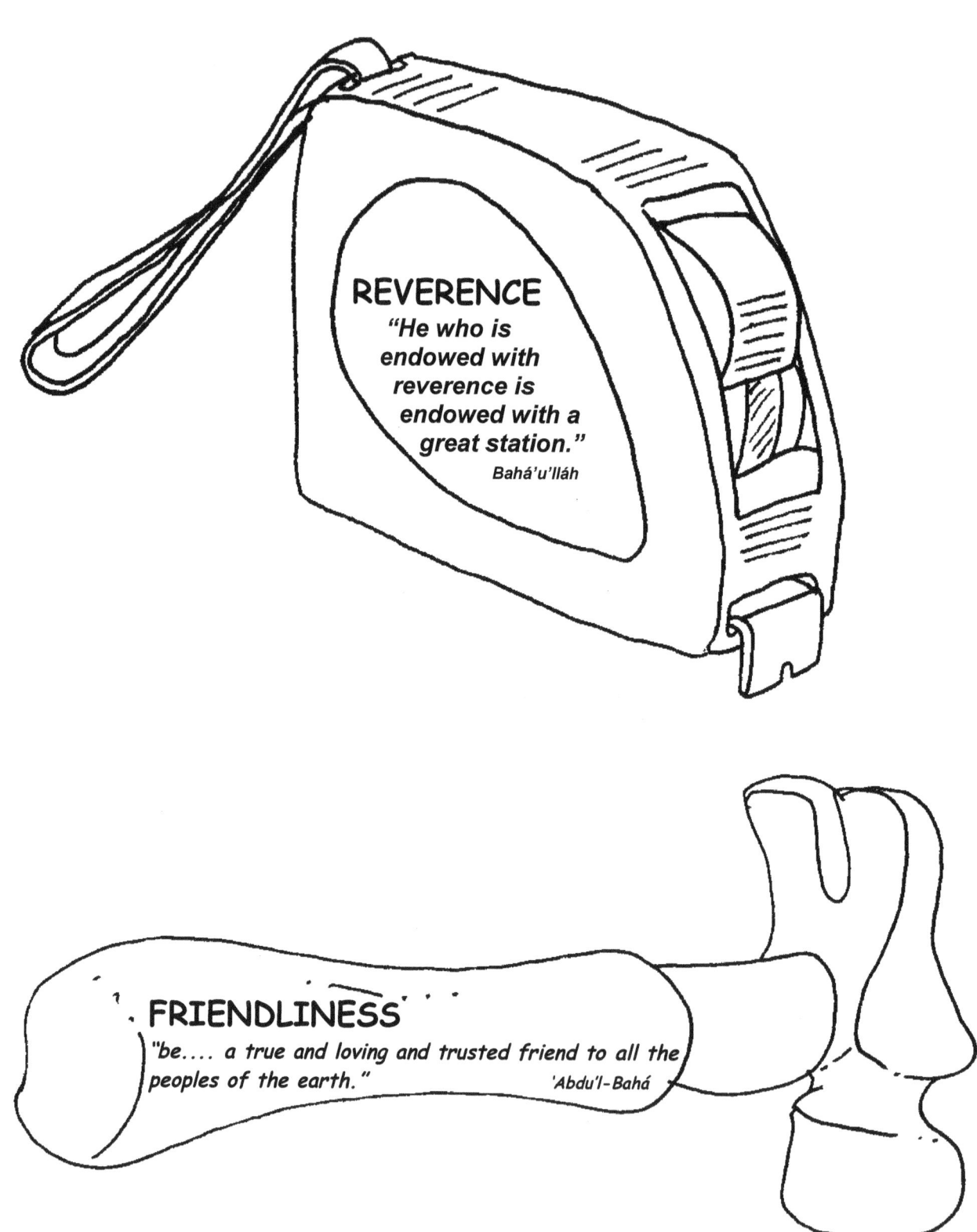

REVERENCE
"He who is endowed with reverence is endowed with a great station."
Bahá'u'lláh

FRIENDLINESS
"be.... a true and loving and trusted friend to all the peoples of the earth."
'Abdu'l-Bahá

EXCELLENCE
"In everything we do we should always try to attain a standard of excellence."
From a letter written by the Universal House of Justice

SCENARIO MATERIALS

TOOLBOX

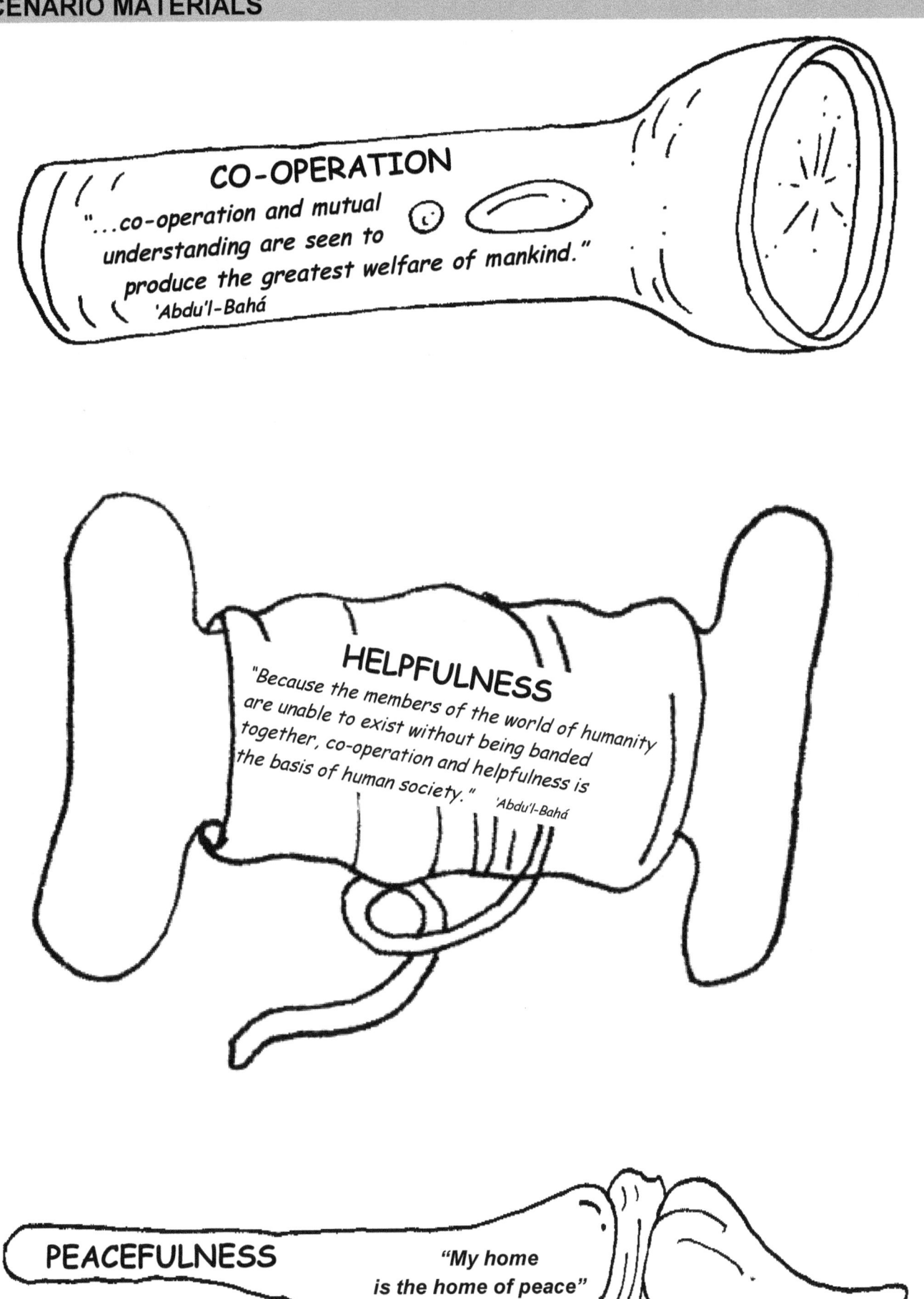

CO-OPERATION
"...co-operation and mutual understanding are seen to produce the greatest welfare of mankind."
'Abdu'l-Bahá

HELPFULNESS
"Because the members of the world of humanity are unable to exist without being banded together, co-operation and helpfulness is the basis of human society."
'Abdu'l-Bahá

PEACEFULNESS
"My home is the home of peace"
'Abdu'l-Bahá

SCENARIO MATERIALS — **TOOLBOX**

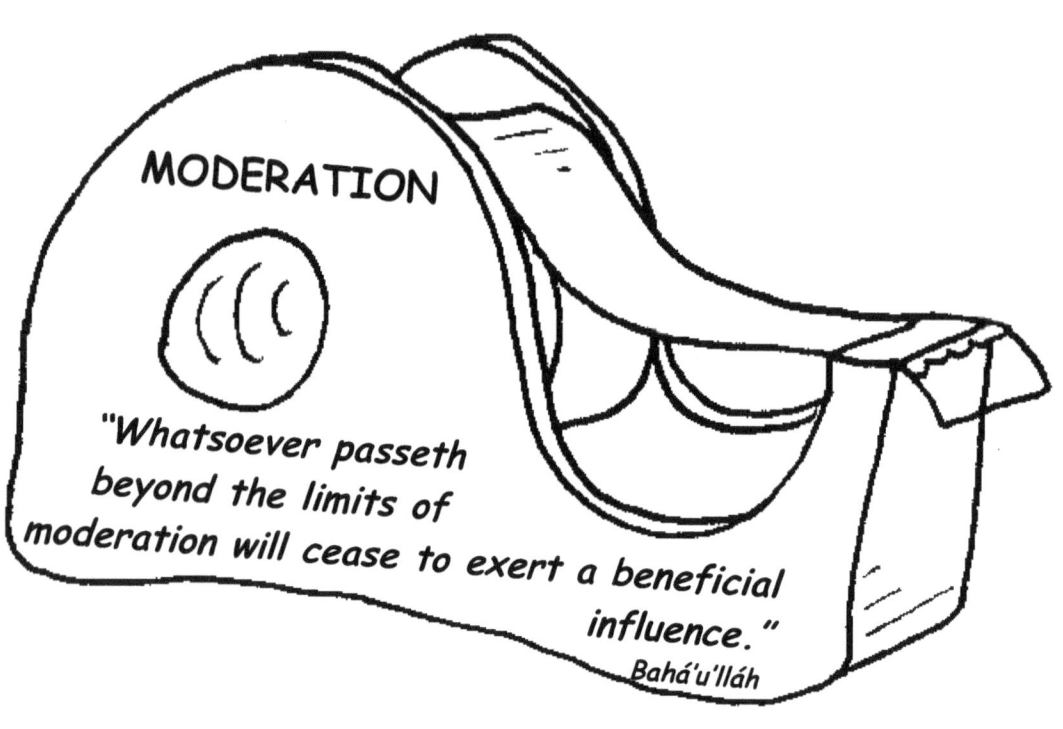

MODERATION

"Whatsoever passeth beyond the limits of moderation will cease to exert a beneficial influence."
— Bahá'u'lláh

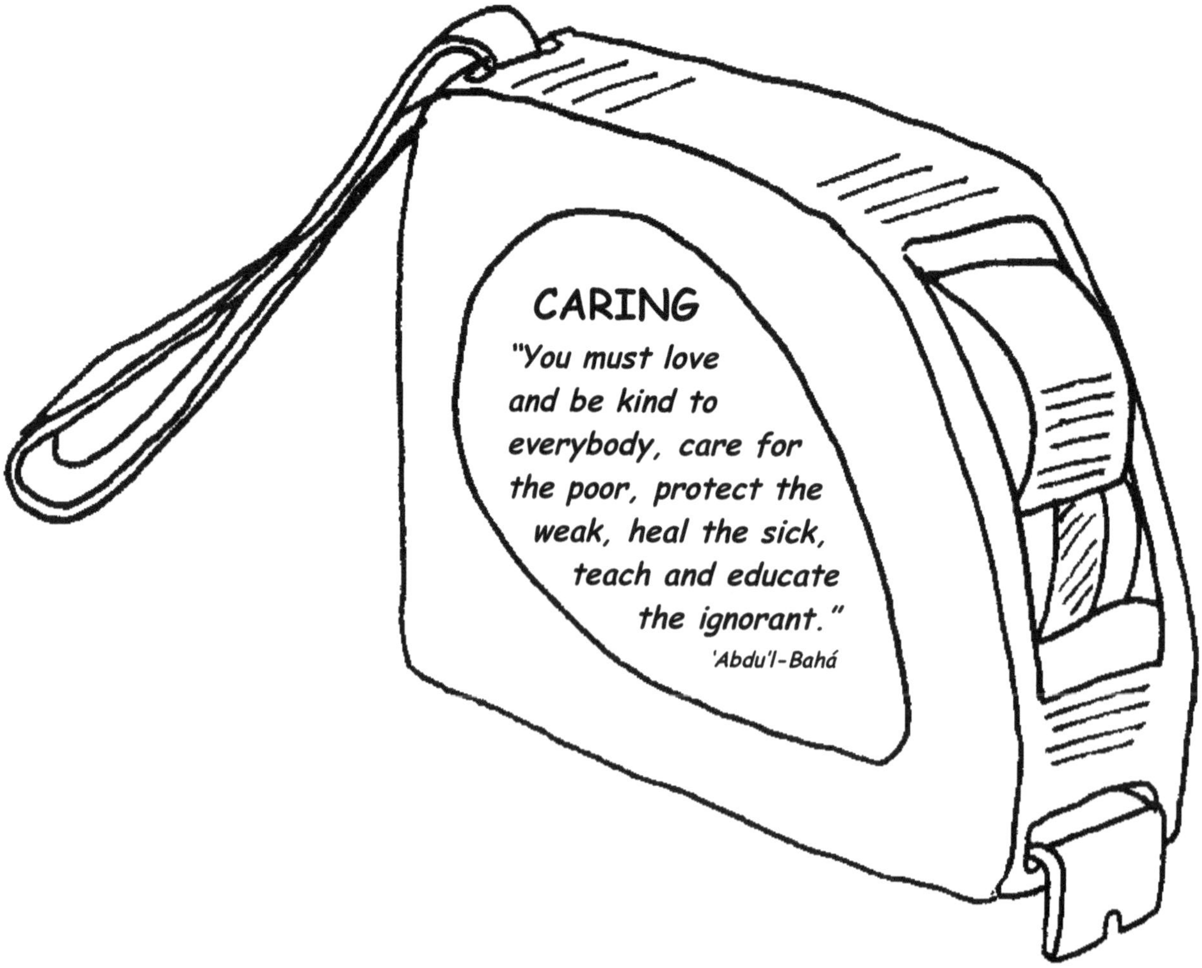

CARING

"You must love and be kind to everybody, care for the poor, protect the weak, heal the sick, teach and educate the ignorant."
— 'Abdu'l-Bahá

SCENARIO MATERIALS

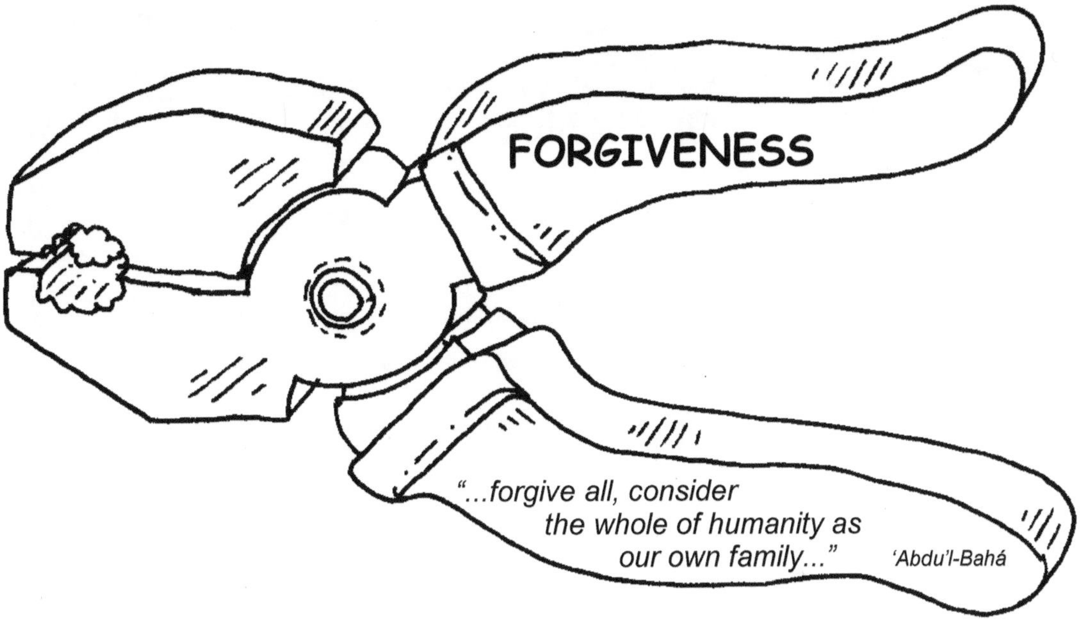

TOOLBOX

FORGIVENESS

"...forgive all, consider the whole of humanity as our own family..." — 'Abdu'l-Bahá

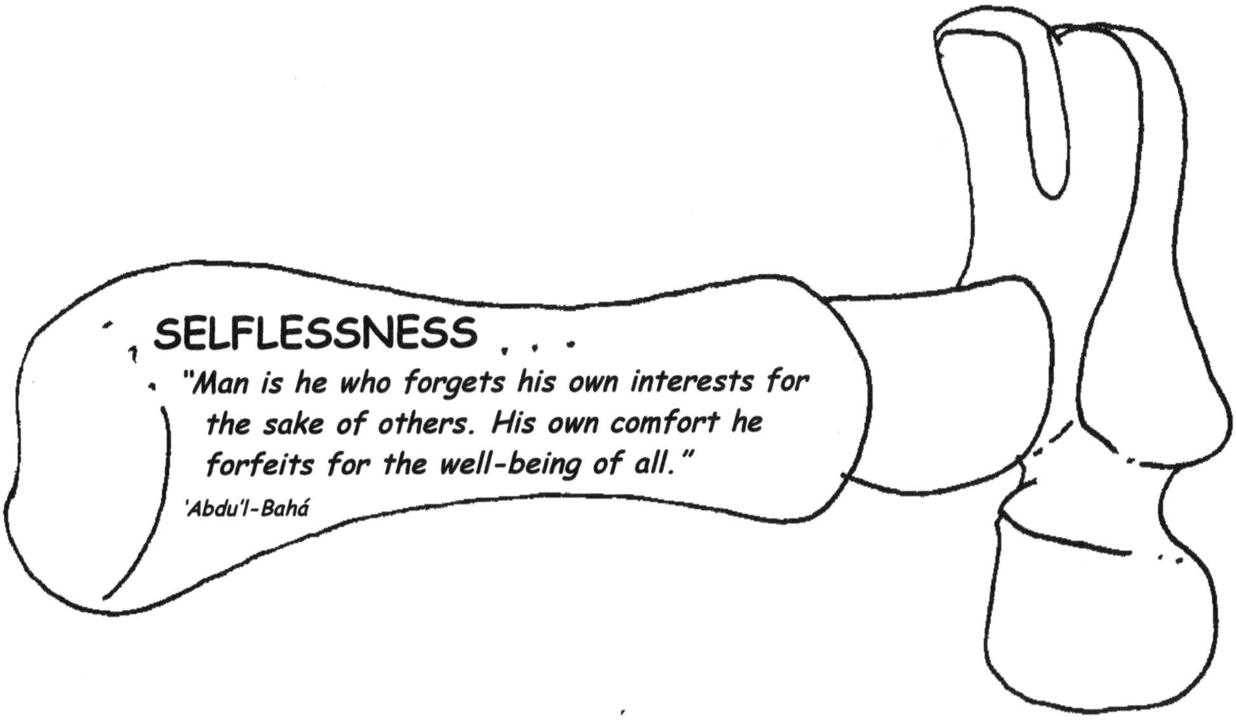

SELFLESSNESS

"Man is he who forgets his own interests for the sake of others. His own comfort he forfeits for the well-being of all."
— 'Abdu'l-Bahá

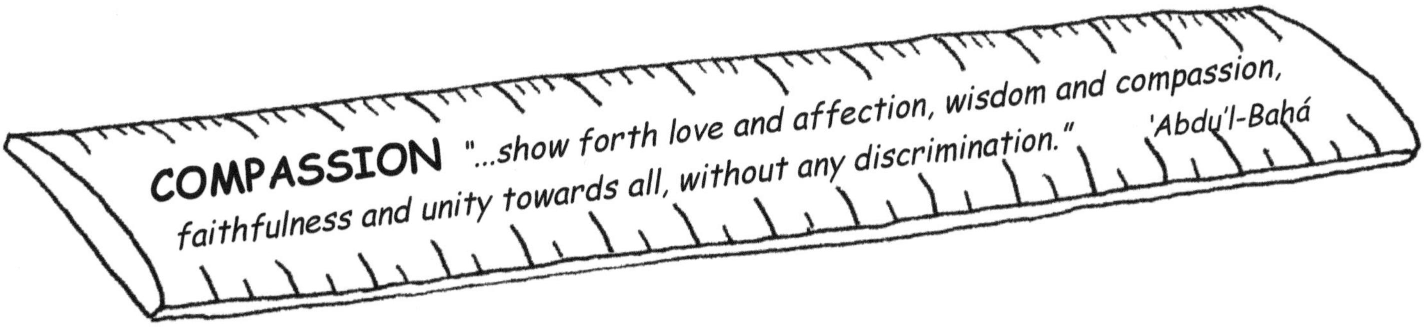

COMPASSION

"...show forth love and affection, wisdom and compassion, faithfulness and unity towards all, without any discrimination." — 'Abdu'l-Bahá

13

SCENARIO MATERIALS   **TOOLBOX**

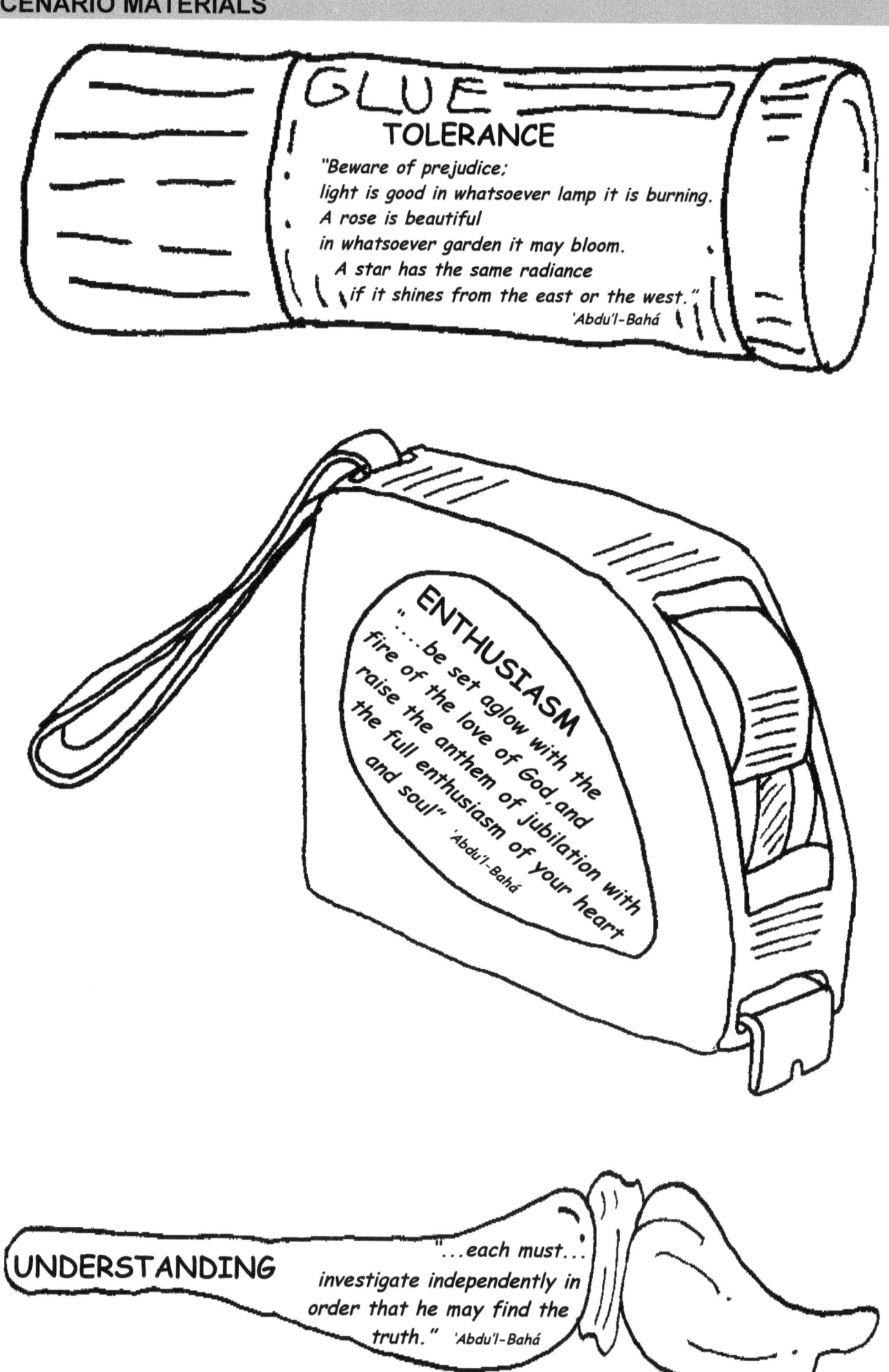

GLUE — TOLERANCE
"Beware of prejudice;
light is good in whatsoever lamp it is burning.
A rose is beautiful
in whatsoever garden it may bloom.
A star has the same radiance
if it shines from the east or the west."
— 'Abdu'l-Bahá

ENTHUSIASM
"...be set aglow with the fire of the love of God, and raise the anthem of jubilation with the full enthusiasm of your heart and soul"
— 'Abdu'l-Bahá

UNDERSTANDING
"...each must... investigate independently in order that he may find the truth."
— 'Abdu'l-Bahá

SCENARIO MATERIALS **TOOLBOX**

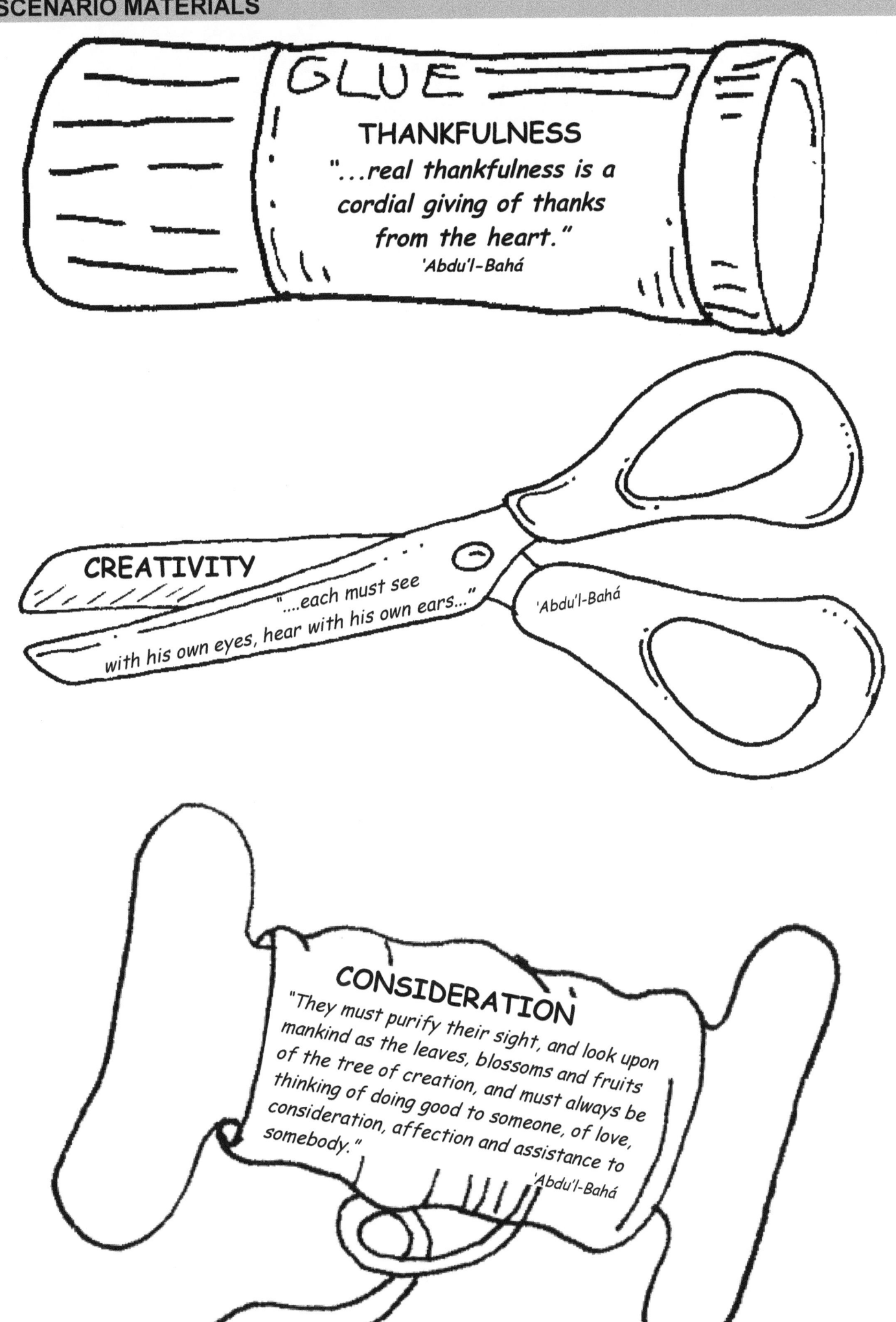

GLUE

THANKFULNESS
"...real thankfulness is a cordial giving of thanks from the heart."
'Abdu'l-Bahá

CREATIVITY
"....each must see with his own eyes, hear with his own ears..."
'Abdu'l-Bahá

CONSIDERATION
"They must purify their sight, and look upon mankind as the leaves, blossoms and fruits of the tree of creation, and must always be thinking of doing good to someone, of love, consideration, affection and assistance to somebody."
'Abdu'l-Bahá

TERM STARTERS

CHOOSE ONE OF THE FOLLOWING
TWO WEEK PLANS TO BEGIN
EACH NEW TERM.

OUR PURPOSE

LESSON PLAN

DAY 1

DISCUSSION: Who is God? God is everywhere although we can't see Him with our eyes. He is always there to help us and protect us.
Why did God create us? God created us to make this world a better place. Sometimes people get sad and angry and need a way to change this so that they can be happy again. To do this God has given us many tools like kindness, love, respect and generosity. These tools are gifts from God to each one of us. We just need to learn how to use them properly so we can make the 'best' choices.

Make up the toolbox described in the beginning of the book and put some virtues inside it. (Do this before class). Show it to the children to demonstrate the above discussion.

PRAYER: God never leaves us alone. He will always be there for us when we need Him and we can ask him for help by saying prayers because prayer is our way of talking to God. God doesn't always help us in the way we expect him to but he will always be there to assist us in making the right choices.
Read out the prayer "Say: O God, my God!"
Use the illustrated prayer provided to discuss the meaning of the prayer. Also briefly explain the meaning of difficult words such as 'attire' and 'temple'.
Justice is one of the tools or gifts God gives us, can you think of some other ones?

SONG: "Say: O God, my God!"
Sing with actions.

ACTIVITY: A Gift – Use activity sheet provided – children can put the gift box in their room to remind them of the gifts God gives us to deal with every difficult situation we have to face.
Purpose – To reflect on the meaning of the prayer and understand that the gifts God gives us help us in every situation.

REVIEW:
Ask the children to colour in the black and white prayer so they have a copy to take home.

DAY 2

PRAYER: "Say: O God, my God!"
Sing with actions.

DISCUSSION: What does God want us to do?
God wants us to change every situation into a happy one. He gives us the tools of love, friendship etc... to do this. We can pray to him, we can ask him for assistance and he will guide us and help us make the right choices.

"When a thought of war comes, oppose it by a stronger thought of peace. A thought of hatred must be destroyed by a more powerful thought of love."
   'Abdu'l-Bahá

STORY: "The Problem"

SONG: "A Better Way" - sing with actions.

ACTIVITY: Happy / Sad Face – Use activity sheet provided.
Purpose – to reflect on how the choices we make have the power to turn sad situations into happy ones.

OUR PURPOSE
GIFT

"Say: O God, my God! ... Thou, verily, art the Possessor of all gifts and bounties."
— Bahá'u'lláh

(quotation repeated 16 times on cut-out cards)

RIBBON — COLOURED PAPER

Each child will need:
- Glue.
- Coloured pieces of paper..
- A copy of a quotation.
- A small box (you can get these from shops like Spotlight).
- A piece of gift rap ribbon.

Instructions:
- Copy this page onto white or coloured paper.
- Cut out the quotation.
- Glue the quotation into the inside of the box.
- Decorate box with coloured pieces of paper.
- Tie a piece of ribbon around box to make it look like a gift.

Instructions:
- Cut out a prayer along the dotted lines
- Cut out a piece of coloured card slightly larger than the prayer.
- Glue the prayer on to the card
- Colour in.

OUR PURPOSE
COLOURING IN

OUR PURPOSE
Happy / Sad Face

EACH CHILD WILL NEED:
• A copy of this page on white card.
• Crayons / pencils
• Scissors
• A paper fastener

"When a thought of war comes, oppose it by a stronger thought of peace. A thought of hatred must be destroyed by a more powerful thought of love."
– Abdu'l-Bahá

PAPER FASTNER

INSTRUCTIONS:
• Copy this page on to white card.
• Cut out the face and the mouth.
• Put a paper fastener through the middle of the mouth so that it can spin around from being sad to happy.
• Colour in (optional)

23

THE PROBLEM

OUR PURPOSE
STORY

Bradley was very good at fixing things. It doesn't matter what was broken or what the problem was, somehow he always managed to make things right again.

One day he was driving in the car with his mum when the car suddenly stopped. "Oh, no," cried his mum. "What could be wrong?" Bradley got out and looked under the hood of the car. "Mmmm," he said. The tool I need to fix this problem is a spanner," he said confidently. He took out a spanner from the back of the car and after a bit of clanging and banging the car started up again. "Wonderful," said his mum, "How do you do it?" "You just need to get the right tool," said Bradley as they drove on down the road.

Later as he walked to school he heard a sudden crash just behind him. He turned around to see Mrs Potts crying and staring at the broken pieces of a bowl. "Oh, no," cried Mrs Potts, "It was my favorite bowl." "Don't worry," said Bradley. "The tool to fix this problem is some glue." Mrs Potts ran in to get some glue from her house while Bradley picked up the pieces. It wasn't long before he had glued the bowl back together again. It was nearly as good as new. Mrs Potts smiled and asked, "How do you do it?" "You just need to get the right tool," said Bradley as he continued down the path on the way to school.

Later at lunchtime in the playground Bradley noticed that his friends were all arguing over a ball. Bradley came up and asked what was wrong. "I had it first," they all cried together. "You can't have all had it first," exclaimed Bradley. "I think the tool to fix this problem is a little bit of sharing. Why don't you share the ball by playing a game together." His friends all started laughing. "That's a good idea," they replied. "How do you do it?" "You just need to get the right tool," said Bradley smiling as he too joined in the game of catch.

MORAL – God has given us many tools to help turn situations from sad ones to happy ones. We just need to know what tool to use.

THE SPIRIT WITHIN

LESSON PLAN

DAY 1

DISCUSSION: Discuss how prayer is our way of talking to God. We can ask for assistance when we need help, thank him for the wonderful things he has already given us and ask for guidance when we feel unsure. God doesn't always help us the way we expect him to. Ask the children what they think they might like to talk to God about.
Read out the prayer "He is God! O God my God"
Use the illustrated prayer provided to discuss the meaning of the prayer.
We need to strive to make our heart pure. Use a glass of water to show that when the water is clean the sun can shine through it but when we put some dust in it the sun cannot. Our heart is the same. When we fill ourselves with nasty thoughts it is like we are making our heart dirty and God cannot shine through us any more. When God does shine through us we become strong inside. We become confident, joyful, loving, respectful.

SONG: "He is God! O God my God"
Sing with actions.

ACTIVITY: Pure Hearts – Use activity sheet provided.
Purpose - to visualize what it means to have a pure heart and let God shine through us.

REVIEW:
Ask the children to colour in the black and white prayer so they have a copy to take home.

DAY 2

PRAYER: "He is God! O God my God"
Sing with actions.

DISCUSSION: Where does love, kindness, respect etc... come from?
Use a small mirror and a torch to show how God has given us the ability to reflect God's qualities just like a mirror reflects the light of a torch or the sun. These virtues do not belong to us just like the light does not belong to the mirror, but we can still carry the virtues with us wherever we go. However, if we stop thinking about God or trying to develop our spiritual qualities it is as if we have turned away from the light and those qualities that make us special will no longer be reflected in our hearts.

"May we indeed become mirrors reflecting the heavenly realities..."
'Abdu'l-Bahá

STORY: "A Purpose for Myrtle"

SONG: "Our Little Mirror" - sing with actions.

ACTIVITY: Person – Use activity sheet provided.
Purpose – visualize quotation – to understand that we are like mirrors. Although we will never be perfect like God, we can reflect his qualities, for example; love, generosity, helpfulness.

THE SPIRIT WITHIN
Pure Hearts

EACH CHILD WILL NEED:
- Scissors, glue
- A heart
- Crayons / pencils
- Sticky tape
- A small piece of coloured cellophane.
- A safety pin.

INSTRUCTIONS:
- Photocopy this page on to white card.
- Cut out the outside of the heart.
- Fold where marked and cut out the small gray heart.
- Glue a small piece of coloured cellophane on to the back of the cut out area.
- Colour in.
- Tape a pin on to the back so that it can be used as a badge.

**He is God!
O God my God
Bestow upon me
a pure heart
like unto
a pearl.**
— 'Abdu'l-Bahá

THE SPIRIT WITHIN
COLOURING IN

Instructions:
- Cut out a prayer along the dotted lines
- Cut out a piece of coloured card slightly larger than the prayer.
- Glue the prayer on to the card
- Colour in.

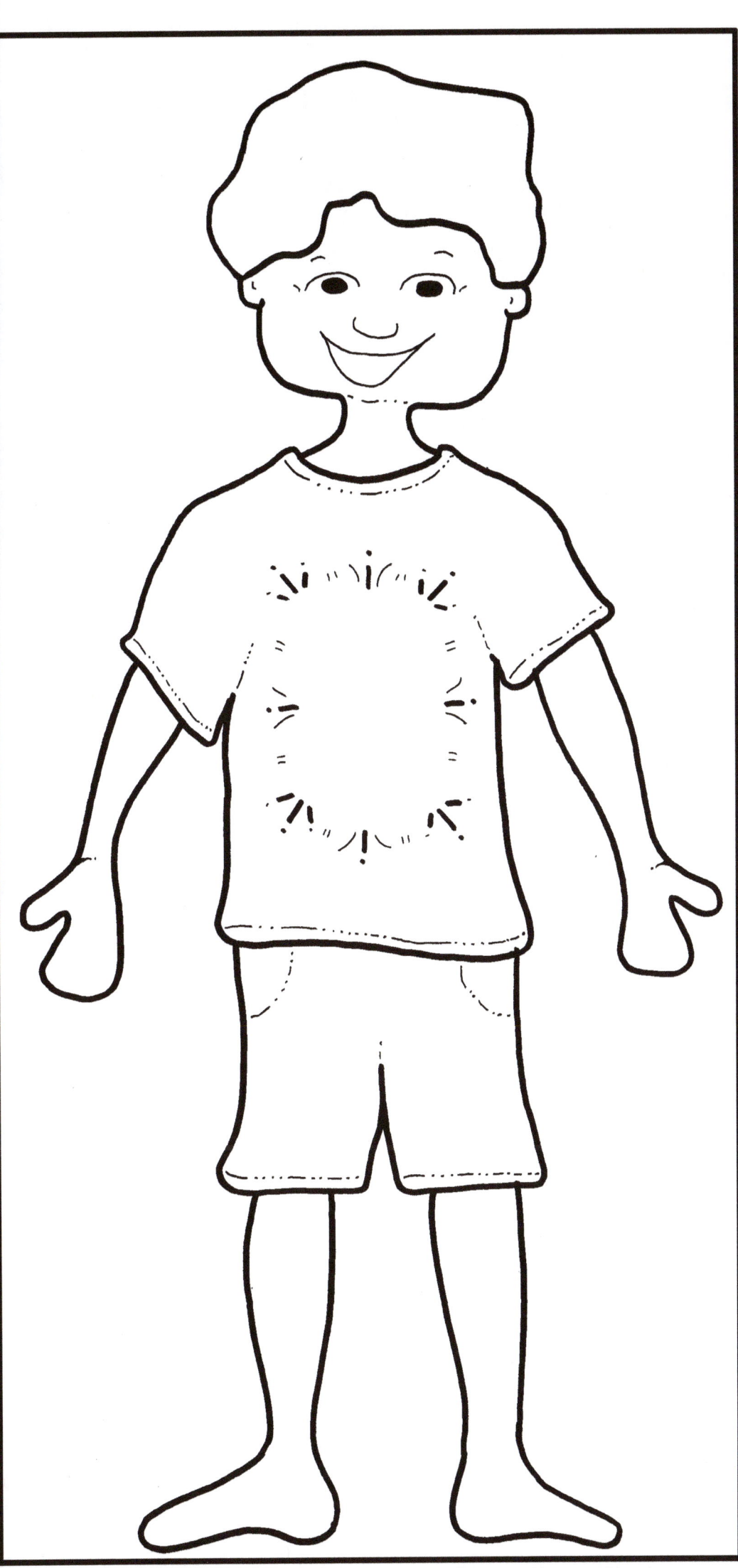

THE SPIRIT WITHIN
PERSON

"May we indeed become mirrors reflecting the heavenly realities..."
'Abdu'l-Bahá

Each child will need:
• Scissors, glue.
• Crayons / Pencils.
• A copy of this page on white paper.
• A small piece of mirror or some shiny paper.

Instructions:
• Cut out the person and the quotation..
• Glue the quotation into the centre of the person.
• Glue the mirror or small shiny piece of paper onto the square under the quotation.
• Colour in.

A PURPOSE FOR MYRTLE

THE SPIRIT WITHIN
STORY

Once upon a time there was a little hand mirror called Myrtle. Myrtle was usually very happy but lately she had become more and more gloomy.

"What can I do?" Myrtle mirror would sigh. "I only reflect people, I will never actually be a person. It's not fair."

"But that is what you do, reflect things," stated Carol comb coming up behind Myrtle.

"What is the use in that," Myrtle sighed again.

"It is what you are created for and people love you when you reflect them. It is your purpose," explained Carol.

"It is a silly purpose," complained Myrtle, "I refuse to do it ever again. I am going to find a real purpose."

Carol didn't bother replying because Myrtle had already disappeared in search of another purpose.

Myrtle went to the kitchen first. "This is an important place where lots of wonderful things get made. I am sure I will find my purpose here," thought Myrtle to herself. She jumped on to the bench and waited to be useful. For a whole day she waited but although cakes and sandwiches and other wonderful food was prepared right next to her nobody used her. She was just no use in the kitchen.

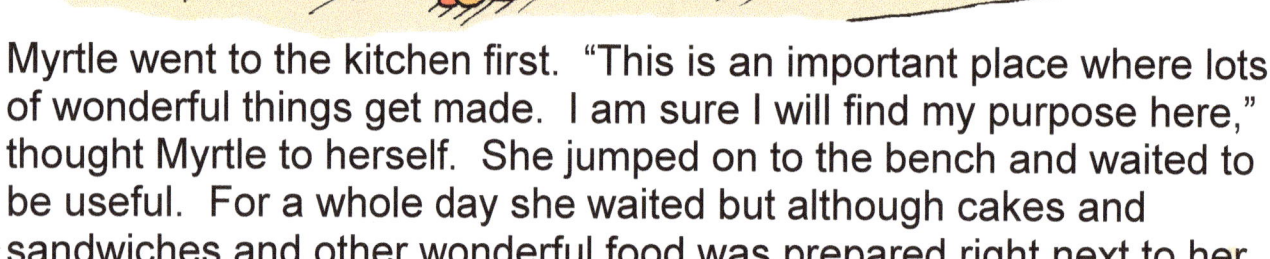

The next day she went out to the garden shed and gazed at all the rakes and spades and gardening equipment. "This is it," thought Myrtle excitedly, this is my purpose. She waited another whole day in the shed but although lawns were raked, weeds were dug out and seeds were planted nobody needed her. She was just not needed in the shed.

THE SPIRIT WITHIN
STORY

Suddenly she spied some washing hanging on the line and decided to try the laundry. She propped herself up next to the detergents and soap then waited to be wanted. She waited a whole day but although clothes were washed and ironed nobody wanted her in the laundry. Sadly she went back to the bathroom and looked sadly at Carol comb.

Just then she was picked up and used by the little girl who lived in the house. The little girl combed her hair and looked in Myrtle mirror to make sure it looked neat and tidy. "I am going to a party," she told Myrtle, "and I want to look my very best."

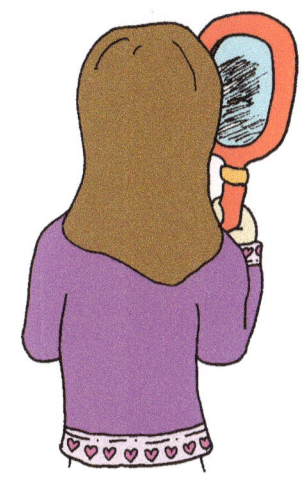

Myrtle was starting to feel important again. Carol was right, this was what she did best. This was her purpose and it felt great to be needed again. She would never be a person but that was alright because she was made to be a mirror and that was what made her special.

MORAL - It is the mirror's job to reflect people, just like it is our purpose to be like a mirror and reflect all the attributes or virtues of God. We will never be perfect like God but just by reflecting those qualities of respect and generosity we become special.

PRAYER

LESSON PLAN

DAY 1

DISCUSSION: Discuss how prayer is our way of talking to God. We can ask for assistance when we need help, thank him for the wonderful things he has already given us and ask for guidance when we feel unsure. God doesn't always help us the way we expect him to. Ask the children what they think they might like to talk to God about.
Read out the prayer "God is sufficient unto me"
Use the illustrated prayer provided to discuss the meaning of the prayer.
Sometimes life is hard and we don't always understand why things have to be the way they are but we still need to trust in God and know that he is looking after us.

SONG: "God is sufficient unto me"
Sing with actions.

ACTIVITY: Bags of trust – Use activity sheet provided.
Purpose - to reflect on what it means to put our trust in God.

REVIEW:
Ask the children to colour in the black and white prayer so they have a copy to take home.

DAY 2

PRAYER: "God is sufficient unto me"
Sing with actions.

DISCUSSION: Why do we pray?
Prayer allows us to be connected to God.

"The wisdom of prayer is this: That it causeth a connection between the servant and the True One..."
'Abdu'l-Bahá

STORY: "Searching for God"

SONG: "Connected" - sing with actions.

ACTIVITY: Chain – Use activity sheet provided.
Purpose – to understand that prayer is the way we can be connected with God.

PRAYER
BAGS OF TRUST

HANDLE

STEP 1. Fold the edges of a piece of paper lengthwise in about 2 cm on each side.

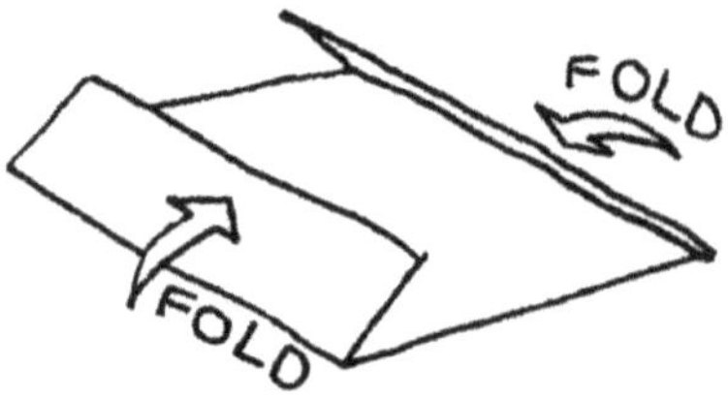

STEP 2. Fold it in half

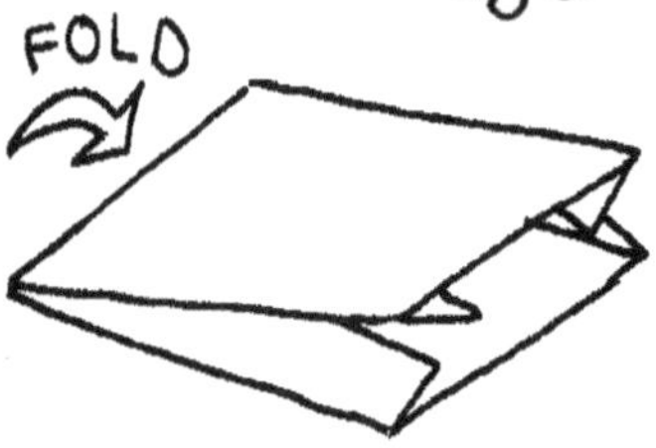

STEP 3. Cut along the dotted lines of this page.

STEP 4. Staple the two folded edges and the handle together. Glue the quotation to the front of the bag.

STEP 5. Children fill in the three cards with three ways we can trust God. These could be written or drawn. Place them in the bag.

EACH CHILD WILL NEED:
- Scissors, glue, crayons
- Stapler (adult use only)
- This page copied on white card.
- A piece of coloured paper.

CUT

God is sufficient unto me.
He verily is the All-Sufficing.
In Him let the trusting trust.
Bahá'u'lláh

I CAN TRUST GOD WHEN:

CUT
CUT

I CAN TRUST GOD WHEN:

I CAN TRUST GOD WHEN:

God is sufficient unto me. He verily is the All-Sufficing. In Him let the trusting trust.

Bahá'u'lláh

PRAYER
COLOURING IN

Instructions:
- Cut out a prayer along the dotted lines
- Cut out a piece of coloured card slightly larger than the prayer.
- Glue the prayer on to the card
- Colour in.

God is sufficient unto me. He verily is the All-Sufficing. In Him let the trusting trust.

Bahá'u'lláh

PRAYER CHAIN

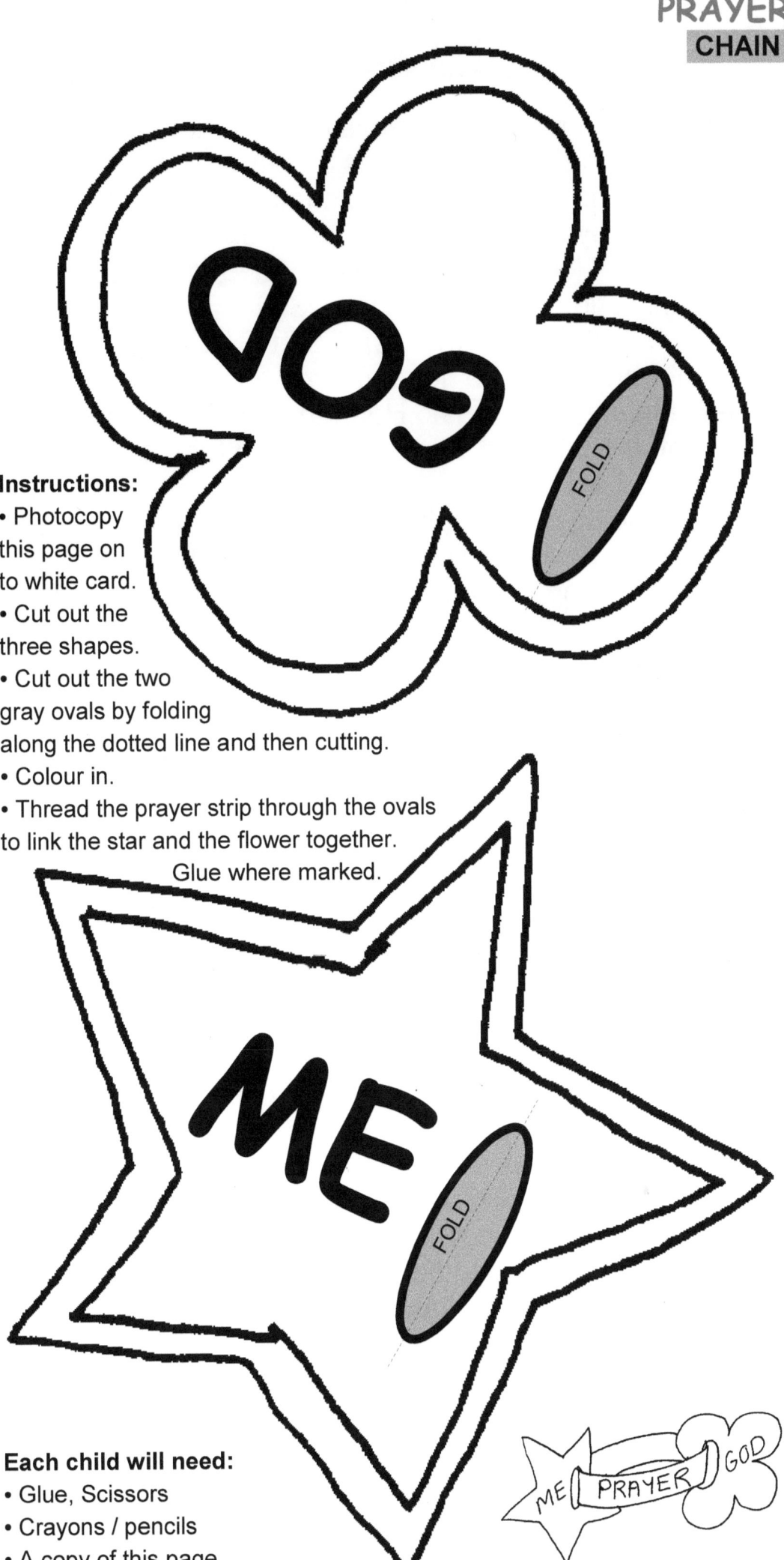

"The wisdom of prayer is this: That it causeth a connection between the servant and the True One..."
'Abdu'l-Bahá

PRAYER

GLUE

Instructions:
- Photocopy this page on to white card.
- Cut out the three shapes.
- Cut out the two gray ovals by folding along the dotted line and then cutting.
- Colour in.
- Thread the prayer strip through the ovals to link the star and the flower together. Glue where marked.

Each child will need:
- Glue, Scissors
- Crayons / pencils
- A copy of this page

SEARCHING FOR GOD

PRAYER STORY

Hannah's room was very messy. Her mum said, "Come and clean up this mess." Hannah looked at the mess and groaned. It would take her ages to put all the toys away again. She sat down on her bed and just looked at the mess for a long time. Suddenly she had a bright idea. She remembered that her mum said that God could help her any time she needed him. "God can help me clean my room," said Hannah excitedly. She leapt off the bed and started searching for God.

First she look in the cupboard, "God! Are you there?" No answer! Then, she looked in the bathroom, "God are you in here?" Still no answer! Next, she looked out in the back yard. "God, are you out here?" But there was only silence. "Where can God be?" Hannah said gloomily. She sat down in a lounge chair and tried to think hard about where else she could search. While she was thinking she suddenly spied a prayer book sitting on the table. She picked it up and flicked through the pages. She remembered her mum saying that she could say a prayer when she needed God to help her, so she sat up straight, closed her eyes and said a prayer for God to help her clean her room. She sat there quietly for a long time and when she opened her eyes she felt that God had left an answer in her heart. She just needed to clean her room one little bit at a time.

Hannah went back to her big mess and this time, instead of looking at all the things that needed doing, she looked first at her dolls and put them away. Then she looked at her blocks and put them back in the box. Next she straightened all the books on the shelf and soon, little bit by little bit, her room became tidy again. When she was finished she looked around proudly just as her mum came to see how she was going. "Well done!" exclaimed her mum. "You have done a lovely job. Are you ready for lunch now?" "I just have one more thing to do," replied Hannah. After her mum had gone she sat down on the bed and said another prayer, this time to thank God for helping her. As she walked out she felt that God left an answer in her heart that said, "Your welcome".

MORAL – **Prayer is our way of talking to God and creates a connection between Him and us.**

DEEDS NOT WORDS

LESSON PLAN

DAY 1

DISCUSSION: Discuss how prayer is our way of talking to God. We can ask for assistance when we need help, thank him for the wonderful things he has already given us and ask for guidance when we feel unsure. God doesn't always help us the way we expect him to. Ask the children what they think they might like to talk to God about.
Read out the prayer "God grant that the light of unity"
Use the illustrated prayer provided to discuss the meaning of the prayer.
God wants the whole world to be in unity and live together peacefully. We are all God's creation and when we all remember this it will help us create this unity. It is not enough for us just to talk about working together. We need to strive to make this really happen.

SONG: "God grant that the light of unity"
Sing with actions.

ACTIVITY: Headbands – Use activity sheet provided.
Purpose - to reflect on the meaning of the prayer.

REVIEW:
Ask the children to colour in the black and white prayer so they have a copy to take home.

DAY 2

PRAYER: "God grant that the light of unity"
Sing with actions.

DISCUSSION: Does it help to talk about doing good things?
We must not just say we are going to do good things. We must also put our words into actions. If we say we will be generous then we should go and give to somebody. If we say we will be confident then we should go and be brave.

"Let deeds, not words, be our adorning!"
'Abdu'l-Bahá

STORY: "What Ryan Said"

SONG: "With Actions" - sing with actions.

ACTIVITY: Action Hat – Use activity sheet provided.
Purpose – to reflect on some of the ways we can put our words into action.

"God grant that the light of unity may envelop the whole earth, and that the seal, 'the Kingdom is God's', may be stamped upon the brow of all its peoples." Bahá'u'lláh

PART 1

PART 2

DEEDS NOT WORDS
HEADBAND

EACH CHILD WILL NEED:
- A stapler (for adult use)
- A copy of the two parts of the head band on white card.
- Scissors, crayons / pencils

INSTRUCTIONS:
- Cut out the two parts of the headband.
- Colour in.
- Staple to fit the size of the child's head. (An extra strip of paper may be needed to extend the length of the hat to fit the size of the head.)

Instructions:
- Cut out a prayer along the dotted lines
- Cut out a piece of coloured card slightly larger than the prayer.
- Glue the prayer on to the card
- Colour in.

DEEDS NOT WORDS
COLOURING IN

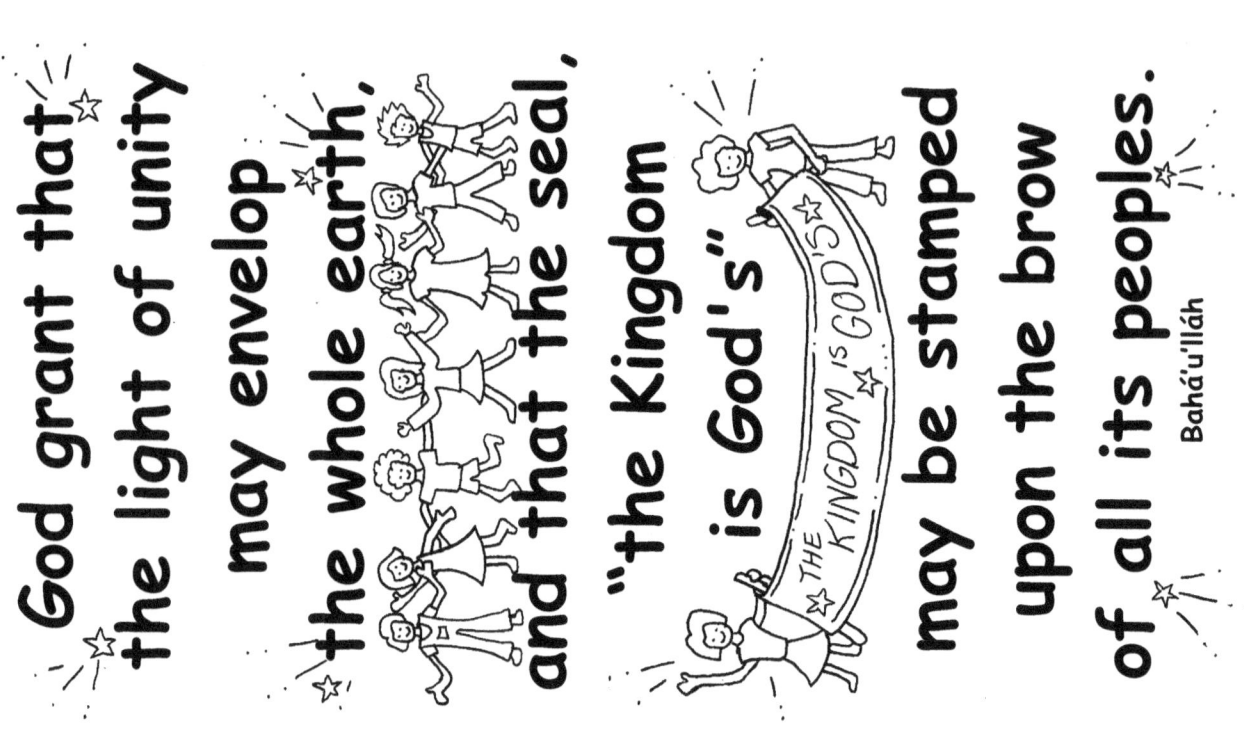

God grant that the light of unity may envelop the whole earth, and that the seal, "the Kingdom is God's" may be stamped upon the brow of all its peoples.

— Bahá'u'lláh

DEEDS NOT WORDS
DEEDS NECKLACE

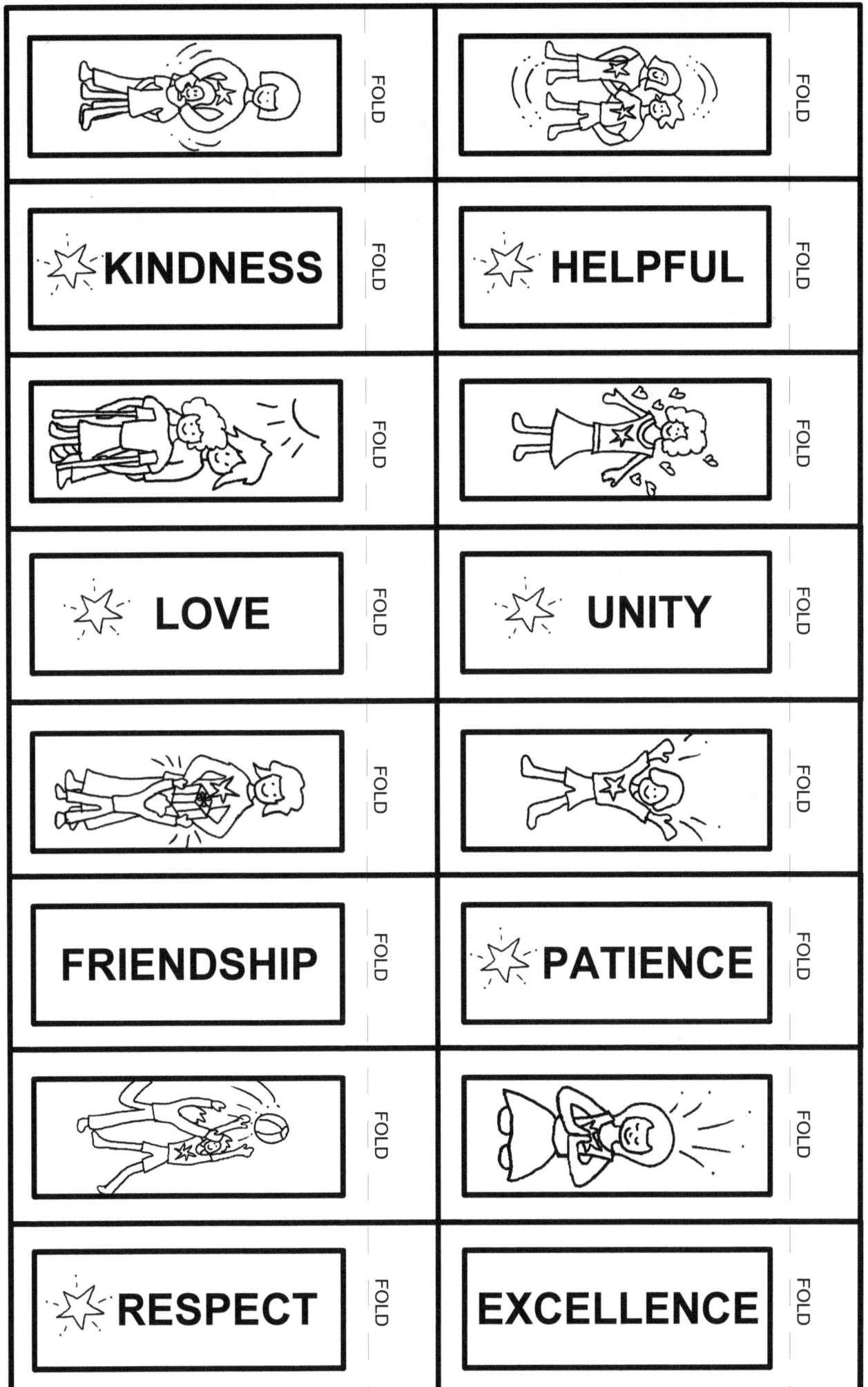

43

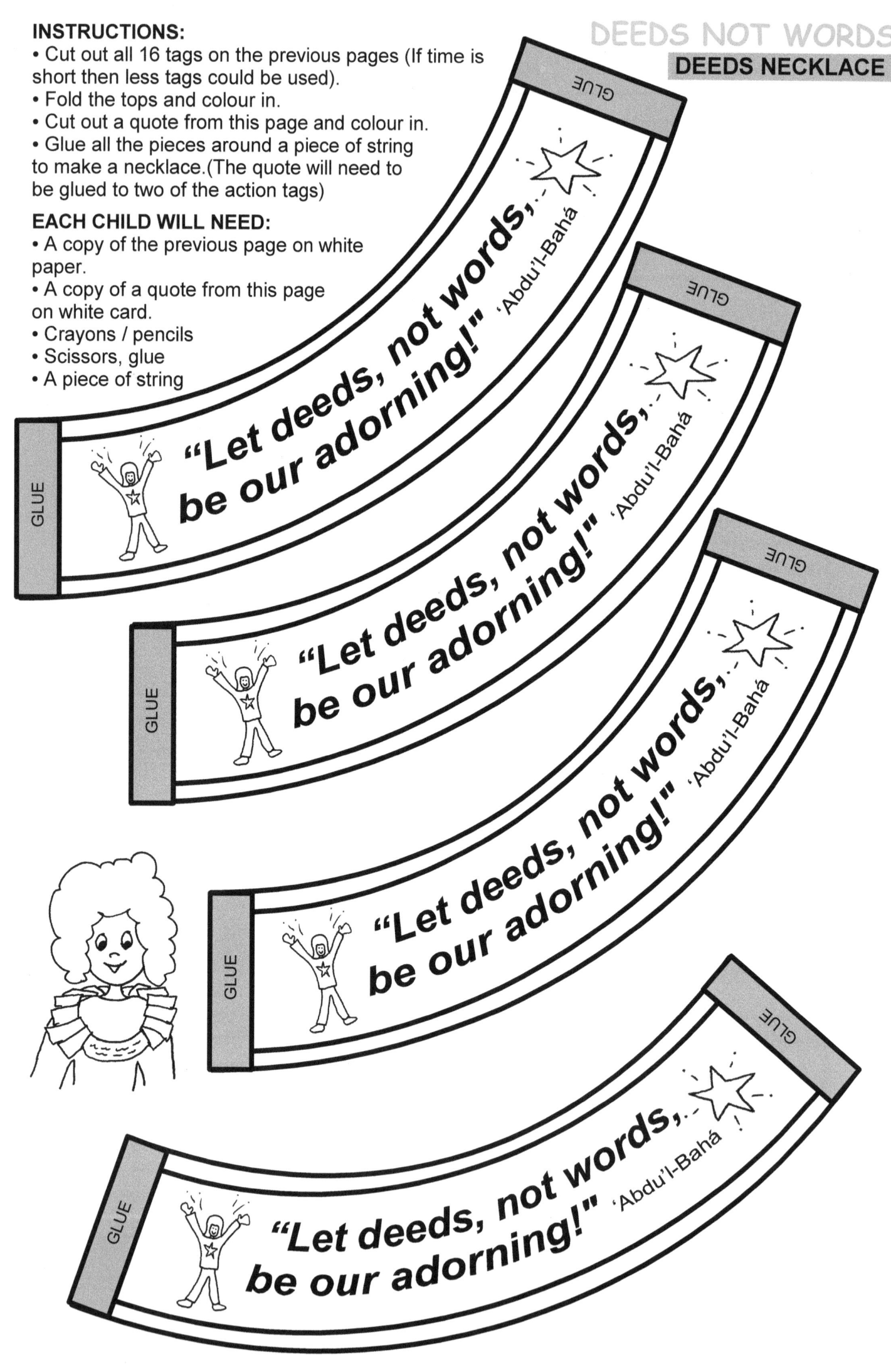

WHAT RYAN SAID

DEEDS NOT WORDS
STORY

Ryan liked going to the beach. He liked swimming, he liked playing in the sand, he like everything about the beach, but today was extra special because he was going to the beach with two of his friends. They had been at the beach for a while when Ryan noticed his friends playing catch with the ball. "Can I play catch with you too?" asked Ryan, "I promise I will share the ball." "Sure," said his friends and threw the ball to him. However, Ryan didn't throw the ball back. Instead, he grabbed the ball and ran off with it laughing. "Hey, come back," yelled his friends.

Later Ryan came back to find his friends building a sand castle. "Can I help too?" asked Ryan. They looked at him for a moment. They had not forgotten about the way he had run off with the ball. After a while they said, "sure, you can help." Ryan sat down and filled a bucket with sand. "I think this bucket should go in the middle," he said and knocked down the centre of his friend's castle so that he could put his there. "Hey," said his friends but Ryan didn't listen.

Soon they were all hungry and sat down to eat. Ryan opened up a box of food and started eating. After a while he noticed that his friends were just watching him. "Didn't you bring anything to eat?" he asked. "You said not to bring anything because you were going to bring lunch for everyone." "Well I didn't," said Ryan nastily, "So you will just have to go without."

His friends wandered off crossly but were soon happy again when they started playing games in the water. Ryan wandered down and asked, "Can I play too? I promise I won't spoil the game." "No," said his friends, "we don't believe you any more. You said you would share the ball but you ran off with it. You said you would help us build our sand castle but you knocked it down. You said you would bring lunch for everyone to share but you didn't. We want to play by ourselves now." Ryan walked off sadly and thought about how right they were. He never did anything he said he would do. He hadn't known it was so important but now he did and the next time Ryan went to the beach he made sure that he always did what he said he would do.

MORAL – Words only have meaning when followed by action.

VIRTUES

CHOOSE THE VIRTUES IN ANY ORDER

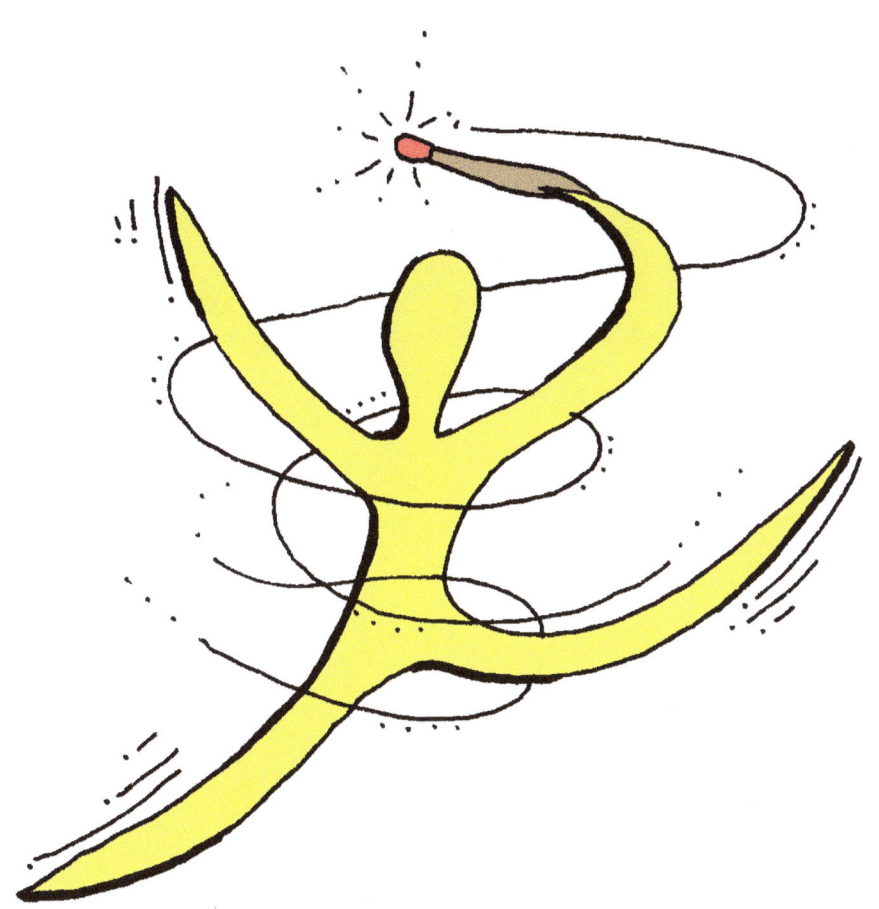

GENEROSITY

LESSON PLAN

SESSION 1

PRAYER: Sing prayers that have been learnt and any others that the children know. Ask them to be reverent because they are talking to God.

SCENARIO:
Read out the scenario, on the next page, to the children.

Use the Happy / Sad Face (as described in the beginning of the book) to discuss what could turn the situation around from a sad one to a happy one. Let the child who comes up with the solution first, turn the mouth from a gloomy face to a smiling one.

Bring out the toolbox (as described in the beginning of the book) and let the children guess which tool (virtue) they could use to fix the situation. Remind the children that these are the tools God gives us to help us in everything we do each day. Choose one child to take out the tool. Read out the virtue and the quotation. Ask the children to say the quotation with you a couple of times. Discuss what the quotation means

"To give and to be generous are attributes of Mine."
    Bahá'u'lláh

Discussion Thoughts - Being giving and generous are qualities of God and they should be qualities of ours too.

SONG: "Give it Away" - sing with actions.

ACTIVITY: Make Special Gifts – Use activity sheet provided.
    Purpose – to reflect on the quotation – to practice being generous.

SESSION 2

PRAYER: Sing prayers that have been learnt and any others that the children know. Ask them to be reverent because they are talking to God.

DISCUSSION REVIEW: What does generosity mean?
    Optional - Use discussion prompts sheet from the beginning of the book to help with the discussion.

SONG: "Give it Away" - sing with actions.

STORY: "Isobella Learns to Share"

GAME: Play a game based on the traditional 'Pass the Parcel' Instead of the person who receives the parcel when the music stops opening it up, they are responsible for giving it to the next person. The person who wins the prize at the end and takes off the last layer of wrapping paper must show generosity by sharing the prize with everyone else in the group. (Make sure the prize is something that can be easily shared around.)
    Purpose – To practice the act of giving.

ACTIVITY:
"To give and to be generous are attributes of Mine."
    Bahá'u'lláh
Use the quote visualization page to review the meaning of the quotation.
Say the quotation with the children a few times. Older children may be able to memorize it.
Give each child a copy of the quotation activity provided. Cut and glue in each part of the quotation in the correct order, colour in and assist the child to write in something that they can do to practice generosity.

GENEROSITY

SCENARIO

Scenario:

I love lollies.
Do you like lollies?
Lollies are really yummy.
Do you ever get sick of eating lollies or could you just eat them and eat them, and eat them?
There was once three boys who loved eating lollies.
Their names were Luke, Lance and Larn. Although they loved eating lollies, they were not allowed to eat them very often so it was a real treat when they were given lollies. One day Lance was given a whole bag of lollies and he ran to meet his friends and tell them about how lucky he was. Luke and Larn didn't look very happy at all. Lance was so busy talking that at first he didn't notice his friends' sad faces. But when he did, he stopped talking and just looked at them.
"What's wrong," asked Lance.
"We do like lollies but we don't have any." replied Larn and the two boys started walking away.
What should Lance do to help make his friends happy?

Possible solution:

He could share the lollies out with his friends so that they can all enjoy the lollies together.

The tool to fix the problem is: **Generosity**.

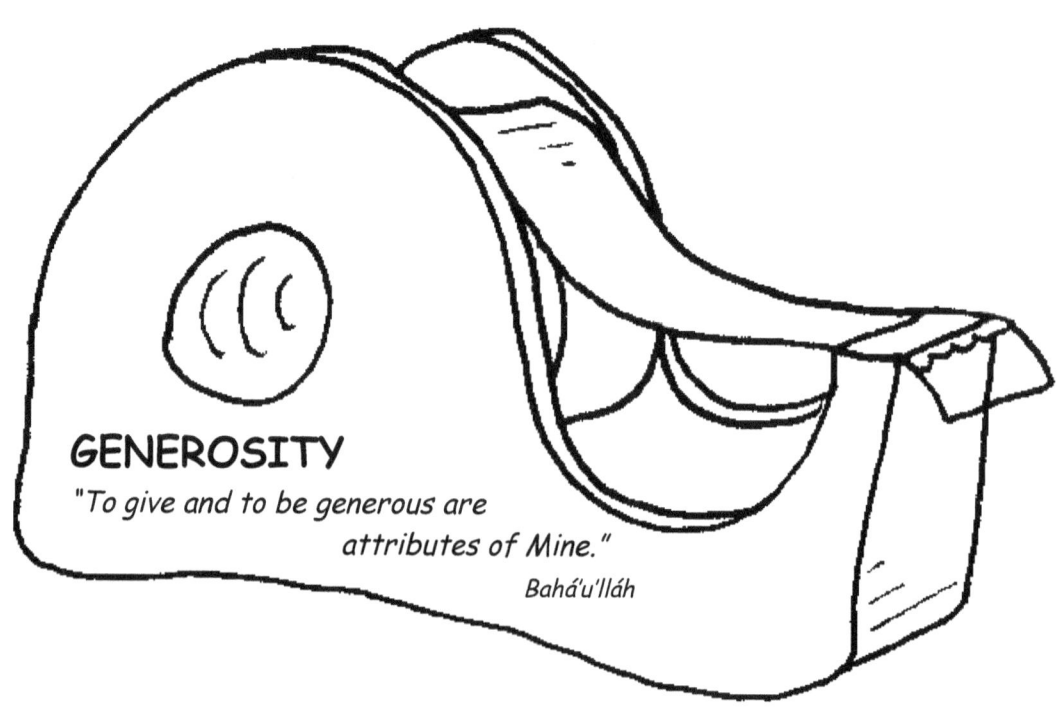

GENEROSITY
"To give and to be generous are attributes of Mine."
Bahá'u'lláh

GENEROSITY
SPECIAL GIFTS

INSTRUCTIONS:
- Copy this page on to white card.
- Cut out flower and quotation.
- Glue the quotation into the centre of the back of the flower.
- Punch holes into the tip of each petal.
- Colour in.
- Place a special gift, for example; a small soap, on top of the quotation.
- Curve the petal up to the centre and thread gift rap ribbon through the holes and tie together.
- Give to someone special.

EACH CHILD WILL NEED:
- Scissors, glue.
- Crowns / pencils.
- A copy of this page.
- A piece of ribbon.
- Access to a hole punch (children may need assistance)
- A small gift.

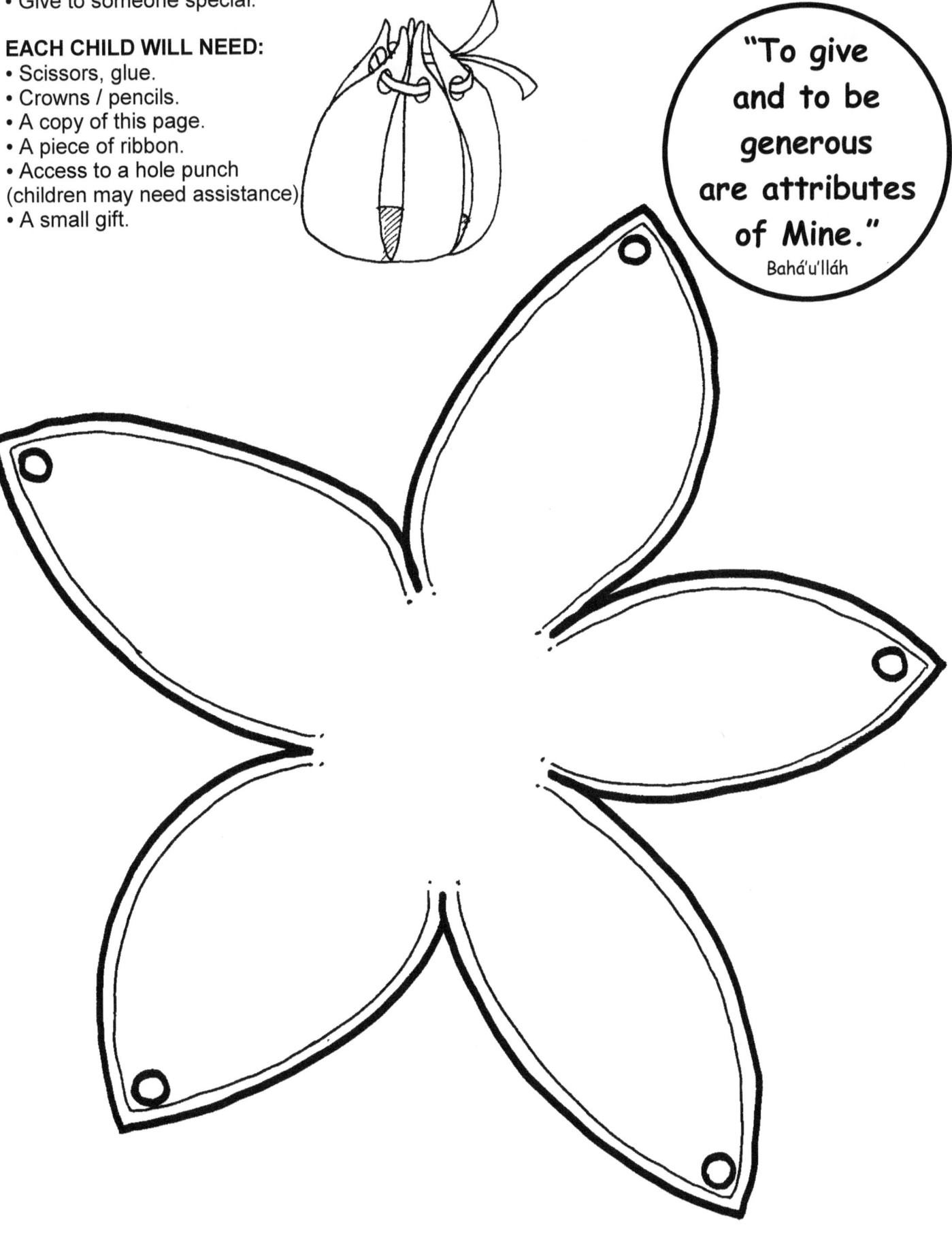

"To give and to be generous are attributes of Mine."
Bahá'u'lláh

Quote Visualization

GENEROSITY

"To give and to be generous are attributes of Mine."

Bahá'u'lláh

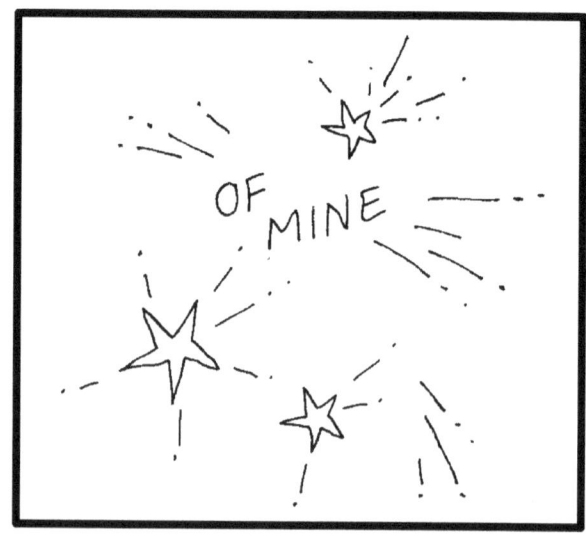

Quotation activity worksheet

GENEROSITY

GENEROSITY

"To give and to be generous are attributes of Mine."

Bahá'u'lláh

☐ ☐ ☐ ☐

I can show generosity by.................................
....

GENEROSITY

"To give and to be generous are attributes of Mine."

Bahá'u'lláh

☐ ☐ ☐ ☐

I can show generosity by.................................
....

GENEROSITY

Quotation activity worksheet

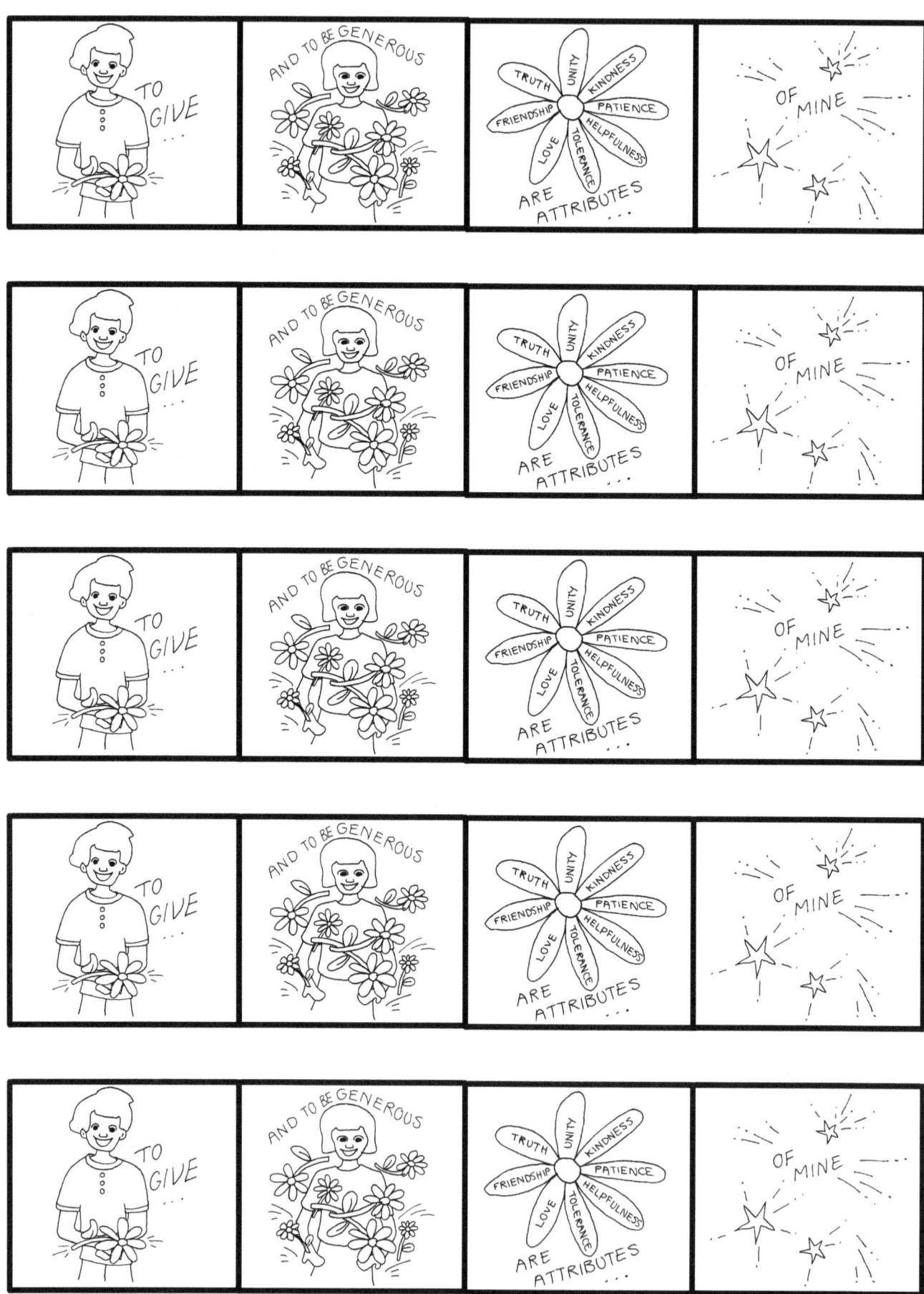

ISOBELLA LEARNS TO SHARE

GENEROSITY STORY

Isobella was very excited because she was going to have a birthday party. She had sat all morning just thinking about all the wonderful toys and presents and food. It was the first real birthday party she had ever had.

Finally the time came and her friends started arriving. First Vanessa, then David and finally Peta. They all had a present for her wrapped in beautiful shiny paper. Vanessa brought her some Lego. David gave her a book and Peta presented her with her very own paint set. Isobella was delighted and grabbed them all up. She ran to her bedroom and shut the door so no-one else could use them. Then she sat there and thought, "These are all mine."

She looked at them admiringly for a long time until, after a while, she started to feel kind of lonely with just her toys for company.

Slowly she opened the door and peeked out. She could just see her friends in the lounge playing party games. They were laughing and singing and having a wonderful time. Isobella closed the door and sat down next to her new toys again. Instead of them making her feel happy she now just felt sad.

"This is no fun," she said to herself. So she picked them all up, took them out to the lounge and for the rest of the afternoon all four friends shared the new toys. They delighted in opening new packages and generally had a wonderful time. At the end of the day, when everyone was leaving, Isobella thought that it was the best day she had ever had. The part that made it the best was not the food or the toys or the presents. It was the wonderful friends she had to share it with.

MORAL – Being generous is good for others but it is also good for us.

HELPFULNESS

LESSON PLAN

SESSION 1

PRAYER: Sing prayers that have been learnt and any others that the children know. Ask them to be reverent because they are talking to God.

SCENARIO:
Read out the scenario on the next page to the children.

Use the Happy / Sad Face (as described in the beginning of the book) to discuss what could turn the situation around from a sad one to a happy one. Let the child who comes up with the solution first turn the mouth from a gloomy face to a smiling one.

Bring out the toolbox (as described in the beginning of the book) and let the children guess which tool (virtue) they could use to fix the situation. Remind the children that these are the tools God gives us to help us in everything we do each day. Choose one child to take out the tool. Read out the virtue and the quotation. Ask the children to say the quotation with you a couple of times. Discuss what the quotation means

"Because the members of the world of humanity are unable to exist without being banded together, co-operation and helpfulness is the basis of human society."
'Abdu'l-Bahá

Discussion Thoughts - Helping each other allows the world to run smoothly. If we didn't help each other then we would all feel alone and we would not be able to accomplish anything.

SONG: "Helpfulness" - sing with actions.

ACTIVITY: Helpfulness Pyramids – Use activity sheet provided.
Purpose – to reflect on the quotation – to understand that helpfulness should be the basis on which all humanity functions.

SESSION 2

PRAYER: Sing prayers that have been learnt and any others that the children know. Ask them to be reverent because they are talking to God.

DISCUSSION REVIEW: What does helpfulness mean?
Optional - Use discussion prompts sheet from the beginning of the book to help with the discussion.

SONG: "Helpfulness" - sing with actions.

STORY: "The Four Little Pigs"

GAME: Make a helpful people chain. Everyone sits in a line holding hands with the people next to them. Start at one end of the line with the first person standing up and pulling the person next to them up as well. Then the second person pulls the next up and so on until everyone has been pulled / helped to their feet.
Purpose – to practice being helpful.

ACTIVITY:
"Because the members of the world of humanity are unable to exist without being banded together, co-operation and helpfulness is the basis of human society."
'Abdu'l-Bahá
Use the quote visualization page to review the meaning of the quotation.
Say the quotation with the children a few times. Older children may be able to memorize it.
Give each child a copy of the quotation activity provided. Cut and glue in each part of the quotation in the correct order, colour in and assist the child to write in something that they can do to practice helpfulness.

HELPFULNESS

SCENARIO

Scenario:
There are lots of jobs to do around the house.
Who likes doing jobs?
Sometimes jobs are hard work but they still need to be done.
Milly is a little girl that does not like doing jobs. When anyone says, "Time to clean up," or "Could someone please help me?" Milly runs away and hides.
Do you ever run away when there is a job to do?
One day Milly wanted to go to the park, but her mother said, "I have too many jobs to do, there is not enough time to go to the park today. There are clothes to wash, beds to be made, dishes to be done and floors to sweep." When she heard that there was work to do she ran away and hid in her room as usual. Milly was not happy.
What could Milly do to help herself become happy again?

Possible solution:
Milly could go and help her mum clean up and do the jobs quickly so that they would still have time to go to the park.

The tool to fix the problem is: **Helpfulness**.

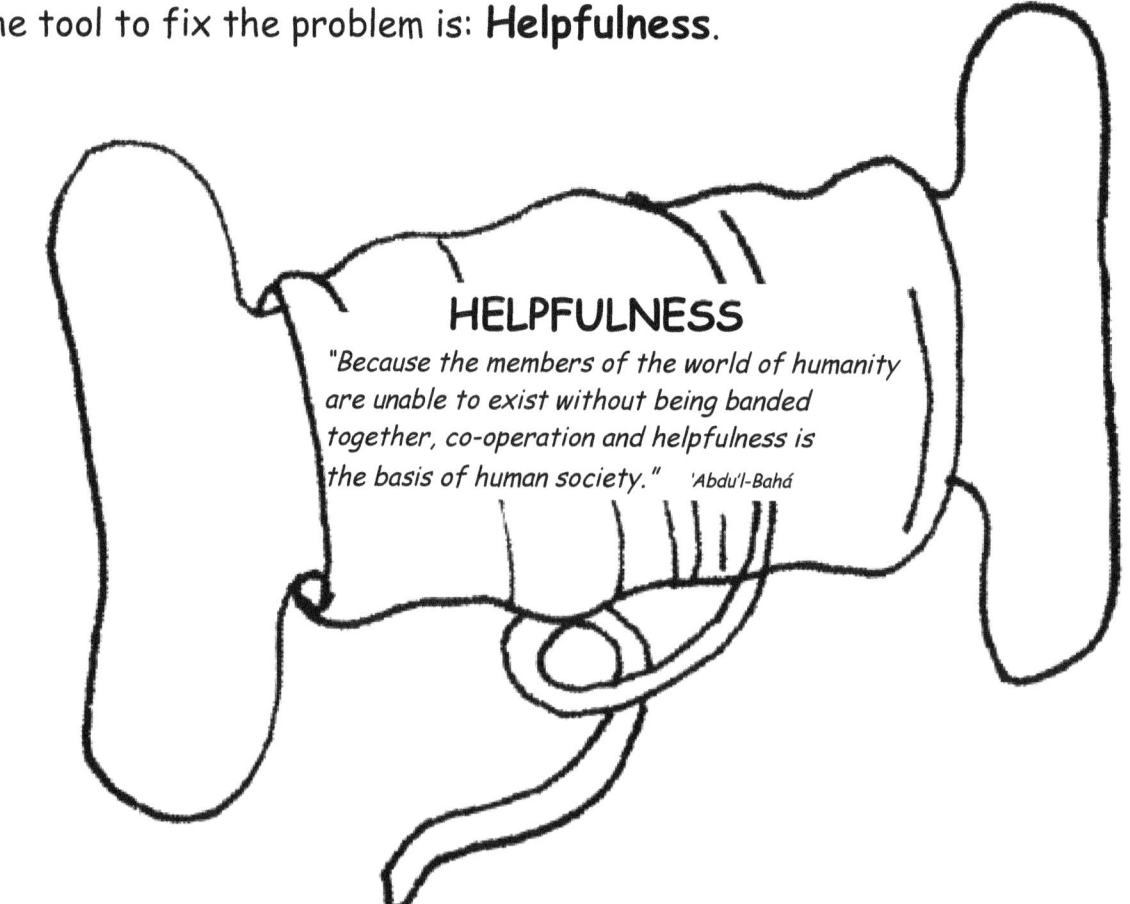

HELPFULNESS
"Because the members of the world of humanity are unable to exist without being banded together, co-operation and helpfulness is the basis of human society." 'Abdu'l-Bahá

HELPFULNESS
HELPFULNESS PYRAMIDS

EACH CHILD WILL NEED:
• Pencils / Crowns, Scissors
• A copy of one pyramid.
• Glue

INSTRUCTIONS:
• Copy this page on to white card.
• Cut out a pyramid.
• Colour in.
• Glue together using area marked 'glue'.

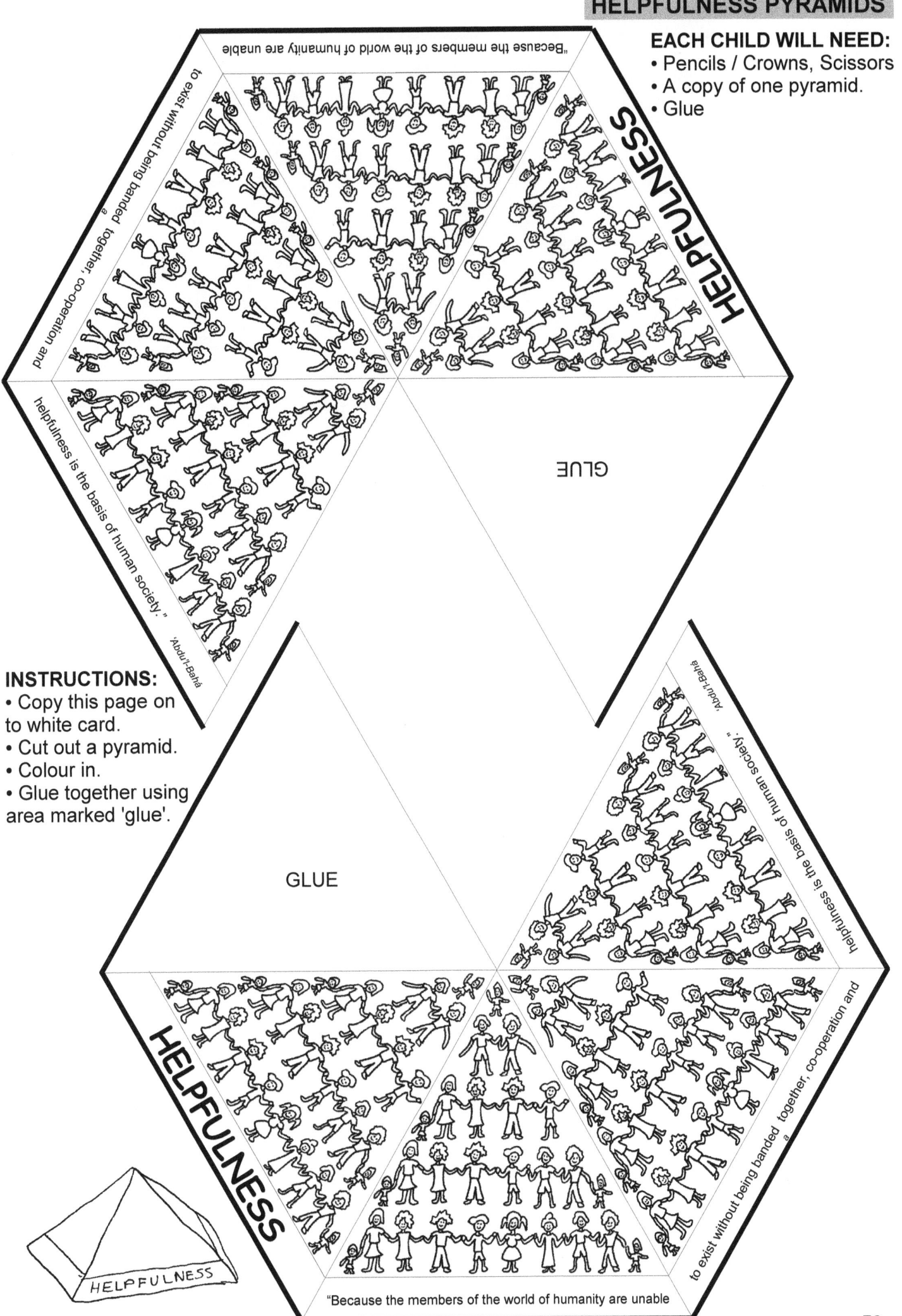

HELPFULNESS

Quote Visualization

HELPFULNESS

"Because the members of the world of humanity are unable to exist without being banded together, co-operation and helpfulness is the basis of human society." — 'Abdu'l-Bahá

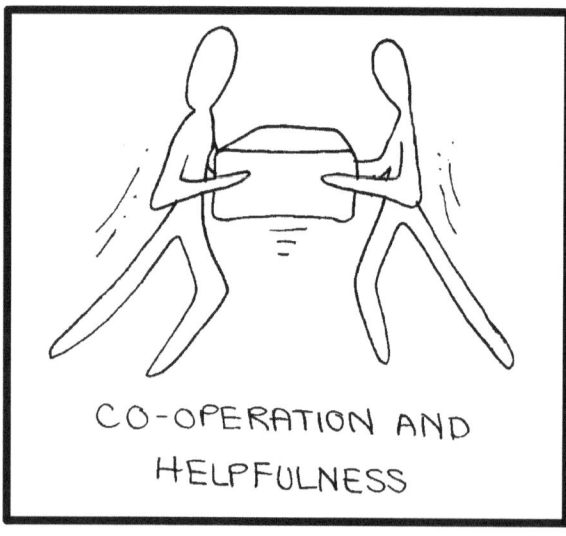

Quotation activity worksheet

HELPFULNESS

HELPFULNESS

"Because the members of the world of humanity are unable to exist without being banded together, co-operation and helpfulness is the basis of human society." — 'Abdu'l-Bahá

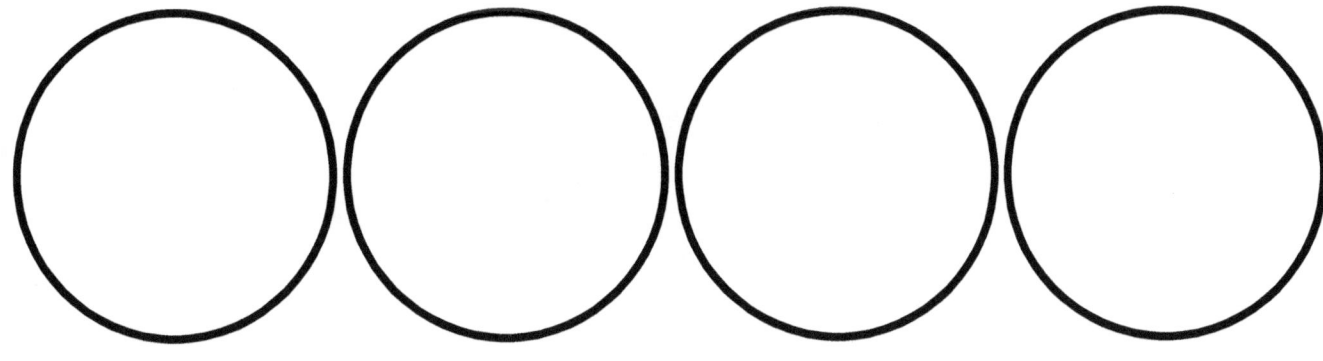

I am helpful when I……………………………………………
………………………………………………………

HELPFULNESS

"Because the members of the world of humanity are unable to exist without being banded together, co-operation and helpfulness is the basis of human society." — 'Abdu'l-Bahá

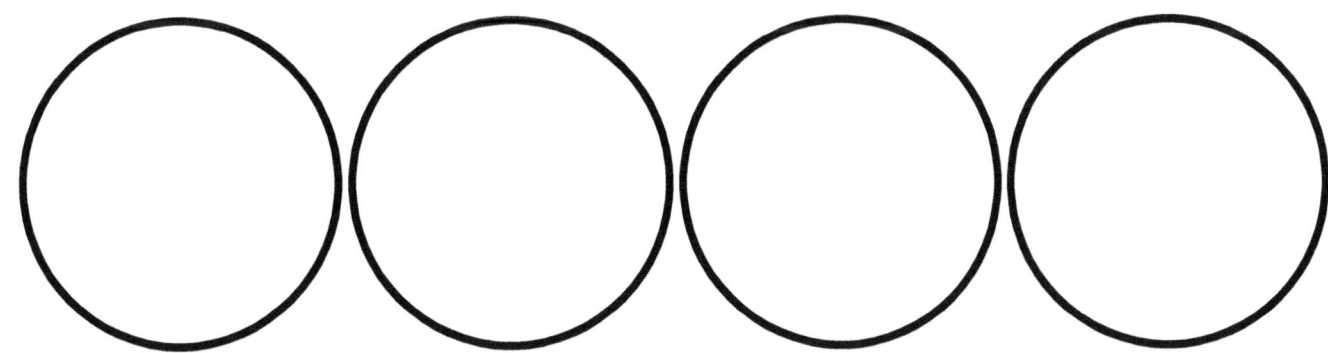

I am helpful when I……………………………………………
………………………………………………………

HELPFULNESS

Quotation activity worksheet

THE FOUR LITTLE PIGS

HELPFULNESS STORY

There was once four little pigs who lived in a beautiful forest with big tall trees and lovely wild flowers. It was very peaceful, most of the time, but there was also a wolf that lived in the forest who would come around every night to look for something to eat. The pigs were always hiding in new places but now they had run out of hiding places so they decided that they needed to build a house that would be strong enough to keep the wolf out.

The first little pig said, "I am going to build a house next to the lake so I will always be able to get water when I need it." He started to build straight away.

The second little pig said, "I am going to build a tree house. The wolf will never be able to get me if I am high up in a tree." So, he started carrying wood up the tree.

The third and fourth little pigs looked up at the sky and saw that the sun was shining very brightly. The third little piggy said, "The sun is shining brightly now, but a day is not a long time to build a house. Let's work together to make a house more quickly and extra strong."
"I agree," said the fourth little piggy and so they began building.

The first little pig was beginning to realize that building a house was a big job. "Whew," he sighed wiping sweat off his face. "This is hard work, I will never get it finished in time. I am going to make things easier for myself. I will make the roof from dried grasses instead of tin to make sure it is finished before dark. The sun went down, the moon came up and who should come prowling through the trees but the wolf. He found the first little pig's house and tried pushing on the wall but it was strong and he couldn't push it down.
He cried out, "My dear little piggy, come out for me.
        I am so hungry, come out and see."
The first little pig replied,
    "My dear big wolf, please let me be.
    I know you are hungry, I don't need to see."
As the wolf felt along the wall he noticed the grass roof and with one swipe of his hand the roof was off and the first little piggy became dinner.

HELPFULNESS
STORY

Meanwhile, the second little pig was starting to feel tired. "I must have a rest, just for a little while," he thought and so he lay down to rest. Before he knew it the sun was going down and the forest was getting dark but he still had no house to hide in. It wasn't long before the wolf came creeping through his part of the forest and who should he find under a half built house, but the second little pig. Again the wolf cried out,

"My dear little piggy, come out for me.
I am so hungry, come out and see."

The second little pig replied,

"My dear big wolf, please let me be.
I know you are hungry, I don't want to see."

The wolf reached behind the tree with his long arms and the second little pig also became the wolf's dinner.

Later, the third and fourth little pigs were just finishing their house. During the day they had both felt tired, but they took turns working while the other had a rest. They finally stood back to look at their house. Because they had worked together, they had made it very strong and as the sun went down and the moon came up they went inside their new house to wait safely for the wolf. It wasn't long before he came and for the third time he cried out,

"My dear little piggys, come out for me.
I am so hungry, come out and see."

The third and fourth little pigs replied together,

"Our dear big wolf, we are clever you will see.
We worked together, we knew you were hungry."

The wolf pushed, and the wolf pulled but no matter how much he tried the walls stayed strong and the roof stayed on and so the wolf went away and that night when the wolf went to bed he was still hungry.

As for the third and fourth little pigs, they spent the night dancing and rejoicing at how well they had helped each other.

MORAL - People were made to help each other. Helping and supporting each other means we can do things much better than if we were just doing it by ourself.

FRIENDLINESS

LESSON PLAN

SESSION 1

PRAYER: Sing prayers that have been learnt and any others that the children know. Ask them to be reverent because they are talking to God.

SCENARIO:
Read out the scenario on the next page to the children.

Use the Happy / Sad Face (as described in the beginning of the book) to discuss what could turn the situation around from a sad one to a happy one. Let the child who comes up with the solution first turn the mouth from a gloomy face to a smiling one.

Bring out the toolbox (as described in the beginning of the book) and let the children guess which tool (virtue) they could use to fix the situation. Remind the children that these are the tools God gives us to help us in everything we do each day. Choose one child to take out the tool. Read out the virtue and the quotation. Ask the children to say the quotation with you a couple of times. Discuss what the quotation means

"be.... a true and loving and trusted friend to all the peoples of the earth."
    'Abdu'l-Bahá

Discussion Thoughts – To be a good friend to someone is to be someone who can be trusted and who always cares about how others are feeling.

SONG: "True Friends" - sing with actions.

ACTIVITY: Friendship Bracelets – Use activity sheet provided.
Purpose – to reflect on the quotation – to practice being friendly.

SESSION 2

PRAYER: Sing prayers that have been learnt and any others that the children know. Ask them to be reverent because they are talking to God.

DISCUSSION REVIEW: What does friendliness mean?
    Optional - Use discussion prompts sheet from the beginning of the book to help with the discussion.

SONG: "True Friends" - sing with actions.

STORY: "A Friend in Need"

GAME: Divide the children into pairs. Use a shirt or tea towel to blindfold one child in each pair. The other child will be the trusted friend who leads them carefully around the room. The children then swap over so that the other has a turn at being a trusted friend.
Purpose – To reflect on what it means to be a trusted friend.

ACTIVITY:
"be.... a true and loving and trusted friend to all the peoples of the earth."
    'Abdu'l-Bahá
Use the quote visualization page to review the meaning of the quotation.
Say the quotation with the children a few times. Older children may be able to memorize it.
Give each child a copy of the quotation activity provided. Cut and glue in each part of the quotation in the correct order, colour in and assist the child to write in something that they can do to practice friendliness.

FRIENDLINESS

SCENARIO

Scenario:

Playgrounds are a lovely places in which to play.
Do you like playing in playgrounds?
Being with friends makes playgrounds even more fun.
There was once two very good friends who went to school together every day. There names were Larry and Lenny. One day they heard that there was going to be a new flying fox in the playground. The two boys were very excited. When playtime came they ran out to play. Everyone wanted to play on the new flying fox. Larry ran to have a turn but when he turned around he found that Lenny was crying.
"Why are you crying Lenny?" he asked.
"I am not tall enough to reach the flying fox," he said with tears in his eyes.
What could Larry do to make Lenny happy?

Possible solutions:

They could go and play somewhere else together.
Larry could lift Lenny up and help him reach the flying fox.

The tool to fix the problem is: **Friendliness**.

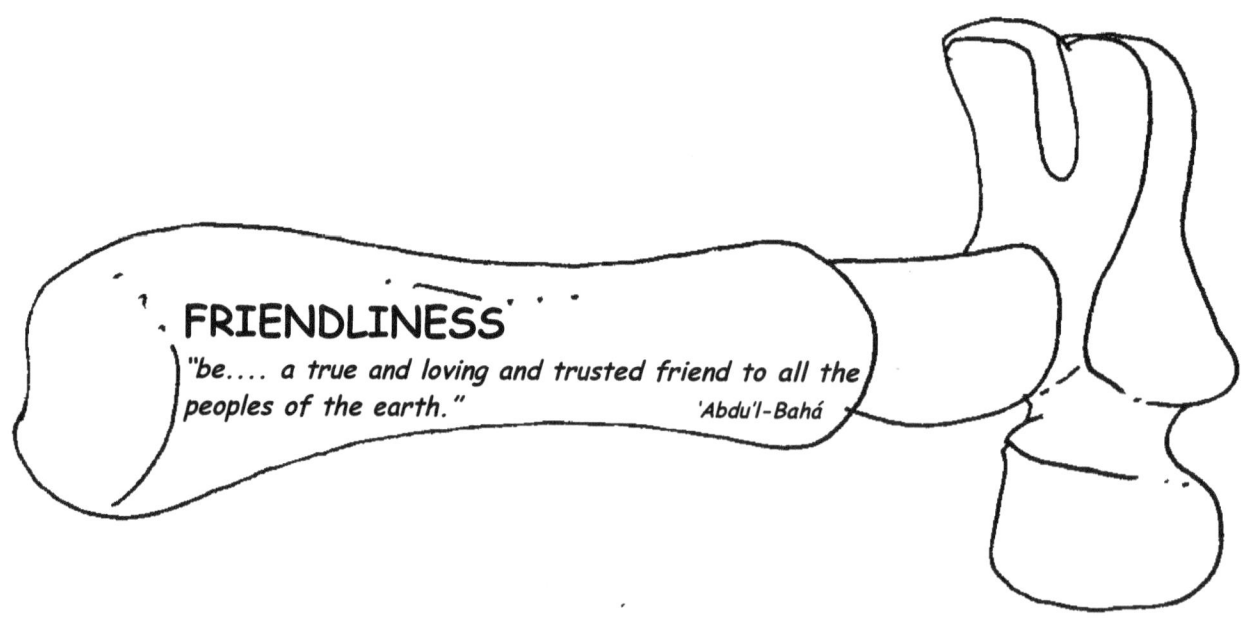

FRIENDLINESS
"be.... a true and loving and trusted friend to all the peoples of the earth."   'Abdu'l-Bahá

FRIENDSHIP BRACELETS

INSTRUCTIONS:

- Copy this page on to coloured card.
- Cut out a quotation.
- Punch two holes in the quotation where marked.
- Thread a piece of string through the holes and then through some beads.
- Tie into a circle to fit around a wrist.
- Repeat the above to make a second friendship Bracelet. Each child should have two each. One to keep and one to give away to a friend. The bracelets are a reminder to the two friends to always love and trust each other.

EACH CHILD WILL NEED:

- Two pieces of string and a hole punch
- Scissors / beads
- Four quotation strips

"be.... a true and loving and trusted friend to all the peoples of the earth." 'Abdu'l-Bahá

"be.... a true and loving and trusted friend to all the peoples of the earth." 'Abdu'l-Bahá

"be.... a true and loving and trusted friend to all the peoples of the earth." 'Abdu'l-Bahá

"be.... a true and loving and trusted friend to all the peoples of the earth." 'Abdu'l-Bahá

"be.... a true and loving and trusted friend to all the peoples of the earth." 'Abdu'l-Bahá

"be.... a true and loving and trusted friend to all the peoples of the earth." 'Abdu'l-Bahá

"be.... a true and loving and trusted friend to all the peoples of the earth." 'Abdu'l-Bahá

"be.... a true and loving and trusted friend to all the peoples of the earth." 'Abdu'l-Bahá

"be.... a true and loving and trusted friend to all the peoples of the earth." 'Abdu'l-Bahá

"be.... a true and loving and trusted friend to all the peoples of the earth." 'Abdu'l-Bahá

"be.... a true and loving and trusted friend to all the peoples of the earth." 'Abdu'l-Bahá

"be.... a true and loving and trusted friend to all the peoples of the earth." 'Abdu'l-Bahá

"be.... a true and loving and trusted friend to all the peoples of the earth." 'Abdu'l-Bahá

"be.... a true and loving and trusted friend to all the peoples of the earth." 'Abdu'l-Bahá

"be.... a true and loving and trusted friend to all the peoples of the earth." 'Abdu'l-Bahá

"be.... a true and loving and trusted friend to all the peoples of the earth." 'Abdu'l-Bahá

"be.... a true and loving and trusted friend to all the peoples of the earth." 'Abdu'l-Bahá

"be.... a true and loving and trusted friend to all the peoples of the earth." 'Abdu'l-Bahá

"be.... a true and loving and trusted friend to all the peoples of the earth." 'Abdu'l-Bahá

"be.... a true and loving and trusted friend to all the peoples of the earth." 'Abdu'l-Bahá

"be.... a true and loving and trusted friend to all the peoples of the earth." 'Abdu'l-Bahá

"be.... a true and loving and trusted friend to all the peoples of the earth." 'Abdu'l-Bahá

"be.... a true and loving and trusted friend to all the peoples of the earth." 'Abdu'l-Bahá

"be.... a true and loving and trusted friend to all the peoples of the earth." 'Abdu'l-Bahá

Quote Visualization — FRIENDLINESS

FRIENDLINESS
"be.... a true and loving and trusted friend to all the peoples of the earth." — 'Abdu'l-Bahá

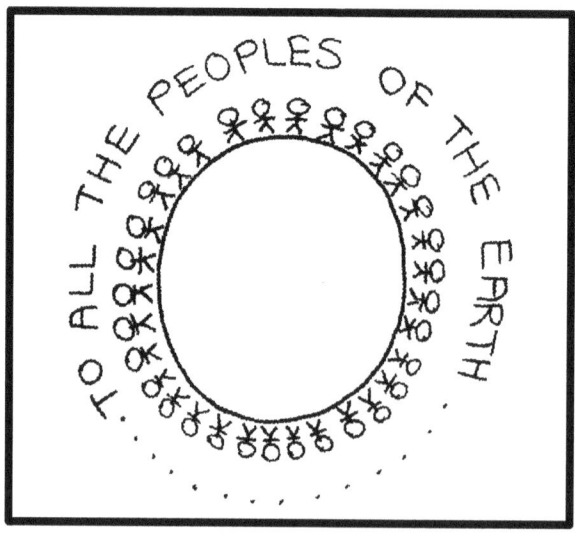

Quotation activity worksheet FRIENDLINESS

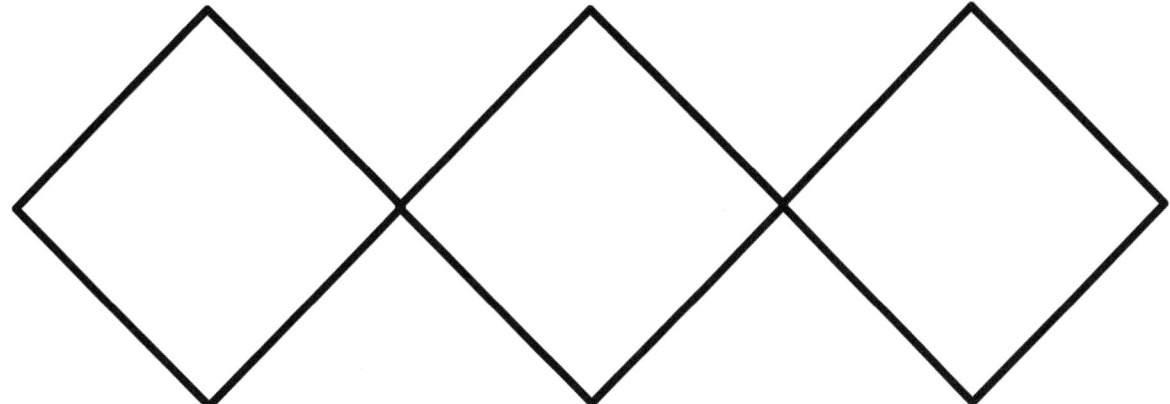

FRIENDLINESS
"be.... a true and loving and trusted friend to all the peoples of the earth." 'Abdu'l-Bahá

I am being a good friend when I....................
....

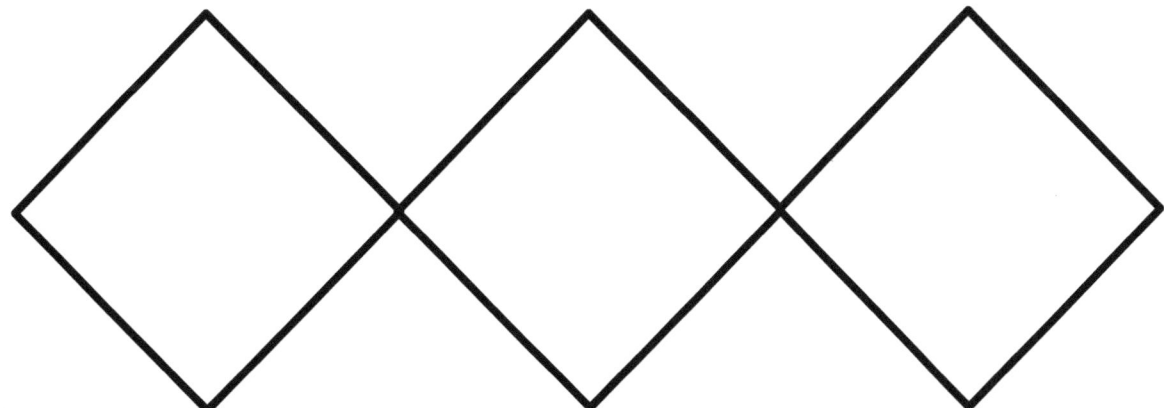

FRIENDLINESS
"be.... a true and loving and trusted friend to all the peoples of the earth." 'Abdu'l-Bahá

I am being a good friend when I....................
....

FRIENDLINESS

Quotation activity worksheet

A FRIEND IN NEED

FRIENDLINESS
STORY

Pip and Pop were flowers who loved nothing better than gazing up at the sky and soaking up the warm sun. They would stretch out their petals and sway backwards and forwards in the soft breeze. Summer was a lovely time with no worries and nothing to do but relax. One day while they were doing nothing at all they heard a little voice calling to them.
"Excuse me," said the voice, "could you please move one of your petals so that I can have some sunlight."

Pip and Pop looked around them but could see no-body around. Then they looked down and there growing in the shadow of their petals, was a tiny sunflower plant. Pop was annoyed. "What are you doing disturbing the peace. Can't you see we are busy doing nothing."
"I just need a little sunlight or I will not be able to grow and instead will die."
Pop was not interested and went back to soaking up the sun, ignoring the protests from the little sunflower plant.
Pip however, looked at the little sunflower plant and then at the sun. "Here you go," Pip said adjusting his petals to let some light through, "There is plenty of sunlight for all of us."
The three plants spent the rest of the summer bathing in the warm sun.

FRIENDLINESS
STORY

Winter came and with it the rain. The sunflower plant had grown very tall and so had many of the other plants. Pip and Pop however were only small plants and now were under the shadow of larger ones. The rain came down on the taller plants which caught the rain first. They drank the water up before Pip or Pop could get any.

"Water, water," cried Pop.
"Excuse me, could someone spare some water," called Pip.

At first it seemed that no-one had heard them and then the little sunflower who was now very tall bent down and gazed at them. Then, using one of his petals as a cup he caught some water and poured it over the two little flowers.
"You gave me sunlight Pip, when I was small. Now I can be a friend to you and give you water." explained the sunflower.
"Next time, you should remember, little Pop, that friends come in all sizes."
Pop didn't say anything, but he thankfully drank up the rain water.

MORAL – Good friends are those that you can trust to help you out when you need it the most.

GENTLENESS

LESSON PLAN

SESSION 1

PRAYER: Sing prayers that have been learnt and any others that the children know. Ask them to be reverent because they are talking to God.

SCENARIO:
Read out the scenario on the next page to the children.

Use the Happy / Sad Face (as described in the beginning of the book) to discuss what could turn the situation around from a sad one to a happy one. Let the child who comes up with the solution first turn the mouth from a gloomy face to a smiling one.

Bring out the toolbox (as described in the beginning of the book) and let the children guess which tool (virtue) they could use to fix the situation. Remind the children that these are the tools God gives us to help us in everything we do each day. Choose one child to take out the tool. Read out the virtue and the quotation. Ask the children to say the quotation with you a couple of times. Discuss what the quotation means

"Should anyone wax angry with you, respond to him with gentleness...."
    Bahá'u'lláh

Discussion Thoughts - If someone pushes us or makes us feel upset we should not push or hurt them back. Instead we should speak and act gently. If we show anger back then that will only make them more upset and things will get worse and worse.

SONG: "Gentle Hands" - sing with actions.

ACTIVITY: Gentle Hands – Use activity provided.
    Purpose – to reflect on the quotation and practice being friendly.

SESSION 2

PRAYER: Sing prayers that have been learnt and any others that the children know. Ask them to be reverent because they are talking to God.

DISCUSSION REVIEW: What does gentleness mean?
    Use some toy animals to demonstrate what gentleness looks like. Let each child have a turn. Use a real pet if possible.
    Optional - Use discussion prompts sheet from the beginning of the book to help with the discussion.

SONG: "Gentle Hands" - sing with actions.

STORY: "Gentle Ginger"

GAME: Get into pairs. Ask one child to make silly faces as if they are making the other person angry. The other person then responds with gentleness by gently patting the other person. Swap roles so everyone has a turn at being gentle and angry / annoying.
    Purpose – To reflect on the quotation – to understand what it means to be gentle.

ACTIVITY:
    "Should anyone wax angry with you, respond to him with gentleness...."
        Bahá'u'lláh
Use the quote visualization page to review the meaning of the quotation.
Say the quotation with the children a few times. Older children may be able to memorize it.
Give each child a copy of the quotation activity provided. Cut and glue in each part of the quotation in the correct order, colour in and assist the child to write in something that they can do to practice gentleness.

GENTLENESS

SCENARIO

Scenario:
Who likes to play with people who push other people around?
I don't think anyone would like to play with someone who scratched, bit, hit or grabbed things.
There was once a girl who did all these things. No-body wanted to play with her but the little girl couldn't understand why. No-one ever said anything to her, they just walked away and went to play with someone else when they saw her coming. The little girl felt very lonely and would usually sit alone eating her lunch and play a game by herself in the corner of the playground. She felt very sad.
What do you think you could do to help the little girl make friends?

Possible solutions:
You could kindly explain why people didn't like playing with her and help to teach her how to play gently.

The tool to fix the problem is: **Gentleness**.

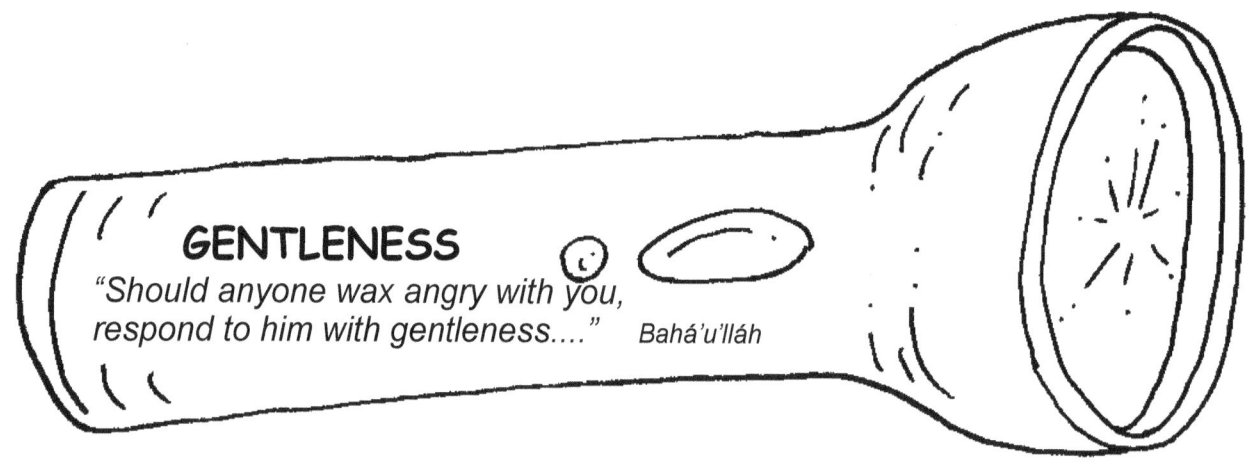

GENTLENESS
"Should anyone wax angry with you, respond to him with gentleness...." *Bahá'u'lláh*

GENTLENESS
GENTLE HANDS

INSTRUCTIONS:
- Ask each child to trace around their hand and then cut it out.
- Glue shiny pieces of paper over the hand to decorate and then trim the edges.
- Cut out a quotation and glue into the centre of the hand.
- Colour in.

EACH CHILD WILL NEED:
- Scissors, glue
- Crayons / pencils
- A copy of a quotation.
- Half a sheet of coloured card.
- Shiny pieces of paper.

"Should anyone wax angry with you, respond to him with gentleness...."
Bahá'u'lláh

Quote Visualization

GENTLENESS

GENTLENESS
"Should anyone wax angry with you, respond to him with gentleness...."
Bahá'u'lláh

Quotation activity worksheet

GENTLENESS

GENTLENESS
"Should anyone wax angry with you, respond to him with gentleness...."
Bahá'u'lláh

I am being gentle when I ....
....

GENTLENESS
"Should anyone wax angry with you, respond to him with gentleness...."
Bahá'u'lláh

I am being gentle when I ....
....

GENTLENESS

Quotation activity worksheet

GENTLE GINGER

GENTLENESS STORY

There was once an orange cat named ginger who loved scaring people. She would wait behind a bush where she couldn't be seen and then suddenly with a loud, "Miaoww," she would jump out and pounce on somebody unexpectedly. Ginger would often scratch them and sometimes even bite. People would then run away and not come back. Ginger liked her game; that is, she liked it all except for the bit where they never came back.

Ginger wanted a friend but no-one wanted to stay and play with her. It was a lovely summer day when she hid behind a bush in her usual spot ready to pounce on someone. It wasn't long before someone came by and Ginger rushed out, miaowing loudly. The little boy she jumped on, instead of running away, stood there laughing. "Hello little cat," he said, "you gave me such a fright."

The cat and the little boy walked down the road together chatting away. The boy was rubbing his arm and the cat looked up to see a long scratch which he had made when he pounced on the boy. The little boy looked at the cat thoughtfully. "You need to be gentle little cat or you might really hurt someone one day." Ginger just purred and rubbed against the little boy's leg until it was time for the boy to go home.

The next day Ginger hid in his usual spot behind the bush and waited for someone to come by. This time however, instead of scratching and biting them, he just miaowed and purred and ran about between their legs. Each time the person, instead of running away, stopped and patted him, talked to him and sometimes gave him something to eat. By the end of the week Gentle Ginger had lots and lots of friends.

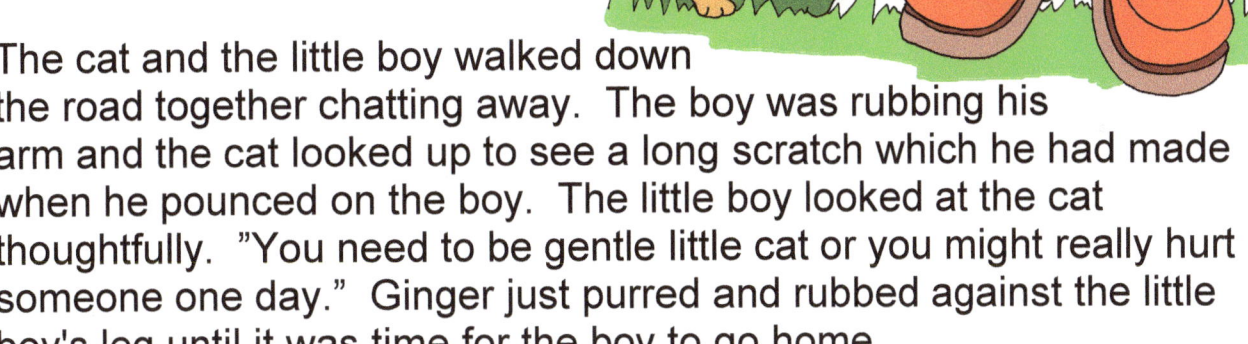

MORAL – We can easily hurt others when we play but we all like a friend who play's gently with us.

REVERENCE

LESSON PLAN

SESSION 1

PRAYER: Sing prayers that have been learnt and any others that the children know. Ask them to be reverent because they are talking to God.

SCENARIO:
Read out the scenario on the next page to the children.

Use the Happy / Sad Face (as described in the beginning of the book) to discuss what could turn the situation around from a sad one to a happy one. Let the child who comes up with the solution first turn the mouth from a gloomy face to a smiling one.

Bring out the toolbox (as described in the beginning of the book) and let the children guess which tool (virtue) they could use to fix the situation. Remind the children that these are the tools God gives us to help us in everything we do each day. Choose one child to take out the tool. Read out the virtue and the quotation. Ask the children to say the quotation with you a couple of times. Discuss what the quotation means

"He who is endowed with reverence is endowed with a great station."
    Bahá'u'lláh

Discussion Thoughts - Reverence connects us to God which makes us stronger inside. Even a king is only a person but a connection with God can make us even greater than a king giving us a station and strength that we could never have if we were just on our own.

SONG: "Reverence Makes Me Stronger" - sing with actions.

ACTIVITY: A Place of Reverence – Give each child a piece of paper. Put on some relaxing music and ask the children to draw a picture of a place that makes you feel reverent or peaceful. Ask the children to do this without talking.
Purpose – to reflect on the meaning of reverence - to practice being reverent

SESSION 2

PRAYER: Sing prayers that have been learnt and any others that the children know. Ask them to be reverent because they are talking to God.

DISCUSSION REVIEW: What does reverence mean?
    Optional - Use discussion prompts sheet from the beginning of the book to help with the discussion.

SONG: "Reverence Makes Me Stronger" - sing with actions.

STORY: "A Place of Peace"

GAME: Ask the children to lie down and close their eyes. Read out the meditation provided.
    Purpose – To reflect on the meaning of reverence – to practice being reverent..

ACTIVITY:
"He who is endowed with reverence is endowed with a great station."
    Bahá'u'lláh
Use the quote visualization page to review the meaning of the quotation.
Say the quotation with the children a few times. Older children may be able to memorize it.
Give each child a copy of the quotation activity provided. Cut and glue in each part of the quotation in the correct order, colour in and assist the child to write in something that they can do to practice reverence.

REVERENCE

SCENARIO

Scenario:
Have you ever been to a cemetery?
Cemeteries can be very sad places. People sometimes go there to remember people who have died.
There was once a boy called Peter who had a young brother named Tim. Tim was very energetic and loved to run. One day their mother took them to a cemetery to see the grave of their grandmother. Their mother knelt down and placed some flowers on the gravestone. Peter started to kneel down too when he suddenly noticed that Tim was running around the gravestones laughing. He thought it was all a game.
Other people at the cemetery started to frown in Tim's direction. What could Peter do to help?

Possible solutions:
He could walk Tim back to his grandmother's graveside and explain to him that cemeteries are places where you need to be quiet to show respect to those who have died and to those who are visiting.

The tool to fix the problem is: **Reverence**.

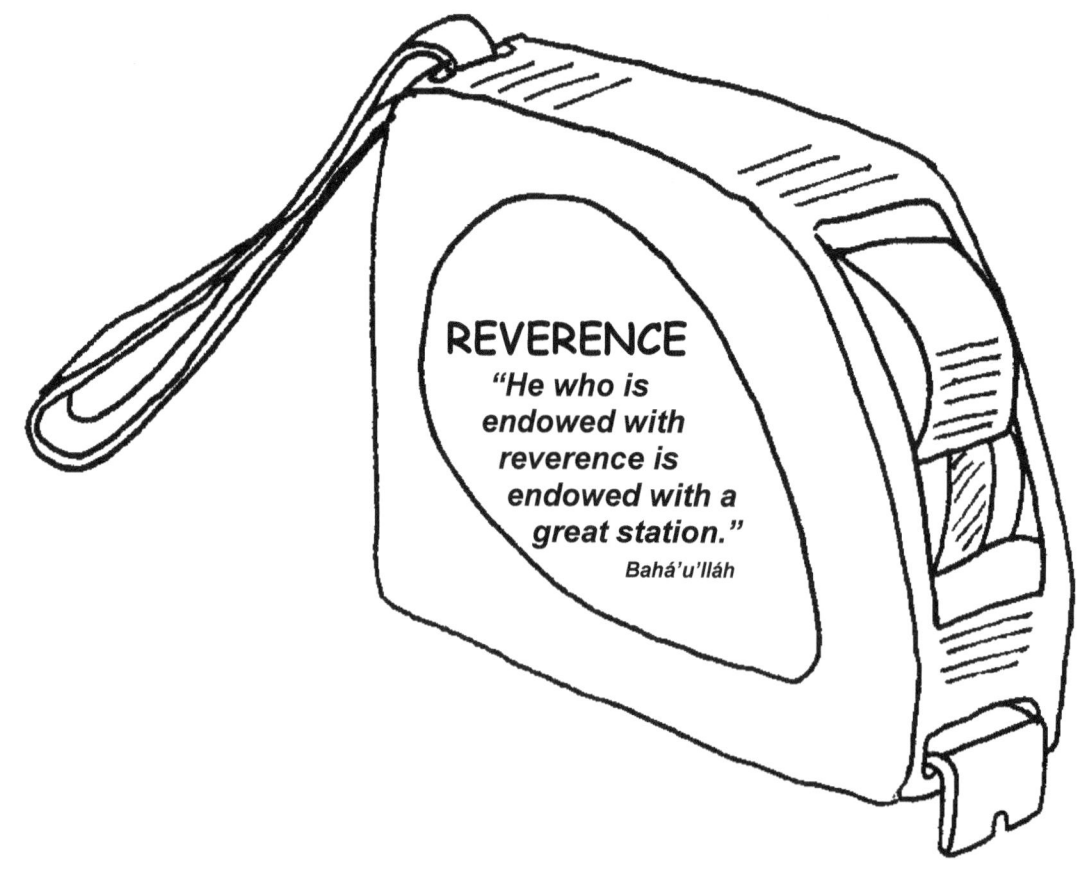

REVERENCE
"He who is endowed with reverence is endowed with a great station."
Bahá'u'lláh

Quote Visualization

REVERENCE

REVERENCE

"He who is endowed with reverence is endowed with a great station."

Bahá'u'lláh

REVERENCE

Quotation activity worksheet

REVERENCE
"He who is endowed with reverence is endowed with a great station."
Bahá'u'lláh

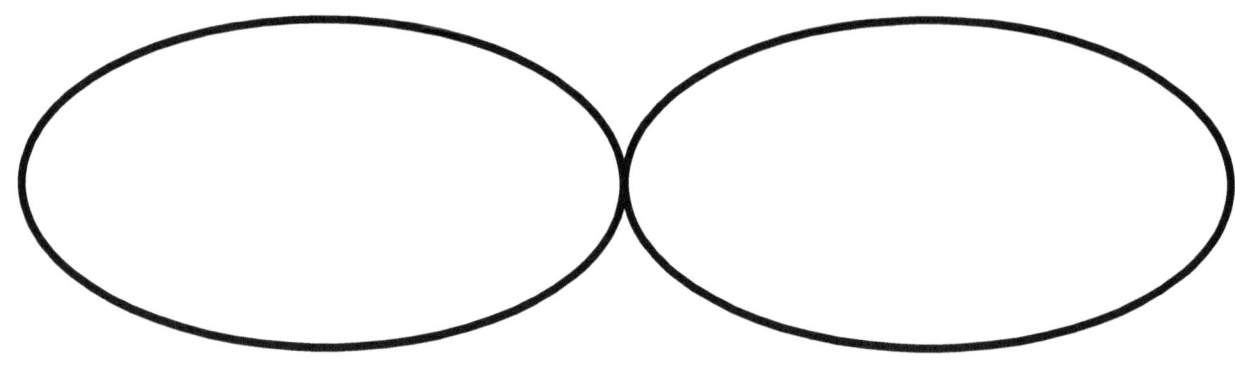

Reverence is when I ....
....

REVERENCE
"He who is endowed with reverence is endowed with a great station."
Bahá'u'lláh

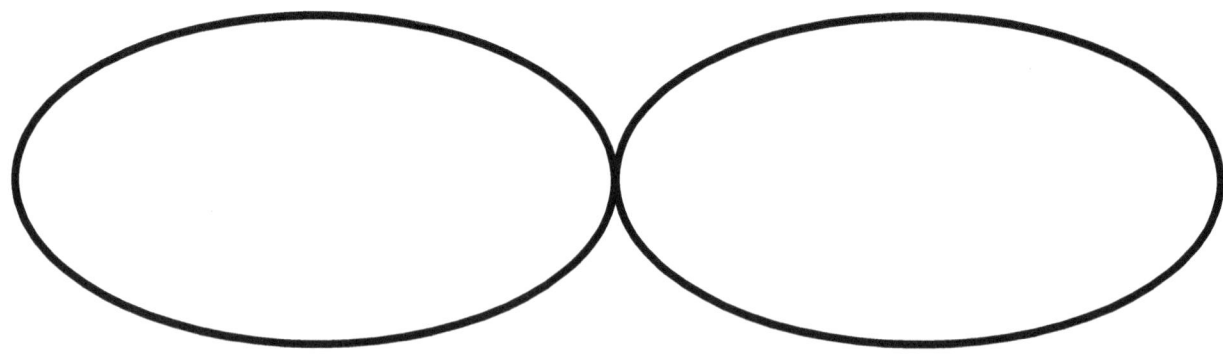

Reverence is when I ....
....

REVERENCE

Quotation activity worksheet

A PLACE OF PEACE

REVERENCE STORY

Sandra was learning some new prayers. Sandra was very good at learning prayers but she was finding it very hard to concentrate because her younger brother Billy was practicing his drums. She just could not hear herself think.

She complained to her mother about the noise but her mother just replied by saying that she needed to find a place of peace. "What is a place of peace?" asked Sandra frowning. "It is somewhere where you can think," explained her mum. "Somewhere where you can think," thought Sandra to herself.

She decided to try her father's study as he seemed to do a lot of thinking in there. She sat down in an armchair near the bookshelf and started to read through the prayers she was learning, but her father was busy typing and the noise kept interrupting her thoughts.

Next she tried going outside but as soon as she had opened her book her dog started licking her.

Sandra was starting to feel very frustrated when she suddenly spied her cubby house. She climbed the ladder and crawled in. Sandra fluffed up some old cushions in one corner and settled herself down. All she could hear was the soft rustle of the trees. It was very peaceful. She started reading and then closed her eyes tight to say the prayers over in her head. She was so involved in what she was doing that she didn't notice that it was getting dark until her mother called her to dinner. Sandra had found her place of peace.

MORAL – When we say prayers we need to shut out other thoughts and sounds, then put our whole focus on the prayer. Sometimes we need a place of peace to help us do this.

ASSERTIVENESS

LESSON PLAN

SESSION 1

PRAYER: Sing prayers that have been learnt and any others that the children know. Ask them to be reverent because they are talking to God.

SCENARIO:
Read out the scenario on the next page to the children.

Use the Happy / Sad Face (as described in the beginning of the book) to discuss what could turn the situation around from a sad one to a happy one. Let the child who comes up with the solution first turn the mouth from a gloomy face to a smiling one.

Bring out the toolbox (as described in the beginning of the book) and let the children guess which tool (virtue) they could use to fix the situation. Remind the children that these are the tools God gives us to help us in everything we do each day. Choose one child to take out the tool. Read out the virtue and the quotation. Ask the children to say the quotation with you a couple of times. Discuss what the quotation means

"be thou of them... who are steadfast in their purpose and confident in their belief."
   Bahá'u'lláh

Discussion Thoughts - We should always stand up for what we believe in and not get influenced by what other people think, do and say.

SONG: "Stand Up" - sing with actions.

ACTIVITY: Assertive Person – Use activity sheet provided.
   Purpose – to reflect on the quotation – to visualize the act of assertiveness.

SESSION 2

PRAYER: Sing prayers that have been learnt and any others that the children know. Ask them to be reverent because they are talking to God.

DISCUSSION REVIEW: What does assertiveness mean?
   Optional - Use discussion prompts sheet from the beginning of the book to help with the discussion.

SONG: "Stand Up" - sing with actions.

STORY: "Standing Up"

GAME: Play an assertiveness game called Stand Up, Sit Down. Read out the situations provided one at a time and ask the children to decide whether the situation is a time to be assertive or accepting. If they think they should be assertive then the child should stand up. If they think the answer is acceptance then they should sit down.
   Purpose – to reflect on what assertiveness means – to understand that assertiveness means standing up for what you believe in.

ACTIVITY:
   "be thou of them... who are steadfast in their purpose and confident in their belief."
      Bahá'u'lláh
   Use the quote visualization page to review the meaning of the quotation.
   Say the quotation with the children a few times. Older children may be able to memorize it.
   Give each child a copy of the quotation activity provided. Cut and glue in each part of the quotation in the correct order, colour in and assist the child to write in something that they can do to practice assertiveness.

ASSERTIVENESS

SCENARIO

Scenario:
Who likes playing marbles?
Do you have special games that you play with them?
Do you like to collect all different colours?
Bradley liked playing with marbles and he liked collecting them too. One day as he was playing marbles with his friend James he noticed some shiny green marbles lying on the ground. James picked them up and put them in his pocket. Not far away were some boys searching everywhere for some marbles they had lost. They were very upset that they had lost them. Bradley knew that the marbles James had put into his pocket were really the lost marbles.
What could Bradley do to help return the marbles to the boys who had lost them?

Possible solution:
Bradley could inform James that the marbles actually belonged to the other boys and ask him to return them.

The tool to fix the problem is: **Assertiveness**.

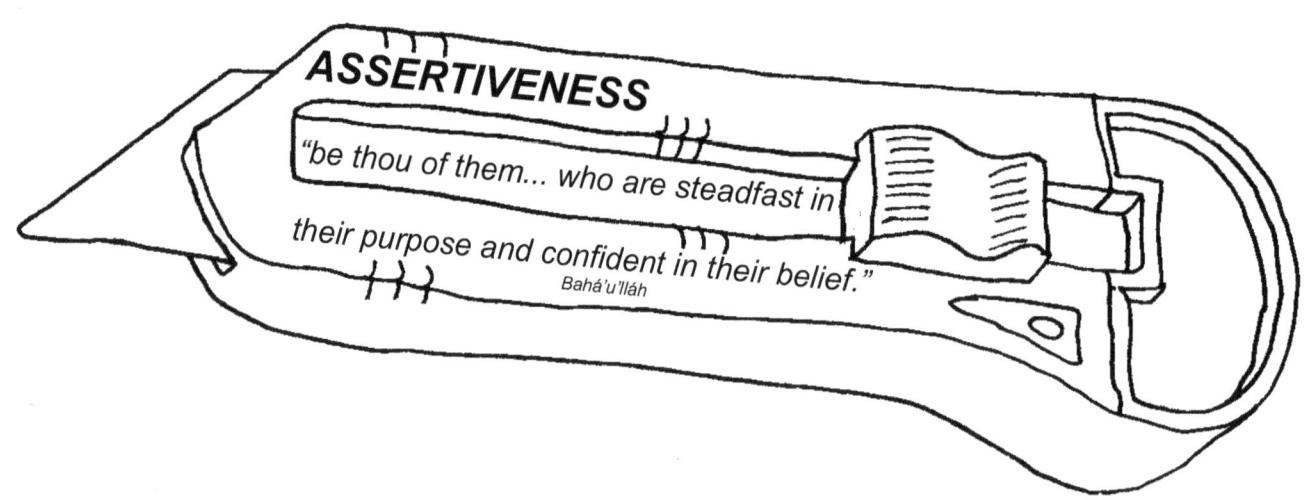

ASSERTIVENESS
"be thou of them... who are steadfast in their purpose and confident in their belief."
Bahá'u'lláh

ASSERTIVE PERSON

Instructions:

- Cut around a person and fold where marked.
- Cut out the hole in the base and put a popstick through the hole.
- Tape the popstick to the back of the person.
- Colour in.
- When you push the popstick upward the person will stand up (be assertive).

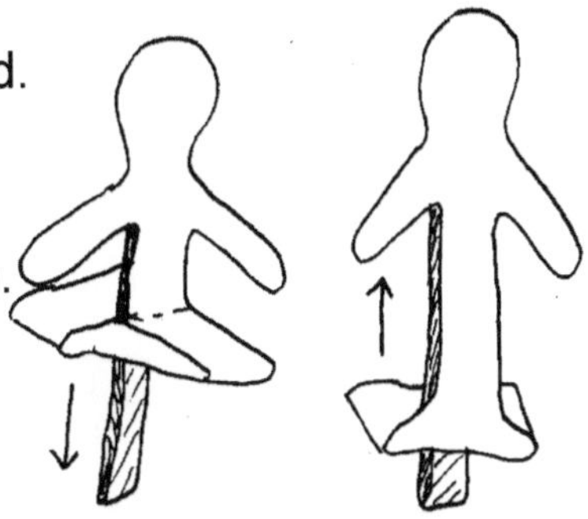

Each child will need:

- Scissors, sticky tape.
- Crayons / Pencils.
- A copy of a person on white card.
- A popstick

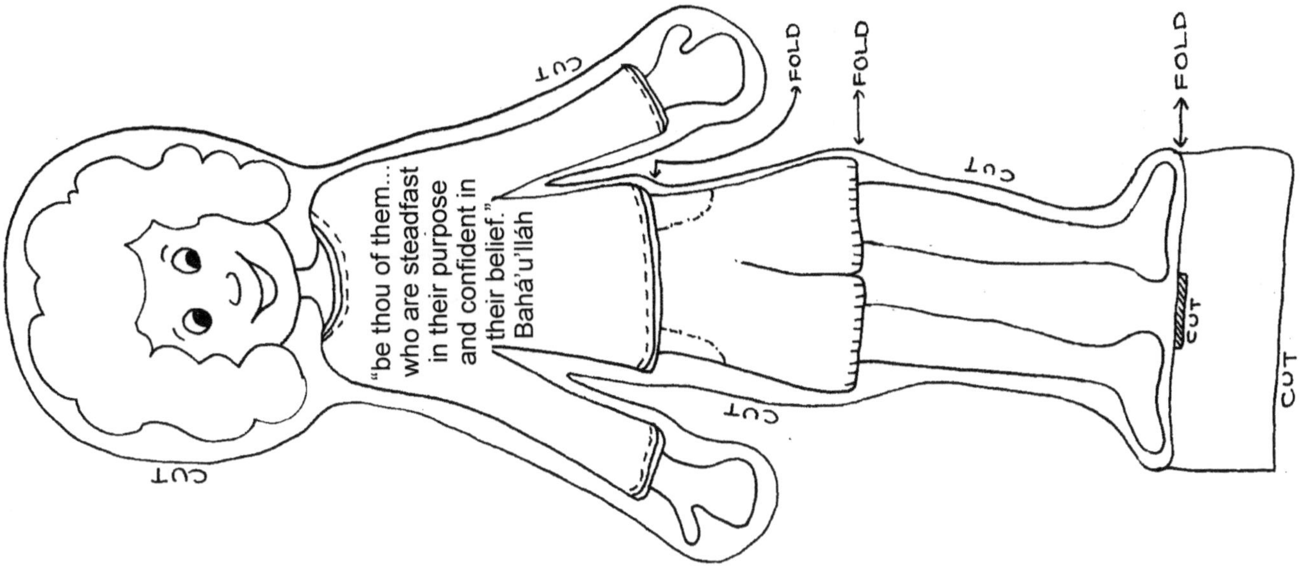

CUT
FOLD
FOLD
FOLD
"be thou of them... who are steadfast in their purpose and confident in their belief."
Bahá'u'lláh
CUT
CUT
CUT
CUT
CUT

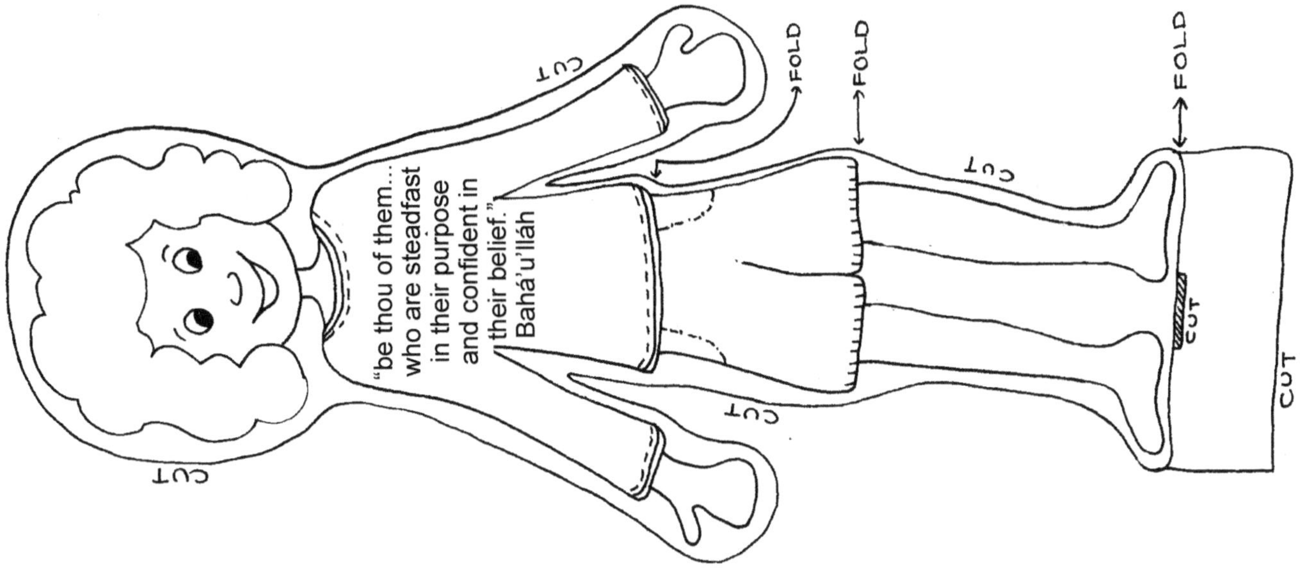

CUT
FOLD
FOLD
FOLD
"be thou of them... who are steadfast in their purpose and confident in their belief."
Bahá'u'lláh
CUT
CUT
CUT
CUT
CUT

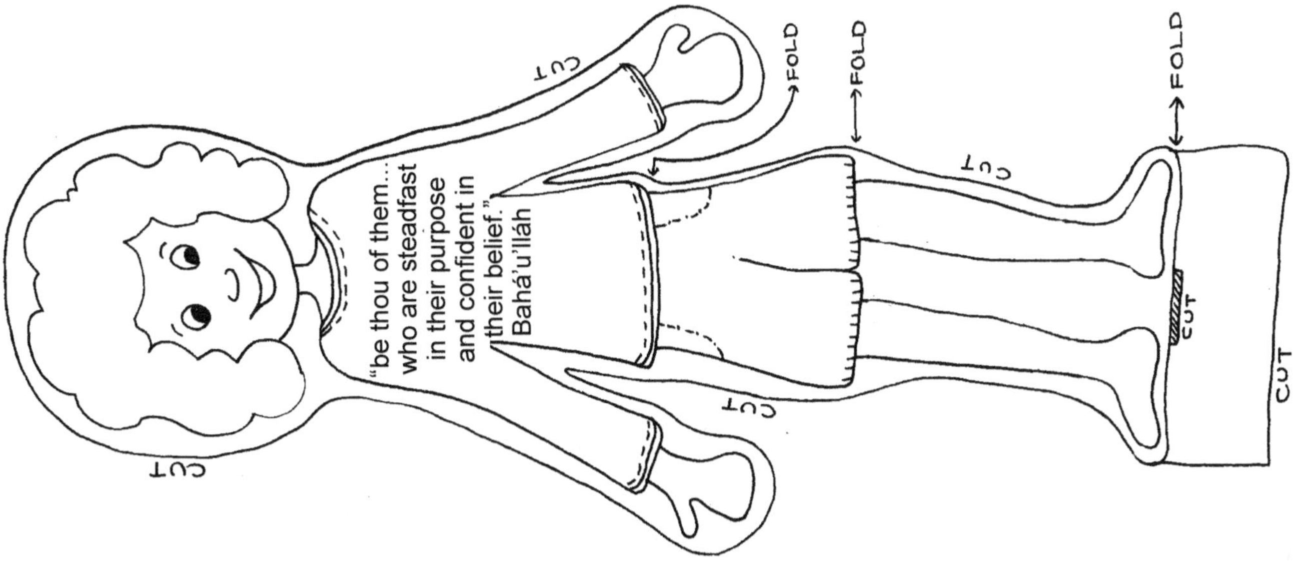

CUT
FOLD
FOLD
FOLD
"be thou of them... who are steadfast in their purpose and confident in their belief."
Bahá'u'lláh
CUT
CUT
CUT
CUT
CUT

Quote Visualization

ASSERTIVENESS

ASSERTIVENESS
"be thou of them...
who are steadfast in their purpose
and confident in their belief."
Bahá'u'lláh

Quotation activity worksheet

ASSERTIVENESS

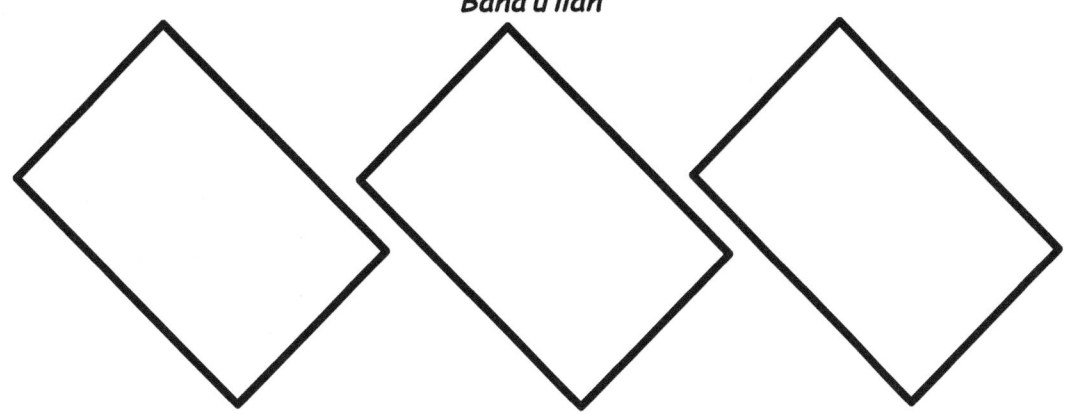

ASSERTIVENESS
"be thou of them...
who are steadfast in their purpose
and confident in their belief."
Bahá'u'lláh

I need to be Assertive when ....
....

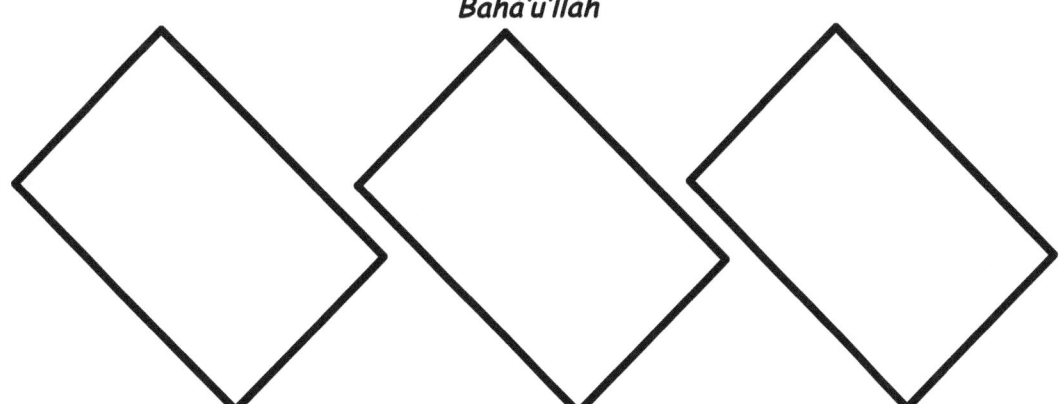

ASSERTIVENESS
"be thou of them...
who are steadfast in their purpose
and confident in their belief."
Bahá'u'lláh

I need to be Assertive when ....
....

ASSERTIVENESS

Quotation activity worksheet

ASSERTIVENESS

GAME

STAND UP, SIT DOWN GAME

What should you do if you are waiting in a queue at the shops and someone pushes into the line in front of you?
STAND UP (Remind the person courteously that they should go to the back of the line)

What should you do if your mum asks you to do your homework?
SIT DOWN (Finish your homework without complaining)

What should you do if your teacher asks you to work quietly?
SIT DOWN (Work quietly)

What should you do if your friend is being criticized for something they are wearing?
STAND UP (Walk away from the bully with your friend and cheer up your friend by saying that you like what they are wearing)

What should you do if your teacher is explaining something to you?
SIT DOWN (Listen quietly and respectfully)

What should you do if someone at school asks you to take something that is not yours?
STAND UP (Tell the person that it is wrong to steal and then walk away)

What should you do if you notice someone is copying your work during a spelling test?
STAND UP (Cover your work up, ask the person not to do it or if they persist, tell the teacher)

What should you do if your friend is trying to spell a word that you can spell easily?
SIT DOWN (Let your friend have time to work it out for themself. If they still need help then maybe give them a clue or help them out a little bit)

What should you do if you get a brand new computer for your birthday but know your friend only has an old one?
SIT DOWN (Don't brag about it and make them feel like they are missing out, but maybe you could share it with them)

What should you do if you notice someone drop fifty dollars on the ground and your friend picks it up and puts it in their pocket?
STAND UP (Tell your friend it does not belong to them and take them to the person so that the money can be given back)

What should you do if one of your friends tells you something nasty about someone else that they don't know very well?
STAND UP (Tell your friend not to spread rumors about other people when they don't really know the truth)

STANDING UP

ASSERTIVENESS STORY

Ralph and Micky were walking through the toy shop. They were looking at all the wonderful trains and cars and spaceships. There was one space ship that was particularly wonderful. It had lights that flashed and doors that opened. Ralph and Micky gazed at it longingly. "If only we had one of those," sighed Ralph. The two boys put all their pocket money together to see if they had enough to buy it, but they were short by five dollars.

Micky wandered on to look at the other toys. Ralph followed behind reluctantly. The two boys then headed towards the door to go home. They were just opening the door when Micky noticed that Ralph had something tucked under his arm. Micky stopped and looked at Ralph suspiciously. "What do you have there?" asked Micky.
"Just that spaceship. The man who owns the toy shop let me have it for free," replied Ralph nervously.
"No he didn't, you were with me all the time and nobody else came anywhere near us." stated Micky.
"Shhh," whispered Ralph, "They have lots of toys, they won't miss just one."
"That's stealing," exclaimed Micky and at the same time grabbed up the toy from under Ralph's arm and walked back to place it on its shelf.

On the way out of the shop he noticed some smaller spaceships. They didn't flash or do anything fancy but they didn't cost much either. Micky picked up two and paid for them at the counter. When he was outside he proudly showed Ralph what he had bought. Ralph smiled. "Thank you," he said looking at Micky guiltily. "They are the best."

MORAL – You should always stand up for what you know is right.

EXCELLENCE

LESSON PLAN

SESSION 1

PRAYER: Sing prayers that have been learnt and any others that the children know. Ask them to be reverent because they are talking to God.

SCENARIO:
Read out the scenario on the next page to the children.

Use the Happy / Sad Face (as described in the beginning of the book) to discuss what could turn the situation around from a sad one to a happy one. Let the child who comes up with the solution first turn the mouth from a gloomy face to a smiling one.

Bring out the toolbox (as described in the beginning of the book) and let the children guess which tool (virtue) they could use to fix the situation. Remind the children that these are the tools God gives us to help us in everything we do each day. Choose one child to take out the tool. Read out the virtue and the quotation. Ask the children to say the quotation with you a couple of times. Discuss what the quotation means

"In everything we do we should always try to attain a standard of excellence."
From a letter written by the Universal House of Justice

Discussion Thoughts – It is not enough just to half do something. We should always do everything to the very best of our ability. This doesn't mean it is perfect, it just means that we have done our best.

SONG: "Strive and Try" - sing with actions.

ACTIVITY: A Ruler of Excellence - Use activity sheet provided.
Purpose – to reflect on the quotation – to understand that excellence is the standard we should always strive for..

SESSION 2

PRAYER: Sing prayers that have been learnt and any others that the children know. Ask them to be reverent because they are talking to God.

DISCUSSION REVIEW: What does excellence mean?
Optional - Use discussion prompts sheet from the beginning of the book to help with the discussion.

SONG: "Strive and Try" - sing with actions.

STORY: "A Good Job"

GAME: Give each child a copy of the shapes provided. Show them the shape picture in the book and ask them to cut out their shapes and try to make the picture themselves. Explain that excellence means not being satisfied until a task is completed to the very best of your ability.
Purpose – to practice excellence.

ACTIVITY:
"In everything we do we should always try to attain a standard of excellence."
From a letter written by the Universal House of Justice
Use the quote visualization page to review the meaning of the quotation.
Say the quotation with the children a few times. Older children may be able to memorize it.
Give each child a copy of the quotation activity provided. Cut and glue in each part of the quotation in the correct order, colour in and assist the child to write in something that they can do to practice excellence.

EXCELLENCE

SCENARIO

Scenario:
Who has heard someone playing a musical instrument?
What kind of instruments do you like?
It takes a lot of practice to play an instrument well.
There was once a girl called Holly who played the flute. She was going to play in a big concert and her music teacher was helping her to practice. Holly liked playing the flute but she hated practicing. She thought that practicing was boring and preferred to just go and play with her toys instead. A week before the concert she went to have one last practice with her music teacher. Her music teacher was not pleased at all. Holly could not play the music properly. "You have not practiced," said her teacher. Nobody will want to hear you play at the concert if you haven't practiced."
Holly went home and thought about it for a long time. She could imagine people laughing at her or putting their fingers in their ears. She felt very ashamed. What could Holly do to fix the situation.

Possible solutions:
Practice every day until the concert.

The tool to fix the problem is: **Excellence**.

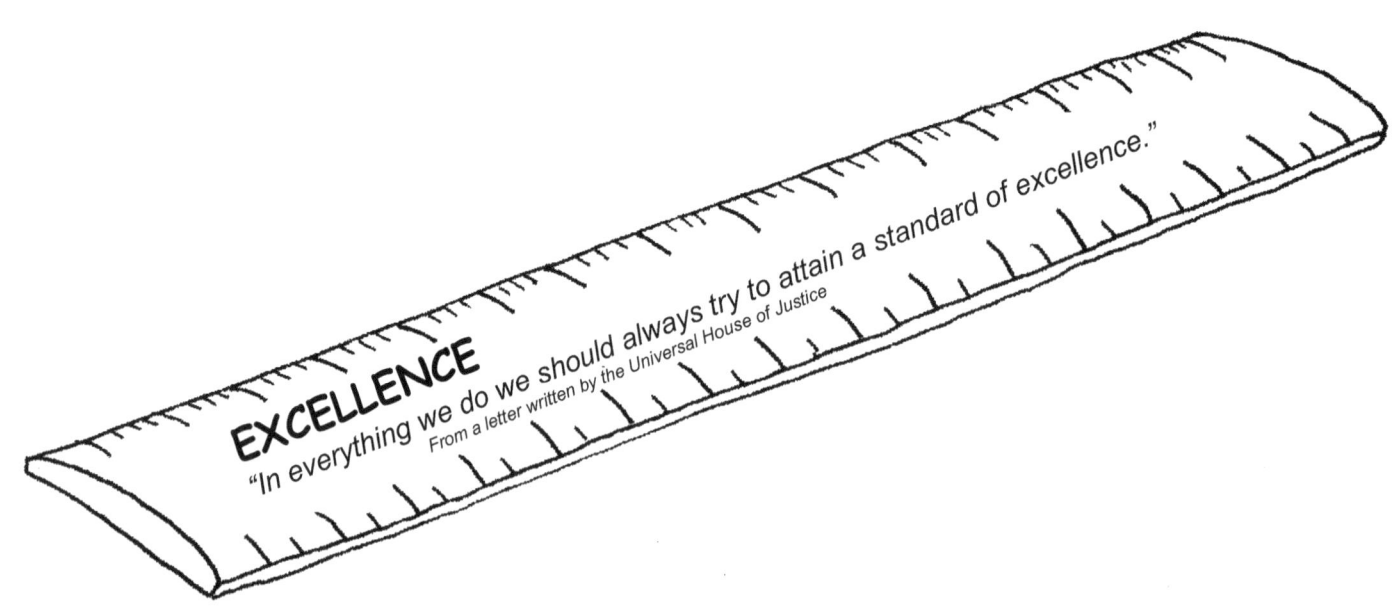
EXCELLENCE "In everything we do we should always try to attain a standard of excellence." From a letter written by the Universal House of Justice

EXCELLENCE
A Ruler of Excellence

EACH CHILD WILL NEED:
- Scissors
- Crayons / pencils
- A copy of a ruler
- A hole punch.

INSTRUCTIONS:
- Photocopy this sheet on to white card.
- Give each child a copy of a ruler.
- Cut out ruler and colour in.
- Optional – punch a hole in the top for hanging or pinning up.

Quote Visualization

EXCELLENCE

"In everything we do we should always try to attain a standard of excellence."

From a letter written by the Universal House of Justice,

Quotation activity worksheet   EXCELLENCE

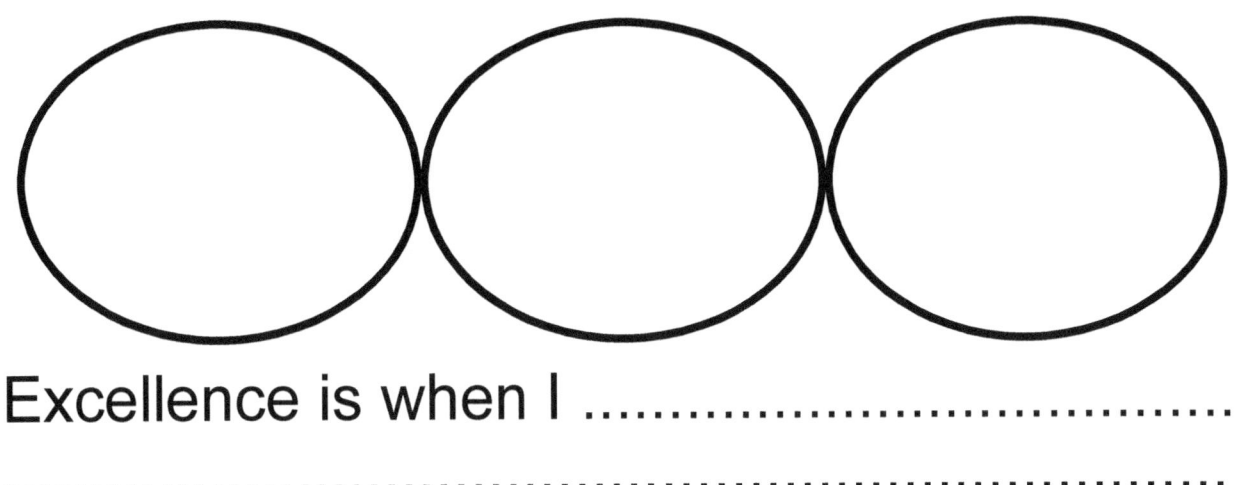

EXCELLENCE
*"In everything we do
we should always try to attain
a standard of excellence."*
From a letter written by the Universal House of Justice,

Excellence is when I ....
....

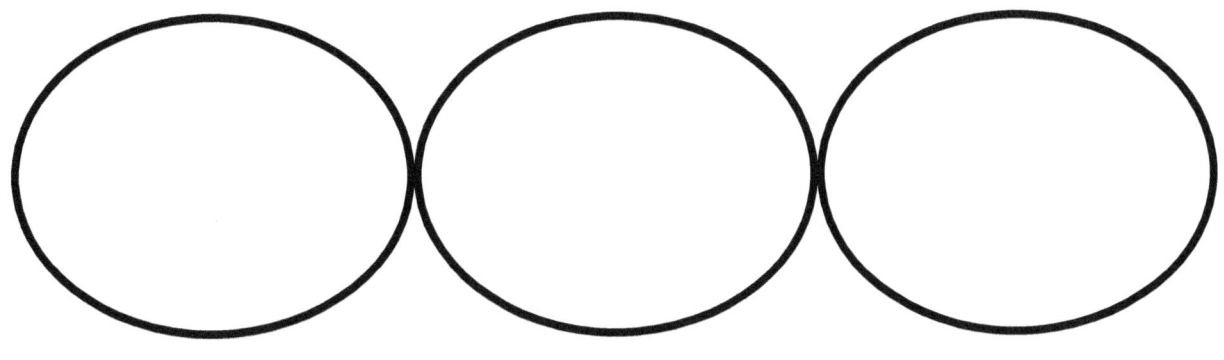

EXCELLENCE
*"In everything we do
we should always try to attain
a standard of excellence."*
From a letter written by the Universal House of Justice,

Excellence is when I ....
....

EXCELLENCE

Quotation activity worksheet

EXCELLENCE

Game

Game

EXCELLENCE

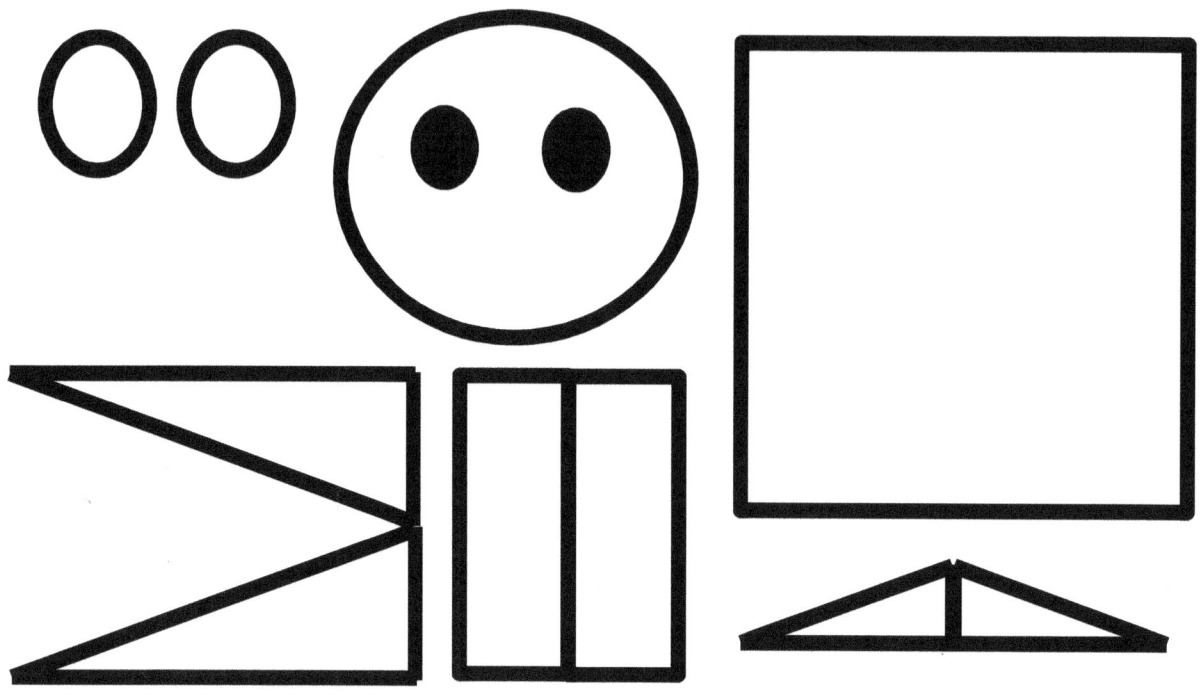

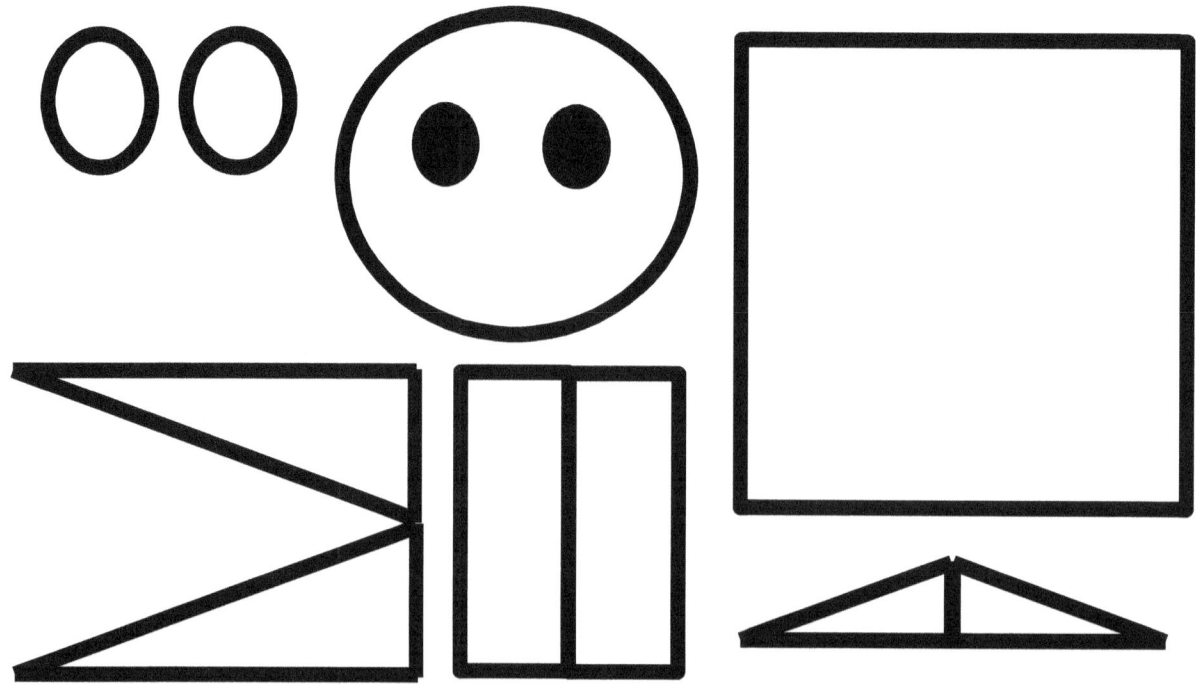

A GOOD JOB

EXCELLENCE STORY

At school one day the teacher announced that they were going to have a colouring in competition. The whole school was going to enter but only one person would win the prize. Ellie liked colouring in, as did all her friends and they started the task with a lot of enthusiasm. After a while Ellie looked at her friends' work, then she looked at her own. Her work was good but her friends' work was so much better. She new she would not win the competition. Ellie thought, "What is the point of trying if I know I am not going to win". She started scribbling over her drawing miserably.

The teacher noticed and came over to talk to her.
"What are you doing Ellie? You are destroying your lovely colouring in," she exclaimed.
"I'm not going to win, it is not good enough," moaned Ellie.
"Instead of competing against everyone else," suggested the teacher, "Compete against yourself. Try to make this the very best colouring you have ever done. Here, have another try." The teacher placed another page on Ellie's desk.

Ellie just looked at it sadly for a long time. Then, picking up a yellow pencil, she slowly started again. This time she went very slowly and very carefully.

The next day it was announced that an older boy in one of the other classes had won the competition. Ellie wasn't surprised but her face did light up when she walked past the school notice board. Displayed for all the school to see were 20 colouring in pages that were picked out as some of the best in the school. Ellie stared at the one in the middle of the bottom row. It was hers. She did not win the competition but she had put in her best effort and other people thought she had done a good job too.

MORAL – Excellence is striving to always do your best and being proud of your work even if it is not as good as someone else's.

PEACEFULNESS

LESSON PLAN

SESSION 1

PRAYER: Sing prayers that have been learnt and any others that the children know. Ask them to be reverent because they are talking to God.

SCENARIO:
Read out the scenario on the next page to the children.

Use the Happy / Sad Face (as described in the beginning of the book) to discuss what could turn the situation around from a sad one to a happy one. Let the child who comes up with the solution first turn the mouth from a gloomy face to a smiling one.

Bring out the toolbox (as described in the beginning of the book) and let the children guess which tool (virtue) they could use to fix the situation. Remind the children that these are the tools God gives us to help us in everything we do each day. Choose one child to take out the tool. Read out the virtue and the quotation. Ask the children to say the quotation with you a couple of times. Discuss what the quotation means

"My home is the home of peace"
    'Abdu'l-Bahá

Discussion Thoughts - Our homes can be a place of peace, but we can also have peace inside us that we can carry everywhere we go. If we are feeling angry or upset we can always close our eyes, take deep breaths and feel peaceful inside again.

SONG: "Nice and Slow" - sing with actions.

ACTIVITY: A House of Peace – Use activity sheet provided.
    Purpose – to reflect on the quotation – to learn about some of the things that make us feel peaceful.

SESSION 2

PRAYER: Sing prayers that have been learnt and any others that the children know. Ask them to be reverent because they are talking to God.

DISCUSSION REVIEW: What does peacefulness mean?
    Optional - Use discussion prompts sheet from the beginning of the book to help with the discussion.

SONG: "Nice and Slow" - sing with actions.

STORY: "The Big Ship"

GAME: Ask the children to think about something that makes them feel angry or upset. Then ask the children to say aloud or in their heads "My home is the home of Peace". Ask them to take deep breaths. Breathe in peaceful thoughts and blow out all the angry thoughts until they feel relaxed. Purpose – For children to understand that just because something upsets them and they feel angry doesn't mean that they have to stay feeling that way. At any time they have the choice to take a deep breath and feel peaceful.

ACTIVITY:
"My home is the home of peace"
    'Abdu'l-Bahá
Use the quote visualization page to review the meaning of the quotation.
Say the quotation with the children a few times. Older children may be able to memorize it.
Give each child a copy of the quotation activity provided. Cut and glue in each part of the quotation in the correct order, colour in and assist the child to write in something that they can do to practice peacefulness.

PEACEFULNESS

SCENARIO

Scenario:

Do you feel angry sometimes?

Do you feel frustrated when things don't work out the way you would like them to?

Everyone feels sad or upset sometimes.

Johnny was a little boy who felt upset quite often. One day Johnny was playing outside on a very hot day and when he came inside he was very sweaty. "Could I please have a nice cold icecream," he asked his mum courteously. "I am very hot and I need to cool down."

"I am sorry Johnny but we don't have any icecream. Would you like a cold drink instead?" replied his mum.

Johnny did not feel happy at all. He felt angry and upset and threw himself on the floor. He shouted and yelled very loudly.

What do you think Johnny could do to help himself feel better?

Possible solution:

Johnny could take some deep breaths and close his eyes for a little while to help himself calm down, then ask for a cold drink or something else instead.

The tool to fix the problem is: **Peacefulness**.

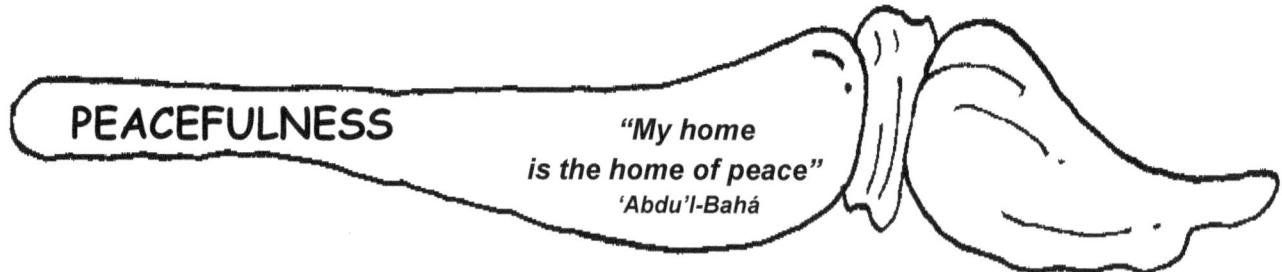

PEACEFULNESS

"My home is the home of peace"
'Abdu'l-Bahá

PEACEFULNESS
A HOUSE OF PEACE

EACH CHILD WILL NEED:
- Scissors
- Crayons / pencils
- A hole punch (shared)
- A copy of a house
- A piece of string / ribbon.

INSTRUCTIONS:
- Copy this page on to white card.
- Give each child a copy of a house.
- Colour in and punch a hole in the top of the roof.
- Tie a string to the top so it can be hung on the wall.

PEACEFULNESS

Quote Visualization

PEACEFULNESS

"My home is the home of peace."

'Abdu'l-Bahá

Quotation activity worksheet

PEACEFULNESS

Peacefulness is when I ....
....

Peacefulness is when I ....
....

PEACEFULNESS

Quotation activity worksheet

THE BIG SHIP

PEACEFULNESS STORY

Tillion, an alien from the planet Laton, took off in his space ship and headed out into the stars. It was beautiful floating through space, watching the stars whizz past and gazing down at the far away glow that marked out where his home was.

Tillion flew for a long time until suddenly he caught sight of a strange space ship he had never seen before. What was this strange ship? Who did it belong to? The ship looked very powerful and didn't appear to want to be friendly. Tillion also realized that he was now a lot further from home than he had thought. In fact, he could not see any far away glow at all to mark out where his home was. He was lost and with a strange ship coming towards him.

Tillion started to panic. He jumped up and down in his seat, covered his face with his hands and started shaking uncontrollably. What was he to do? What could he do? He was just a little ship, he couldn't fight a big one or he would be destroyed.

Slowly Tillion took a deep breath. In and out he breathed, in and out. He took his hands away from his face and made himself calm down. He thought about what his choices were and then made a decision. He picked up the space phone and connected through to the big ship. "Hello, hello," he said calmly. "I have lost my way. Could you please give me directions to the planet Laton."
A very friendly voice answered, "Hello, we are from the planet Giston and have come to visit some friends who are staying on your planet. Follow us and we will take you home."
"Thank you," replied Tillion gratefully.
He had been worried for nothing. They were just friendly neighbors coming to visit. Tillion took another deep breath and then followed the big ship as it showed him the way home.

MORAL – Being peaceful helps us to let go of our anger and fear so that we can deal with think clearly.

CREATIVITY

LESSON PLAN

SESSION 1

PRAYER: Sing prayers that have been learnt and any others that the children know. Ask them to be reverent because they are talking to God.

SCENARIO:
Read out the scenario on the next page to the children.

Use the Happy / Sad Face (as described in the beginning of the book) to discuss what could turn the situation around from a sad one to a happy one. Let the child who comes up with the solution first turn the mouth from a gloomy face to a smiling one.

Bring out the toolbox (as described in the beginning of the book) and let the children guess which tool (virtue) they could use to fix the situation. Remind the children that these are the tools God gives us to help us in everything we do each day. Choose one child to take out the tool. Read out the virtue and the quotation. Ask the children to say the quotation with you a couple of times. Discuss what the quotation means

"....each must see with his own eyes, hear with his own ears..."
    'Abdu'l-Bahá

Discussion Thoughts - Just because someone else does something, it doesn't mean we should do it the same way. We should use our own eyes to decide what we think is beautiful and use our own mind to come up with our own ideas.

SONG: "Many Ways" - sing with actions.

ACTIVITY: Glasses – Use activity sheet provided.
    Purpose – to visualize the quotation and understand that being creative means that we need to see things with our own eyes instead of copying what other people are doing.

SESSION 2

PRAYER: Sing prayers that have been learnt and any others that the children know. Ask them to be reverent because they are talking to God.

DISCUSSION REVIEW: What does creativity mean?
    Optional - Use discussion prompts sheet from the beginning of the book to help with the discussion.

SONG: "Many Ways" - sing with actions.

STORY: "A Friend in Need"

GAME: Give each child a pile of cotton wool balls or craft matchsticks and ask them to use their creativity to make a picture with them. Remind the children that they need to use their own eyes and not copy anyone else.
    Purpose – To practice being creative.

ACTIVITY:
"....each must see with his own eyes, hear with his own ears..."
    'Abdu'l-Bahá
Use the quote visualization page to review the meaning of the quotation.
Say the quotation with the children a few times. Older children may be able to memorize it.
Give each child a copy of the quotation activity provided. Cut and glue in each part of the quotation in the correct order, colour in and assist the child to write in something that they can do to practice creativity.

SCENARIO

Scenario:
Who likes writing and drawing?
What do you like to draw?
Jane, Sandra and Peter all loved drawing and writing. One day they were all given special books to draw and write in. They were very proud of their books but they all looked exactly the same. Every time they put down their books they forgot which one belonged to which person. What could these three friends do to change things so that they wouldn't keep mixing up the books?

Possible solution:
They could use their creativity to decorate the front of each book so that each one looked different.

The tool to fix the problem is: **Creativity**.

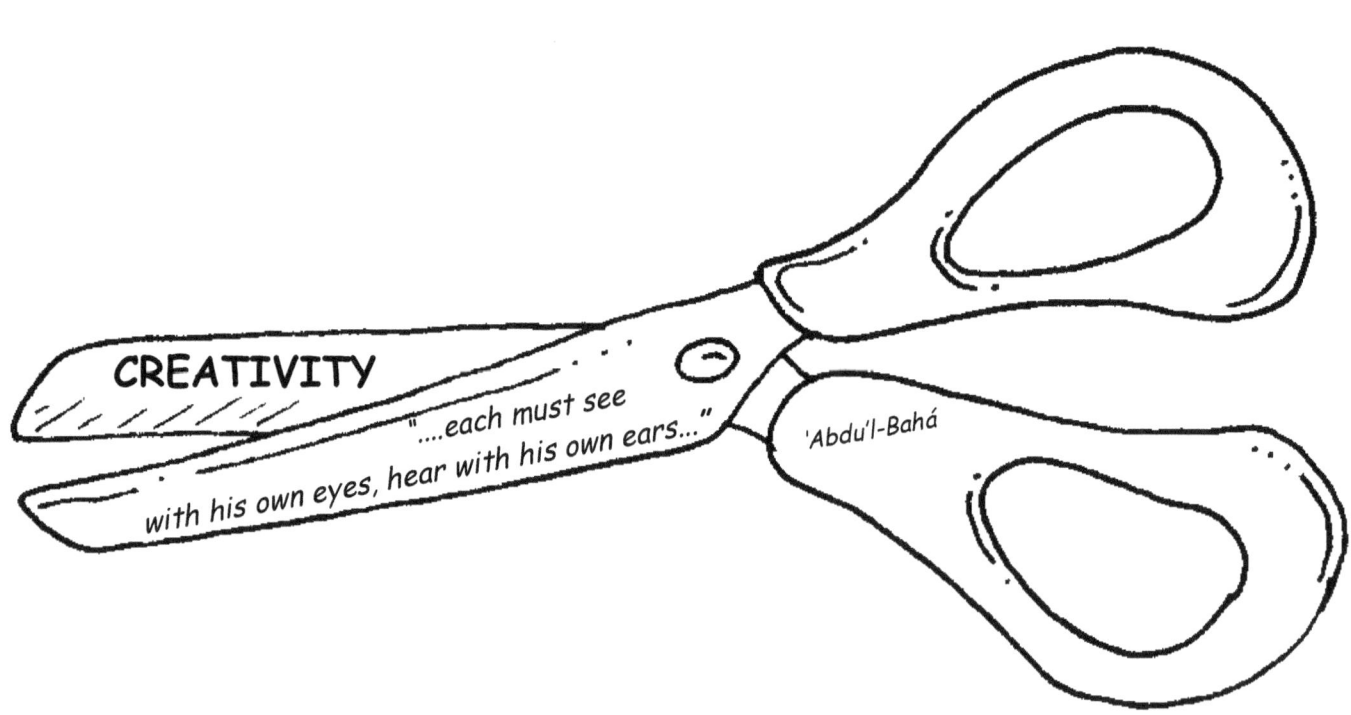

CREATIVITY
GLASSES

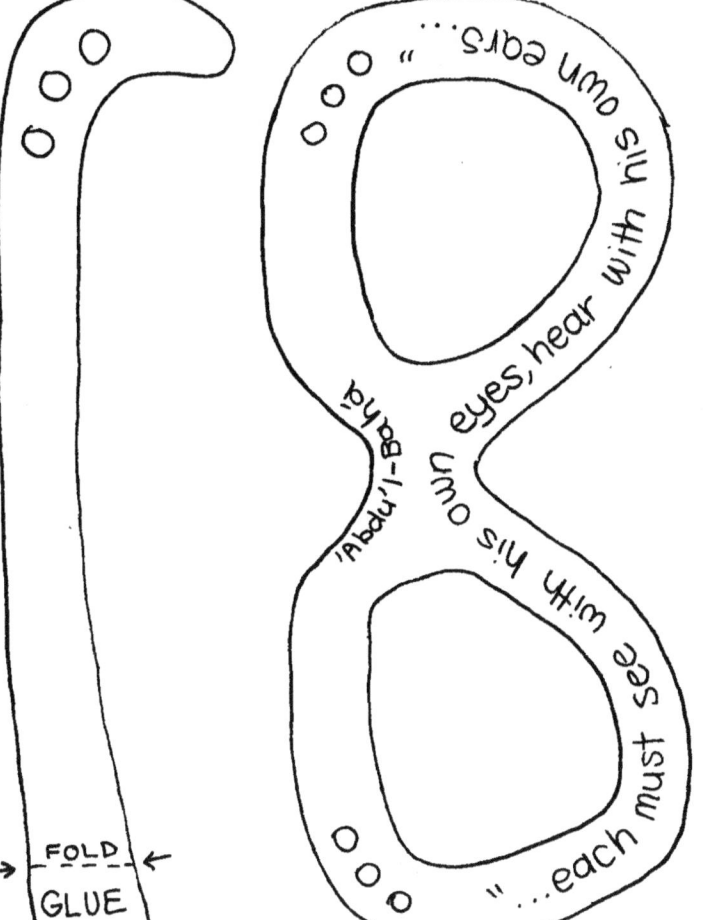

EACH CHILD WILL NEED:
- A copy of the three parts of the glasses on white card.
- Scissors, glue
- Two small pieces of coloured cellophane.
- Crayons / pencils

INSTRUCTIONS:
- Colour in.
- Cut out the three parts of the glasses. Children will probably need help cutting the eye holes. These could be done beforehand with a craft knife.
- Glue the glasses together where marked.
- Glue small pieces of coloured cellophane on to the back of the glasses to cover the eye holes.
- Fold back the sides to fit around the ears.

"...each must see with his own eyes, hear with his own ears..." -Bahá'í-Abdu'l-Bahá

Quote Visualization — CREATIVITY

CREATIVITY

*"....each must see with his own eyes,
hear with his own ears..."*

'Abdu'l-Bahá

Quotation activity worksheet   CREATIVITY

CREATIVITY
"....each must see with his own eyes, hear with his own ears..."
'Abdu'l-Bahá

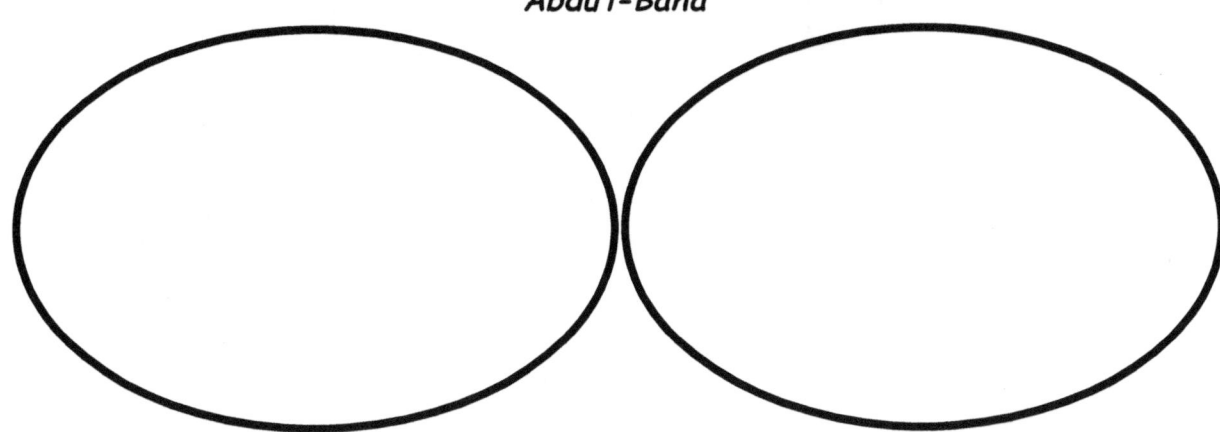

I can use creativity when I ....
....

CREATIVITY
"....each must see with his own eyes, hear with his own ears..."
'Abdu'l-Bahá

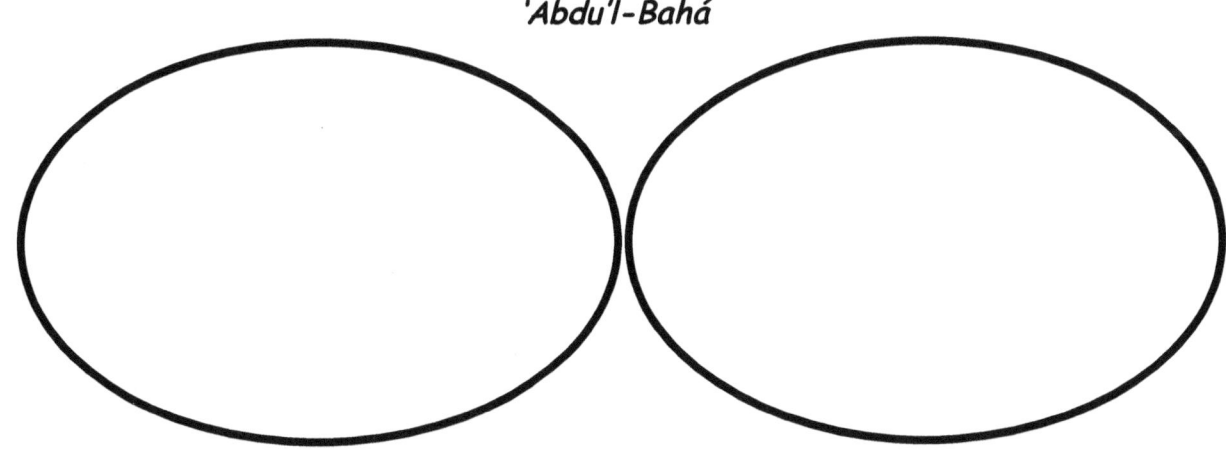

I can use creativity when I ....
....

CREATIVITY

Quotation activity worksheet

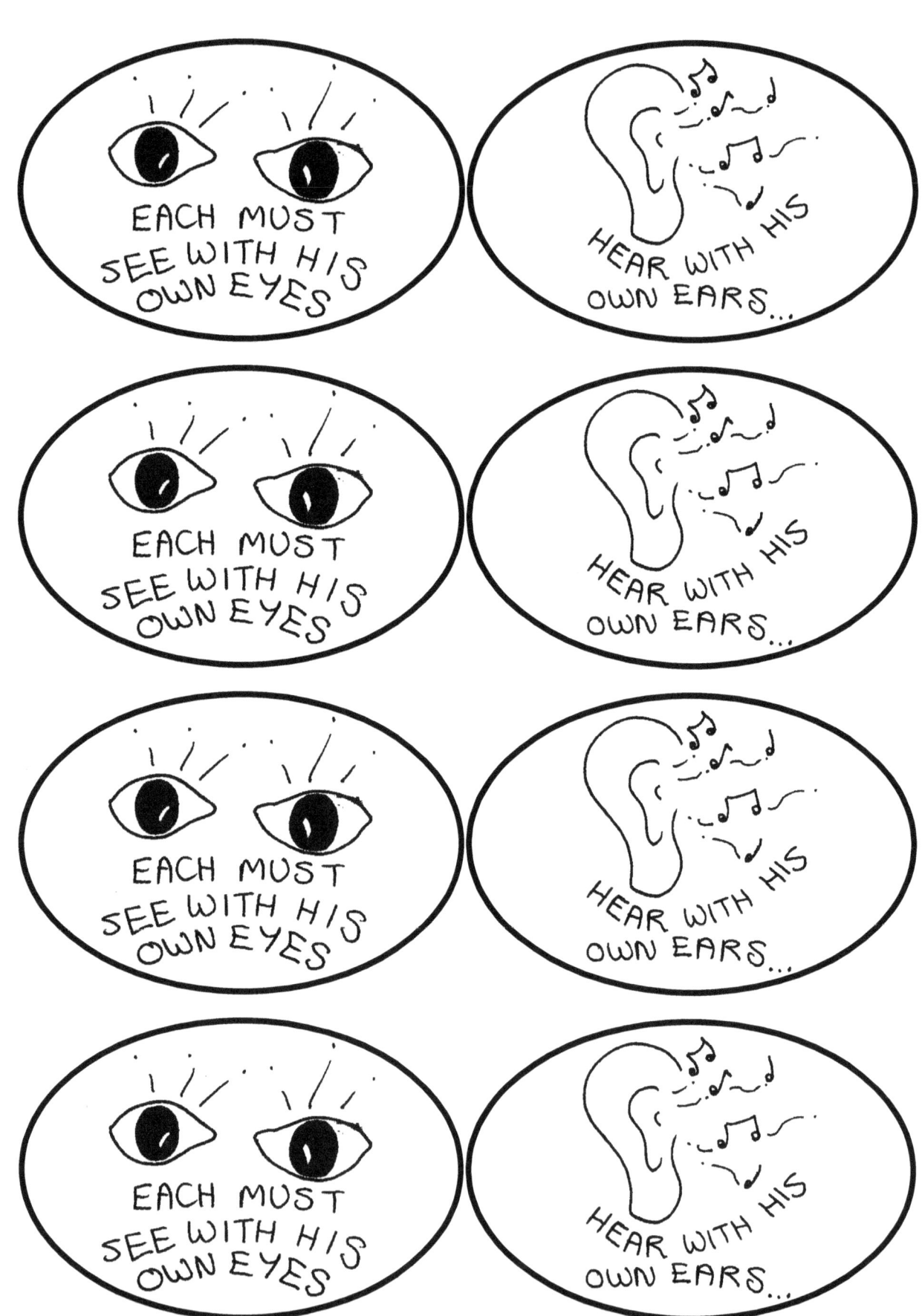

SOMETHING DIFFERENT

CREATIVITY STORY

Elizabeth was invited to a school dance party but she was not feeling very happy about it because she had nothing special to wear. Her friends were all going shopping to buy something really special at the shops but Elizabeth didn't have any money. She was sitting very sadly on the steps of her house when her mum came home.
"Why are you so sad?" her mum asked.
"I want to go to the dance party but I have nothing special to wear." said Elizabeth gloomily.
"Why don't you make something special," her mum suggested, "come inside and let's see what material we have in the cupboard."
Elizabeth followed her inside feeling very doubtful.

They looked inside the cupboard and found some shiny pink material but there wasn't enough for a dress. Then, tucked right at the back, Elizabeth found some purple silk. That afternoon Elizabeth and her mum cut and sewed the shiny pink material and the purple silk to make a dress. Elizabeth put it on and was very pleased. They had done a great job.

When the time of the dance came, Elizabeth put on her dress and picked some flowers from the garden to decorate her hair. She proudly walked to the dance, but when she got there she was very surprised. All her friends were wearing exactly the same dress. They had all gone to the shop to buy the best dress and had ended up with the same thing. Her friends all admired her dress and asked, "Where did you get it from?"
"From the back of the cupboard," said Elizabeth mischievously then added, "I used my creativity."
Then they all went to join the dance and Elizabeth felt she had more fun than anyone else.

MORAL – Creativity is using your own mind to make something that is special and different from everything else.

FORGIVENESS

LESSON PLAN

SESSION 1

PRAYER: Sing prayers that have been learnt and any others that the children know. Ask them to be reverent because they are talking to God.

SCENARIO:
Read out the scenario on the next page to the children.

Use the Happy / Sad Face (as described in the beginning of the book) to discuss what could turn the situation around from a sad one to a happy one. Let the child who comes up with the solution first turn the mouth from a gloomy face to a smiling one.

Bring out the toolbox (as described in the beginning of the book) and let the children guess which tool (virtue) they could use to fix the situation. Remind the children that these are the tools God gives us to help us in everything we do each day. Choose one child to take out the tool. Read out the virtue and the quotation. Ask the children to say the quotation with you a couple of times. Discuss what the quotation means

"...forgive all, consider the whole of humanity as our own family..."
   'Abdu'l-Bahá

Discussion Thoughts – Sometimes people can hurt us or do something we don't like. We should see each person like a member of our family and forgive them. Forgiveness allows your friendship to grow again.

SONG: "I Forgive You" - sing with actions.

ACTIVITY: Family Picture – Use activity sheet provided.
   Purpose – to reflect on the quotation.

SESSION 2

PRAYER: Sing prayers that have been learnt and any others that the children know. Ask them to be reverent because they are talking to God.

DISCUSSION REVIEW: What does forgiveness mean?
   Optional - Use discussion prompts sheet from the beginning of the book to help with the discussion.

SONG: "I Forgive You" - sing with actions.

STORY: "Secrets"

GAME: Ask the children to close their eyes and think of something that someone has done to them that they didn't like or that they feel angry or upset about (eg. Someone called them a nasty name, pushed them, took something that was special to them or broke a special toy.) Then ask the children to imagine themselves saying "I forgive you" to that person. Now ask them to try to take some deep breaths and try to let go of any anger or sadness towards that person.
   Purpose – To practice being forgiving.

ACTIVITY:
"...forgive all, consider the whole of humanity as our own family..."
   'Abdu'l-Bahá
Use the quote visualization page to review the meaning of the quotation.
Say the quotation with the children a few times. Older children may be able to memorize it.
Give each child a copy of the quotation activity provided. Cut and glue in each part of the quotation in the correct order, colour in and assist the child to write in something that they can do to practice forgiveness.

FORGIVENESS

SCENARIO

Scenario:

Does anyone have a special toy that they like more than any other toy? Sometimes it is hard to share a toy that is very special to you.

Rebecca was a little girl who had a special toy. She had been given a doll for her birthday and she spent many hours every day playing with it. She would dress the doll up, put the doll to bed, pretend to feed it and even sleep with it at night. One day Rebecca had a friend come to play. Her friend's name was Amy. Rebecca proudly showed Amy her doll. Amy wanted to play with the doll too but Rebecca wouldn't even let her touch it. They played lots of other games but Amy could not forget about the beautiful doll she was not allowed to play with. When Rebecca was not looking Amy picked up the doll. Rebecca turned around and yelled at her to put it down. Amy said, "No, I won't." Rebecca tried to take it from her and as she pulled one of the arms ripped off. Rebecca burst into tears and held the broken doll in her arms. What could the girls do to fix the situation.

Possible solutions:

Amy could say sorry to Rebecca for taking the doll and Rebecca could say sorry for showing her the doll and then not sharing it. They could also ask Rebecca's mother to help them sew the torn arm back on again.

The tool to fix the problem is: **Forgiveness**.

"...forgive all, consider the whole of humanity as our own family..." 'Abdu'l-Bahá

FORGIVENESS
FAMILY PICTURE

EACH CHILD WILL NEED:
- Scissors, glue
- Crayons / pencils
- A copy of a frame and a blank square.

INSTRUCTIONS:
- Photocopy this page on to white card
- Give each child a copy of a frame and a blank square.
- Cut out the square and the frame.
- Colour in the frame and draw a picture of a family in the blank square.
- Glue the picture of the family into the centre of the frame like a photograph.

"*...forgive all, consider the whole of humanity as our own family...*"
'Abdu'l-Bahá

Quote Visualization — FORGIVENESS

FORGIVENESS

"...forgive all, consider the whole of humanity as our own family..."

'Abdu'l-Bahá

Quotation activity worksheet

FORGIVENESS

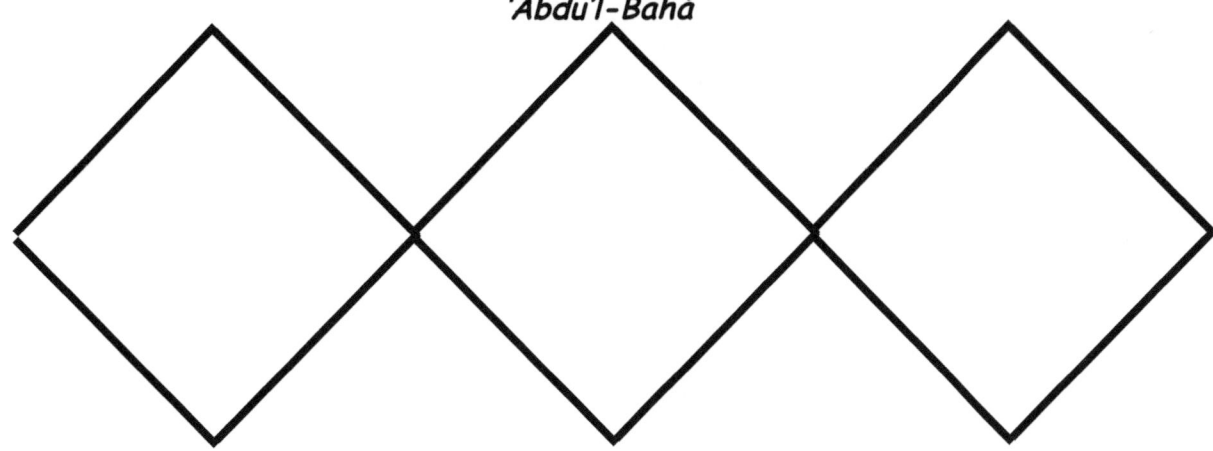

I can show forgiveness by ....
....

I can show forgiveness by ....
....

125

Quotation activity worksheet

FORGIVENESS

SECRETS

FORGIVENESS STORY

Danny and Leon were the best of friends. They would do everything together. They played together at school and after school. One day they were sitting in the school playground when they spied a spider web. Danny stepped back and Leon looked at him surprised.
"What is the matter," asked Leon.
"If I tell you a secret will you promise not to tell any of the other kids." said Danny hesitantly.
"Of course I won't tell," promised Leon.
"I am afraid of spiders," admitted Danny.
"That's alright," Leon said comfortingly. "I am scared of sharks."
The days passed and the two friends kept each other's secrets until one day they were swimming in the pool with some other friends from school. Danny was feeling mischievous and so as Leon swam past him he suddenly called out "Shark, shark." Leon screamed and jumped out of the pool as quickly as he could. When he turned around everyone was laughing including his friend Danny.
Leon walked away sadly and sat by himself. Danny tried to talk to him but Leon wouldn't listen. The next day at school Leon sat by himself again at lunch. When they went into class Leon leant over and gave Danny a small box.
"What is it," Danny asked.
"A present," replied Leon smiling as he walked back to his desk.
As all the other children came into class Danny opened the box. A spider crawled out and Danny jumped on to a desk screaming. Leon caught the spider and put it back into the box but not before the rest of class had seen. Everyone thought it was very funny. Everyone that is except for Danny who was still shaking.
After school Leon ran up to Danny. Danny ignored him.
"Come on, it was just a joke." said Leon.
"You promised you wouldn't tell anyone," sulked Danny.
"Well, you promised you wouldn't tell anyone my secret too," said Leon.
Danny looked at him for a while then said,
"You are right, I didn't keep my promise either."
The two friends smiled at each other and then started walking home. That afternoon they played with each other after school for the first time in many days.

MORAL – Forgiveness means letting go of the bad things you have done to each other so that you can keep being friends.

TOLERANCE

LESSON PLAN

SESSION 1

PRAYER: Sing prayers that have been learnt and any others that the children know. Ask them to be reverent because they are talking to God.

SCENARIO:
Read out the scenario on the next page to the children.

Use the Happy / Sad Face (as described in the beginning of the book) to discuss what could turn the situation around from a sad one to a happy one. Let the child who comes up with the solution first turn the mouth from a gloomy face to a smiling one.

Bring out the toolbox (as described in the beginning of the book) and let the children guess which tool (virtue) they could use to fix the situation. Remind the children that these are the tools God gives us to help us in everything we do each day. Choose one child to take out the tool. Read out the virtue and the quotation. Ask the children to say the quotation with you a couple of times.
Discuss what the quotation means

"Beware of prejudice; light is good in whatsoever lamp it is burning.
A rose is beautiful in whatsoever garden it may bloom.
A star has the same radiance if it shines from the east or the west."
    'Abdu'l-Bahá

Discussion Thoughts - Prejudice means to judge things without really knowing the truth. We should be tolerant and understanding. We should see each person as beautiful in their own way and appreciate them for the way they are. A rose is beautiful no matter where it is and it shares its beauty with everyone no matter who they are. A light is beautiful no matter where it is shining and it shines on all of us no matter who we are. We should be like a lamp and shine and share with everyone.

SONG: "Words Without Sound" - sing with actions.

ACTIVITY: A Bundle of Flowers – Use activity sheet provided.
    Purpose – to reflect on the meaning of the quotation.

SESSION 2

PRAYER: Sing prayers that have been learnt and any others that the children know. Ask them to be reverent because they are talking to God.

DISCUSSION REVIEW: What does tolerance mean?
    Optional - Use discussion prompts sheet from the beginning of the book to help with the discussion.

SONG: "Words Without Sound" - sing with actions.

STORY: "The Fern, the Rose Bush and the Grass"

GAME: Give each child a miscellaneous object (eg. Spoon, ribbon, dirt, carrot etc...) Ask each child to have a turn at saying something positive about their object. Explain that we should always look at the good in things instead of the bad. If we look for the good we will find it. This is what being tolerant means. Looking for the good in each other.
    Purpose – To reflect on what it means to be tolerant.

ACTIVITY:
"Beware of prejudice; light is good in whatsoever lamp it is burning.
A rose is beautiful in whatsoever garden it may bloom.
A star has the same radiance if it shines from the east or the west."
    'Abdu'l-Bahá
Use the quote visualization page to review the meaning of the quotation. Say the quotation with the children a few times. Older children may be able to memorize it. Give each child a copy of the quotation activity provided. Cut and glue in each part of the quotation in the correct order, colour in and assist the child to write in something that they can do to practice tolerance.

TOLERANCE

SCENARIO

Scenario:
Who has friends?
Who likes playing with friends?
What does it feel like if no one wants to play with you?
There was once a girl called Laurin who came from a far off place where everyone dyed their hair green. She looked very strange and when she talked she sounded strange too. Nobody played with her and so Laurin would sit alone every day and eat her lunch. Laurin looked very sad and very lonely.
If you saw Laurin what do you think you could do to cheer her up?

Possible solution:
You could eat your lunch with her.
Talk to her and find out what her favorite games are.
Introduce her to other children.
Invite her to join in the games you are playing.

The tool to fix the problem is: **Tolerance**.

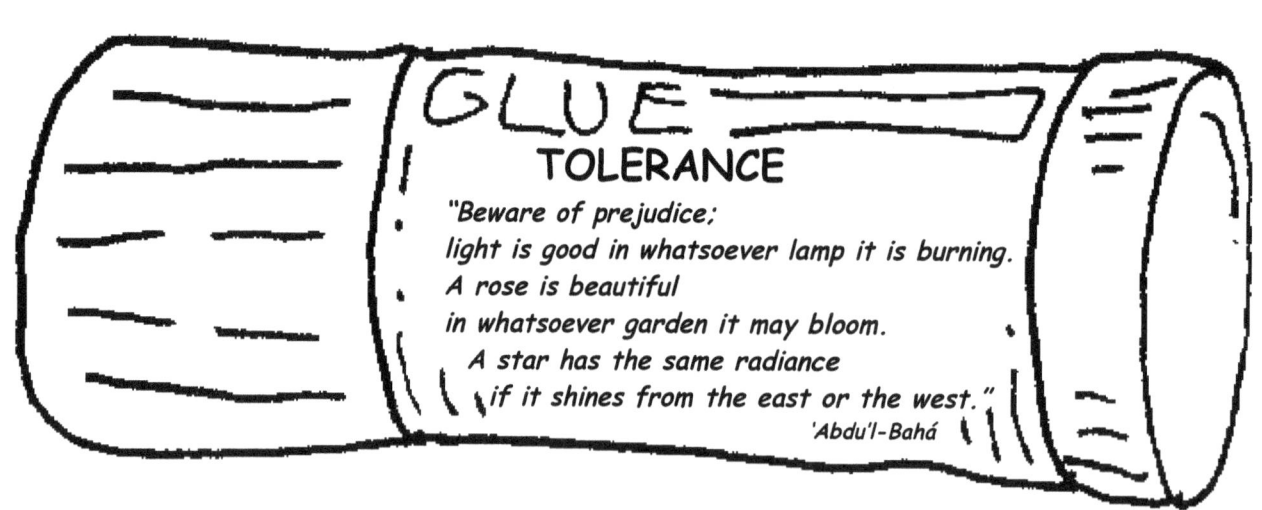

GLUE
TOLERANCE
"Beware of prejudice;
light is good in whatsoever lamp it is burning.
A rose is beautiful
in whatsoever garden it may bloom.
A star has the same radiance
if it shines from the east or the west."
'Abdu'l-Bahá

TOLERANCE
A BUNDLE OF FLOWERS

INSTRUCTIONS:
- Using a strip of coloured crepe paper, scrunch the bottom edge together and tie with a pipe cleaner.
- Attach leaves by folding the green crepe paper in half curling the pipe cleaner around the ends.
- Repeat the above to make a few flowers.
- Place the flowers in a small jar or container.
- Give a copy of the quotation to each child. Glue or sticky tape to the container.

EACH CHILD WILL NEED:
- Scissors / glue / sticky tape
- A copy of the quotation
- Coloured strips of crepe paper about 6cm by 50cm. The colours should be bright; eg. Red, Orange, Yellow, Pink, Purple.
- Strips of green crepe paper about 3cm by 10cm.
- Pipe cleaners (Green or Brown)
- Small jars or containers.

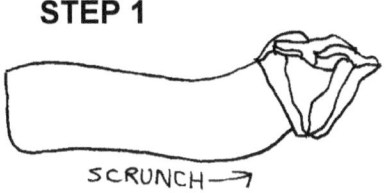

STEP 1 — SCRUNCH

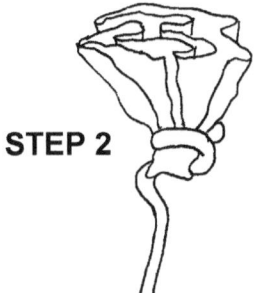

STEP 2

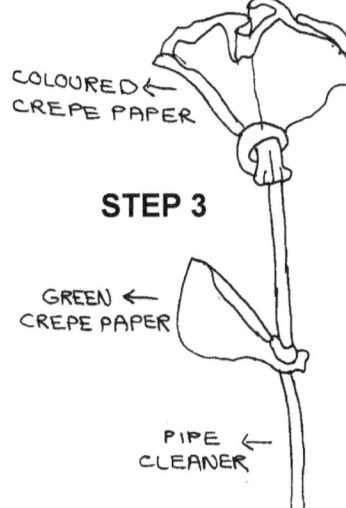

STEP 3 — COLOURED CREPE PAPER, GREEN CREPE PAPER, PIPE CLEANER

*"Beware of prejudice;
light is good
in whatsoever lamp it is burning.
A rose is beautiful
in whatsoever garden it may bloom.
A star has the same radiance
if it shines from the east or the west."*

'Abdu'l-Bahá

TOLERANCE

Quote Visualization

TOLERANCE

*"Beware of prejudice; light is good in whatsoever lamp it is burning.
A rose is beautiful in whatsoever garden it may bloom.
A star has the same radiance if it shines from the east or the west."*

'Abdu'l-Bahá

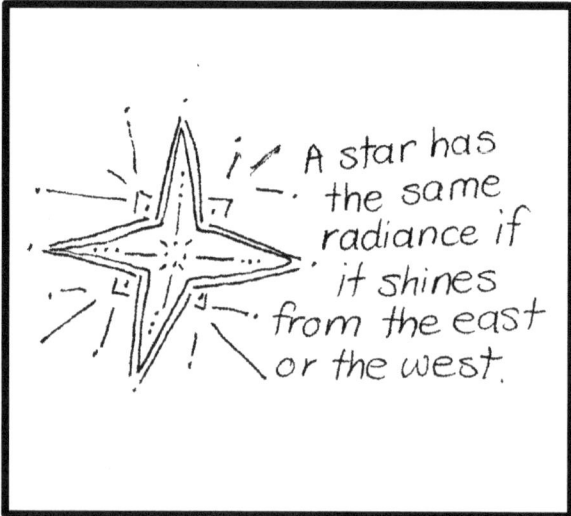

TOLERANCE

Quotation activity worksheet

TOLERANCE
*"Beware of prejudice; light is good in whatsoever lamp it is burning.
A rose is beautiful in whatsoever garden it may bloom.
A star has the same radiance if it shines from the east or the west."*
'Abdu'l-Bahá

I am being tolerant when I ....
....

TOLERANCE
*"Beware of prejudice; light is good in whatsoever lamp it is burning.
A rose is beautiful in whatsoever garden it may bloom.
A star has the same radiance if it shines from the east or the west."*
'Abdu'l-Bahá

I am being tolerant when I ....
....

TOLERANCE

Quotation activity worksheet

THE FERN, THE ROSE BUSH AND THE GRASS

TOLERANCE STORY

There was once three plants. The first was a fern that was grown in a greenhouse at Lilliput Cottage where it was protected from the weather and plant eating bugs. The second was a rose bush that was grown at the back of a shopping centre in the nearby town and prepared for someone to buy. The third was grass and grown outside at Lilliput cottage where it had to brave the weather and struggle against pesty bugs.

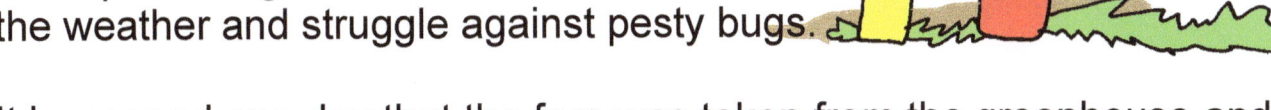

It happened one day that the fern was taken from the greenhouse and put into a garden bed next to the grass and the rose bush was bought from the shop and planted next to the fern. So it was, that the fern, the grass and the rose bush were introduced to each other.

The fern was very proud that it had been raised with the best of everything in the greenhouse. It's leaves had never been eaten by bugs or burnt by the hot sun and therefore felt itself to be superior to all other plants. The fern moaned to the rose bush, "Would you move your branches or your thorns will poke holes in my leaves."
"Move yourself," retorted the rose bush who, having been raised along side many other plants had had to fight for survival. It was the plant that grew the quickest and got the most sun and water that thrived and was eventually bought by someone. The others got tossed away. The rose bush fluffed out its leaves and stretched its roots into the ground. It looked down and saw the grass creeping over the edge and into the garden bed. "Keep on your side," complained the rose bush.
"I need to get the nutrients where I can find them," stated the grass. "I was raised here and I know that good nutrients are not always easy to find so I will take what I can, where I can."

TOLERANCE
STORY

The three plants continued to argue until the sun went down and the world got dark. As each day passed the sun got hotter and hotter. The rose bush had beautiful flowers but each time one would bloom it would get burnt by the sun. The rose bush complained constantly until finally the fern who had had enough of its whining reached out with its thick green leaves to shade the rose bush from the heat of the day. The roses started blooming more and more beautifully. Without the sun burning them the rose bush was able to cover itself in beautiful colourful flowers. "Thank you, thank you," the rose bush repeated again and again. It was so grateful for the fern's help.

The sun continued to be hot and the earth got dry and had less and less nutrients to sustain the plants. The rose bush was so beautiful that it was given special fertilizer to help it grow, but the grass got nothing and slowly its leaves started to turn yellow. The rose bush looked down on the sad yellowed leaves then moved its roots aside so that the grass could creep over to where the soil was rich in nutrients. "Thank you, thank you," repeated the grass gratefully as it sucked up the nutrients it needed
so much.

Still the sun got hotter and the fern got dryer. It had been raised in a greenhouse and did not know how to save water. It's leaves browned and dried out. The grass which took up so much space was given much more water than it really needed so it allowed the fern to reach its roots into its wet soil and drink some of the water thirstily.
"Thank you, thank you," cried the fern who was now feeling much better.

From that day on, although they all looked different and had come from different places they always helped each other out so that all year the grass, the fern and the rose bush were green and healthy. In the whole of the garden these three plants looked the most wonderful.

MORAL – Tolerance means accepting each other for just the way they are and knowing that everyone has something special they can give to others.

THANKFULNESS

LESSON PLAN

SESSION 1

PRAYER: Sing prayers that have been learnt and any others that the children know. Ask them to be reverent because they are talking to God.

SCENARIO:
Read out the scenario on the next page to the children.

Use the Happy / Sad Face (as described in the beginning of the book) to discuss what could turn the situation around from a sad one to a happy one. Let the child who comes up with the solution first turn the mouth from a gloomy face to a smiling one.

Bring out the toolbox (as described in the beginning of the book) and let the children guess which tool (virtue) they could use to fix the situation. Remind the children that these are the tools God gives us to help us in everything we do each day. Choose one child to take out the tool. Read out the virtue and the quotation. Ask the children to say the quotation with you a couple of times. Discuss what the quotation means

"...real thankfulness is a cordial giving of thanks from the heart."
    'Abdu'l-Bahá

Discussion Thoughts – Thankfulness is more than just saying the words 'thank you'. It is also how we feel inside.

SONG: "Thank You" - sing with actions.

ACTIVITY: Thank you card – Use activity sheet provided.
Purpose – to practice being thankful.

SESSION 2

PRAYER: Sing prayers that have been learnt and any others that the children know. Ask them to be reverent because they are talking to God.

DISCUSSION REVIEW: What does thankfulness mean?
Optional - Use discussion prompts sheet from the beginning of the book to help with the discussion.

SONG: "Thank You" - sing with actions.

STORY: "The Sad Song"

GAME: Give each child a turn at saying something that they can thank God for, something they can thank their mum or dad for and something they can thank one of their friends for.

ACTIVITY:
"...real thankfulness is a cordial giving of thanks from the heart."
    'Abdu'l-Bahá
Use the quote visualization page to review the meaning of the quotation.
Say the quotation with the children a few times. Older children may be able to memorize it.
Give each child a copy of the quotation activity provided. Cut and glue in each part of the quotation in the correct order, colour in and assist the child to write in something that they can do to practice thankfulness.

THANKFULNESS

SCENARIO

Scenario:

Who likes getting presents?

Do you like knowing what the present is going to be before you get it or do you like to be surprised when you unwrap it?

There was once a girl called Jane. It was her Birthday and she was turning five years old. She had invited all her friends to a party and was waiting for them to arrive. She had told them all what she wanted for a present - dolls and more dolls because Jane loved dolls more than anything else. When her friends arrived she unwrapped the presents one by one. She unwrapped the first doll, "Too small." she said and gave it back to her friend. She unwrapped the next present, "It doesn't have curly hair," she said and again returned the gift. Each time she unwrapped a present she complained that is was no good and returned it ungratefully. Soon she realized she had no presents left to unwrap but had given all the gifts back and so she was left with nothing at all. Jane was very sad and sorry that she had been so quick to criticize the presents that were really very beautiful even if they weren't exactly what she was hoping for. What could Jane have done to make the situation turn out differently.

Possible solution:

She could have been grateful for what she was given instead of only thinking about what she didn't have.

The tool to fix the problem is: **Thankfulness**

THANKFULNESS
"...real thankfulness is a cordial giving of thanks from the heart."
'Abdu'l-Bahá

THANKFULNESS
THANKYOU CARD

INSTRUCTIONS:
• Fold half a piece of coloured A4 card in half to make a card.
• Cut out the large heart and glue to the front of the card. Smaller hearts could be cut to decorate around the outside.
• Cut out the message square and glue into the centre of the card.
• Write in the message and colour in.

EACH CHILD WILL NEED:
• Scissors, glue
• A large heart and a message square.
• Half a sheet of coloured A4 card.
• Crayons / Pencils
• Optional - Small cut out hearts for decoration.

Quote Visualization

THANKFULNESS

THANKFULNESS
"...real thankfulness is a cordial giving of thanks from the heart."

'Abdu'l-Bahá

Quotation activity worksheet — THANKFULNESS

THANKFULNESS
"...real thankfulness is a cordial giving of thanks from the heart."
'Abdu'l-Bahá

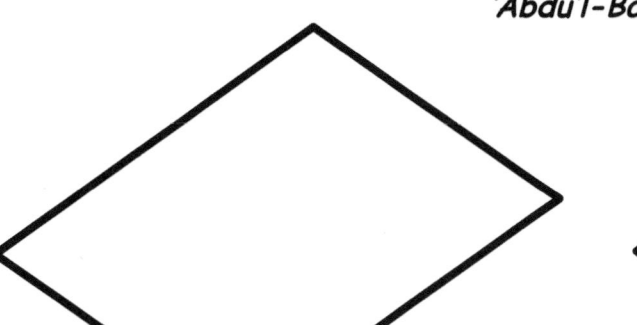
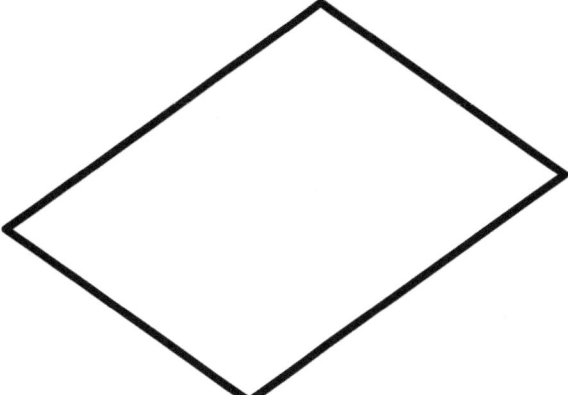

I can be thankful when I..................................
....

THANKFULNESS
"...real thankfulness is a cordial giving of thanks from the heart."
'Abdu'l-Bahá

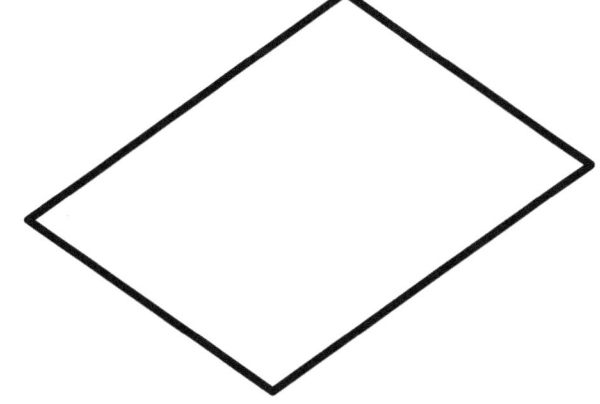
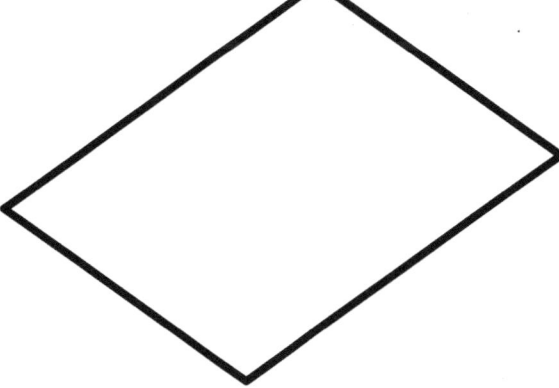

I can be thankful when I..................................
....

THANKFULNESS

Quotation activity worksheet

THE SAD SONG

THANKFULNESS STORY

Jake was a guitar and his best friend was Bobby the drum. They would sit together for hours listening to the other instruments play. "I wish I could play beautiful tunes like the flutes do," said Bobby miserably. Jake wasn't listening. He was too busy thinking about how nice it would be to be able call out really loudly like the horns did. They sat there in silence feeling very sad about all the things they could not do.

Later, Jake the guitar started to play a sad song because sad was how he felt. The notes rang out through the room and bounced off the walls. After a little while Bobby the drum joined in with a soft beat to his tune. They were so absorbed in their music that they did not notice that all the other instruments had fallen silent.

The other instruments listened quietly and some even shed a few tears as they listened to the sad music float around them. When the music stopped, Bobby and Jake looked up and were surprised to see so many attentive listeners.
"Oh, I'm sorry," said Jake, thinking he had disturbed their playing.
"That was beautiful," exclaimed the clarinet.
"Incredible," said the horn.
"I wish I could make people feel the music like that," sighed the Oboe. Slowly the instruments moved away to other parts of the room leaving Bobby and Jake staring after them in astonishment.
"It seems we all have something that other people want or wish they had," said Bobby thoughtfully.
"Yes, it seems we all have something we should be grateful for," replied Jake. He smiled at Bobby and Bobby smiled back.

MORAL – Thankfulness is appreciating the things we do have instead of longing for the things we don't have.

ENTHUSIASM

LESSON PLAN

SESSION 1

PRAYER: Sing prayers that have been learnt and any others that the children know. Ask them to be reverent because they are talking to God.

SCENARIO:
Read out the scenario on the next page to the children.

Use the Happy / Sad Face (as described in the beginning of the book) to discuss what could turn the situation around from a sad one to a happy one. Let the child who comes up with the solution first turn the mouth from a gloomy face to a smiling one.

Bring out the toolbox (as described in the beginning of the book) and let the children guess which tool (virtue) they could use to fix the situation. Remind the children that these are the tools God gives us to help us in everything we do each day. Choose one child to take out the tool. Read out the virtue and the quotation. Ask the children to say the quotation with you a couple of times. Discuss what the quotation means

"....be set aglow with the fire of the love of God, and raise the anthem of jubilation with the full enthusiasm of your heart and soul"
    'Abdu'l-Bahá

Discussion Thoughts – When we feel connected with God we feel happy inside. When we are enthusiastic we let this happiness out and share it with others.

SONG: "Be Free" - sing with actions.

ACTIVITY: Heart of Enthusiasm – Use activity sheet provided.
    Purpose – to reflect on the meaning of the quotation.

SESSION 2

PRAYER: Sing prayers that have been learnt and any others that the children know. Ask them to be reverent because they are talking to God.

DISCUSSION REVIEW: What does enthusiasm mean?
    Optional - Use discussion prompts sheet from the beginning of the book to help with the discussion.

SONG: "Be Free" - sing with actions.

STORY: "A Great Idea"

GAME: Ask the children to stand up and look at the ceiling of the room. Ask them to jump with as much enthusiasm as they can to see if they can touch the roof. Explain that although we can't reach the roof we feel very joyful when we approach things with enthusiasm.
    Purpose – To practice being enthusiastic and understand how enthusiasm can affect how we feel about the things we do.

ACTIVITY:
"....be set aglow with the fire of the love of God, and raise the anthem of jubilation with the full enthusiasm of your heart and soul"
    'Abdu'l-Bahá
Use the quote visualization page to review the meaning of the quotation.
Say the quotation with the children a few times. Older children may be able to memorize it.
Give each child a copy of the quotation activity provided. Cut and glue in each part of the quotation in the correct order, colour in and assist the child to write in something that they can do to practice enthusiasm.

SCENARIO

Scenario:
Who feels excited sometimes?
What are some things that make you excited?
There was once a boy who was nearly always gloomy. When someone had an idea he would always say something like "That won't work," or "How boring." or "What a silly idea." He never seemed to be excited about anything and so he found everything very uninteresting. One day his mum told him that they were going to go camping. The boy immediately groaned and said, "I just want to stay home," but his mum insisted that he must come anyway. The boy felt very annoyed and thought about how boring it was all going to be. What could the boy do to make the camping trip fun and exciting.

Possible solution:
He could think about all the good things he can do when he is camping and decide to make it as much fun as possible instead of dwelling on how bad he thought it would be.

The tool to fix the problem is: **Enthusiasm**

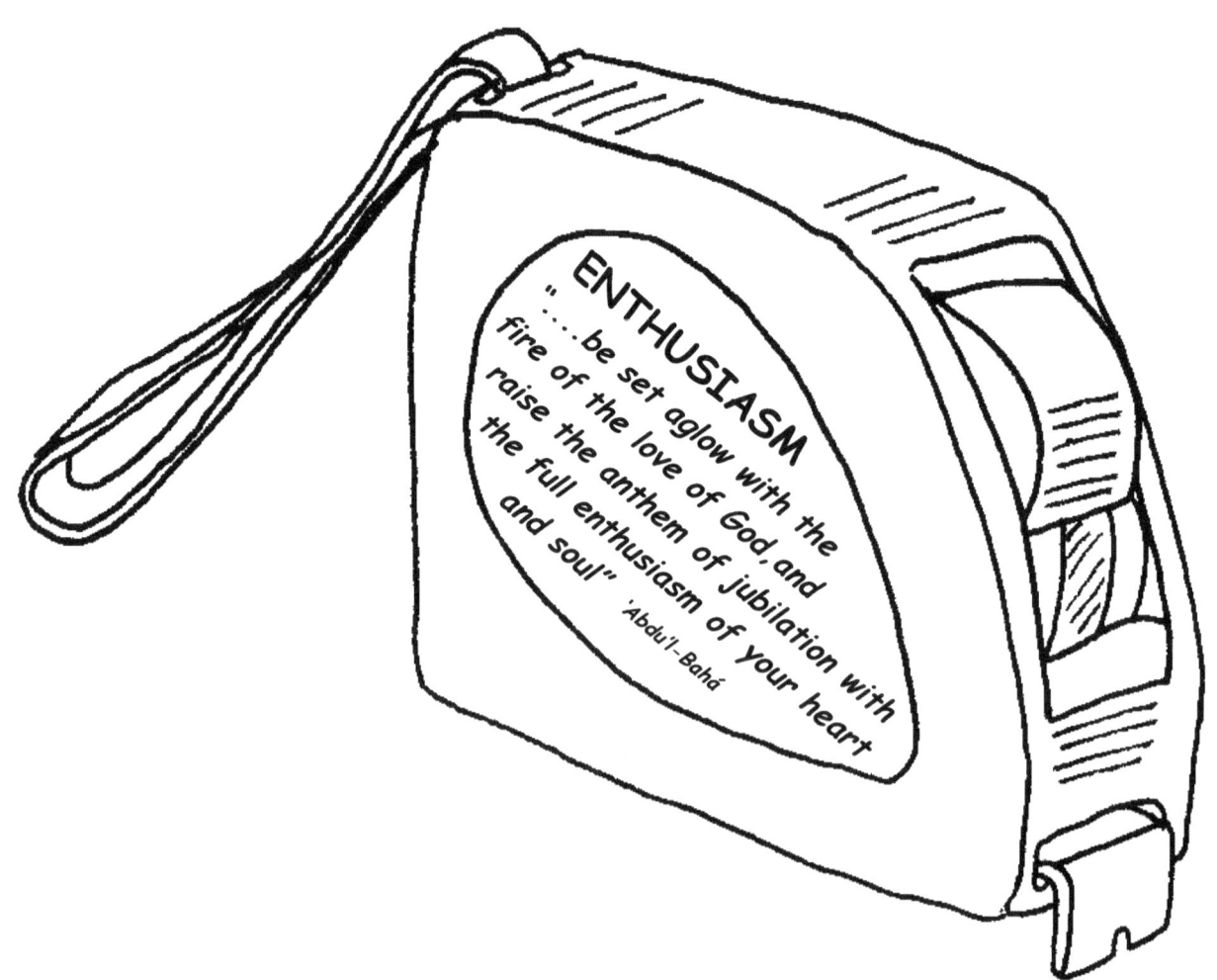

ENTHUSIASM
"....be set aglow with the fire of the love of God, and raise the anthem of jubilation with the full enthusiasm of your heart and soul" 'Abdu'l-Bahá

ENTHUSIASM
HEART OF ENTHUSIASM

"....be set aglow with the fire of the love of God, and raise the anthem of jubilation with the full enthusiasm of your heart and soul"
'Abdu'l-Bahá

"....be set aglow with the fire of the love of God, and raise the anthem of jubilation with the full enthusiasm of your heart and soul"
'Abdu'l-Bahá

"....be set aglow with the fire of the love of God, and raise the anthem of jubilation with the full enthusiasm of your heart and soul"
'Abdu'l-Bahá

"....be set aglow with the fire of the love of God, and raise the anthem of jubilation with the full enthusiasm of your heart and soul"
'Abdu'l-Bahá

EACH CHILD WILL NEED:
- Scissors, glue
- A copy of a heart on white card
- Crayons / pencils
- Some small flame shapes in red / gold / orange / yellow colours.

"....be set aglow with the fire of the love of God, and raise the anthem of jubilation with the full enthusiasm of your heart and soul"
'Abdu'l-Bahá

"....be set aglow with the fire of the love of God, and raise the anthem of jubilation with the full enthusiasm of your heart and soul"
'Abdu'l-Bahá

INSTRUCTIONS:
- Give each child a copy of a heart to cut out.
- Glue flame shapes onto the edge of the back of the heart.
- Colour in.

Quote Visualization

ENTHUSIASM

*"....be set aglow with the fire of the love of God,
and raise the anthem of jubilation with
the full enthusiasm of your heart and soul"*

'Abdu'l-Bahá

Quotation activity worksheet

ENTHUSIASM

ENTHUSIASM
*"....be set aglow with the fire of the love of God,
and raise the anthem of jubilation with
the full enthusiasm of your heart and soul"*
'Abdu'l-Bahá

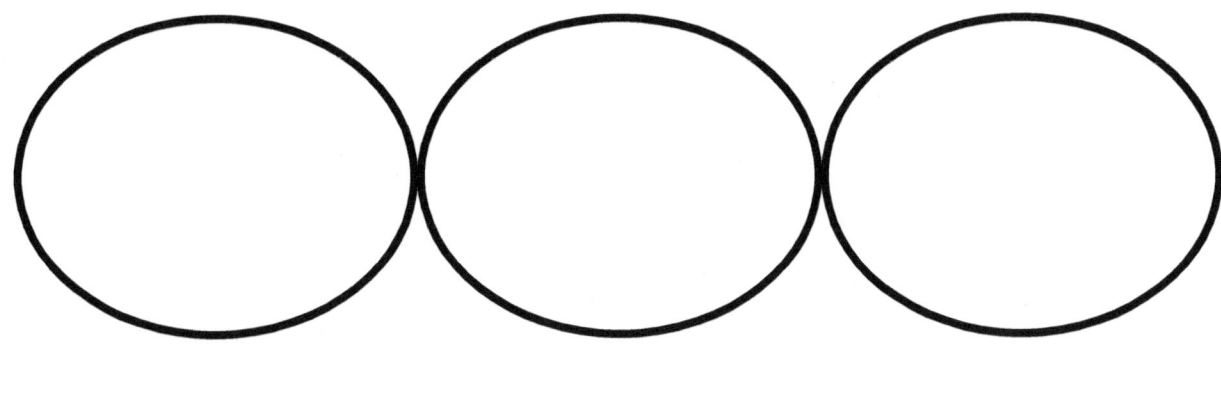

Enthusiasm is when I ....
....

ENTHUSIASM
*"....be set aglow with the fire of the love of God,
and raise the anthem of jubilation with
the full enthusiasm of your heart and soul"*
'Abdu'l-Bahá

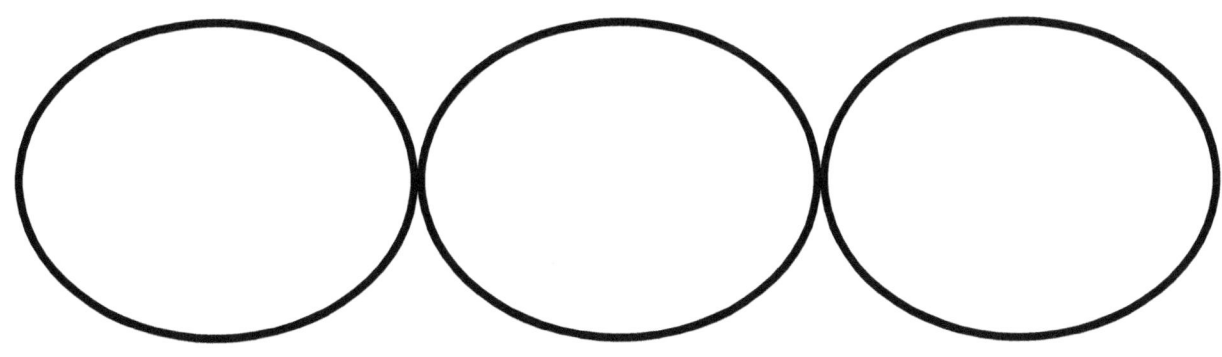

Enthusiasm is when I ....
....

Quotation activity worksheet

ENTHUSIASM

A GREAT IDEA

ENTHUSIASM
STORY

There was once two marbles.
Bright was a shiny marble who was always full of energy and ready for an adventure. Gloom was a plain brown marble who never wanted to do anything except sit in one place and moan. Bright and Gloom were sitting on the grass one day when Bright suddenly came up with one of his bright ideas. "Let's roll through some puddles. It would be great to go splash and zoom through the water," exclaimed Bright excitedly. "Yuk," replied Gloom. "I don't see why getting muddy and dirty and smelly could ever be a good idea."
"Well I am sure someone will like to come with me," said Bright as he rolled off to find a friend to play with. It wasn't long before Gloom could see Bright and some friends splashing through some puddles not far away. Gloom continued to sit by himself doing nothing.
"How does Bright always seem to manage to get so many friends doing so many silly things," Gloom said aloud to himself. "It's because he's always so enthusiastic and happy. That makes him fun to play with," said Rolly, a green and yellow marble who suddenly appeared behind Gloom. Rolly rolled on and joined the other marbles in the puddles.
"I can do that too," Gloom said to himself. He rolled over to the puddles where the other marbles were getting very muddy and then called out as loudly and as enthusiastically as he could. "I am going to roll down some pipes, who would like to come."
Everyone stopped, looked at him surprised for a moment and then all called out "I will," as they jumped out of the puddles and followed Gloom over to some pipes lying on a hill not far away. The marbles spent the afternoon whizzing down the pipes and flying out the other end. "What a great idea that was," called all the marbles as they rolled off home that night. Bright came up beside him.
"It was a great idea," Bright said happily. "What shall we do tomorrow?"
"How about playing hide and seek in the grass," suggested Gloom in a very cheery voice.
"Good idea," Bright said sleepily, "I can't wait."
Then he fell asleep next to Gloom who didn't look gloomy at all. Neither did he look plain or brown. In fact Gloom glowed as if a little light had been turned on inside him.

MORAL – Enthusiasm is choosing to be happy and making the best of everything we do.

CONSIDERATION

LESSON PLAN

SESSION 1

PRAYER: Sing prayers that have been learnt and any others that the children know. Ask them to be reverent because they are talking to God.

SCENARIO:
Read out the scenario on the next page to the children.

Use the Happy / Sad Face (as described in the beginning of the book) to discuss what could turn the situation around from a sad one to a happy one. Let the child who comes up with the solution first turn the mouth from a gloomy face to a smiling one.

Bring out the toolbox (as described in the beginning of the book) and let the children guess which tool (virtue) they could use to fix the situation. Remind the children that these are the tools God gives us to help us in everything we do each day. Choose one child to take out the tool. Read out the virtue and the quotation. Ask the children to say the quotation with you a couple of times. Discuss what the quotation means

"They must purify their sight, and look upon mankind as the leaves, blossoms and fruits of the tree of creation, and must always be thinking of doing good to someone, of love, consideration, affection and assistance to somebody."
    'Abdu'l-Bahá

Discussion Thoughts - We must see each person as a member of the world of humanity. We should show consideration to each one without any discrimination.

SONG: "Brothers and Sisters" - sing with actions.

ACTIVITY: Tree of Creation – Use activity sheet provided.
    Purpose – to reflect on the meaning of the quotation.

SESSION 2

PRAYER: Sing prayers that have been learnt and any others that the children know. Ask them to be reverent because they are talking to God.

DISCUSSION REVIEW: What does consideration mean?
    Optional - Use discussion prompts sheet from the beginning of the book to help with the discussion.

SONG: "Brothers and Sisters" - sing with actions.

STORY: "Sitting Alone"

GAME: Play a game of consideration bingo. Read out a question from those provided or make up your own. The first person to call out the right answer can put a cross in one of their boxes. Whoever fills in all their boxes first and calls out bingo, wins the game. Use the game boards provided.
    Purpose – to increase familiarity with what it means to be considerate.

ACTIVITY:
    "They must purify their sight, and look upon mankind as the leaves, blossoms and fruits of the tree of creation, and must always be thinking of doing good to someone, of love, consideration, affection and assistance to somebody."
        'Abdu'l-Bahá
Use the quote visualization page to review the meaning of the quotation.
Say the quotation with the children a few times. Older children may be able to memorize it.
Give each child a copy of the quotation activity provided. Cut and glue in each part of the quotation in the correct order, colour in and assist the child to write in something that they can do to practice consideration.

CONSIDERATION

SCENARIO

Scenario:
Do you like having friends come over to your house and play?
Do you look after them when they are at your house?
There was once a boy named Shane who couldn't wait to get home from school because he had his friend Steven coming to visit and they were going to play with his new train set. Shane ran home and arrived just as Steven was getting out of his mum's car. It was a very hot day and after the boys had run inside Shane got a cold glass of water from the fridge and gulped it down thirstily. Steven looked at him eagerly as he was very hot and thirsty too but was too shy to ask for a drink so he said nothing. What should Shane do to help make Steven feel welcome?

Possible solution:
Shane should offer Steven a glass of water too.

The tool to fix the problem is: **Consideration**

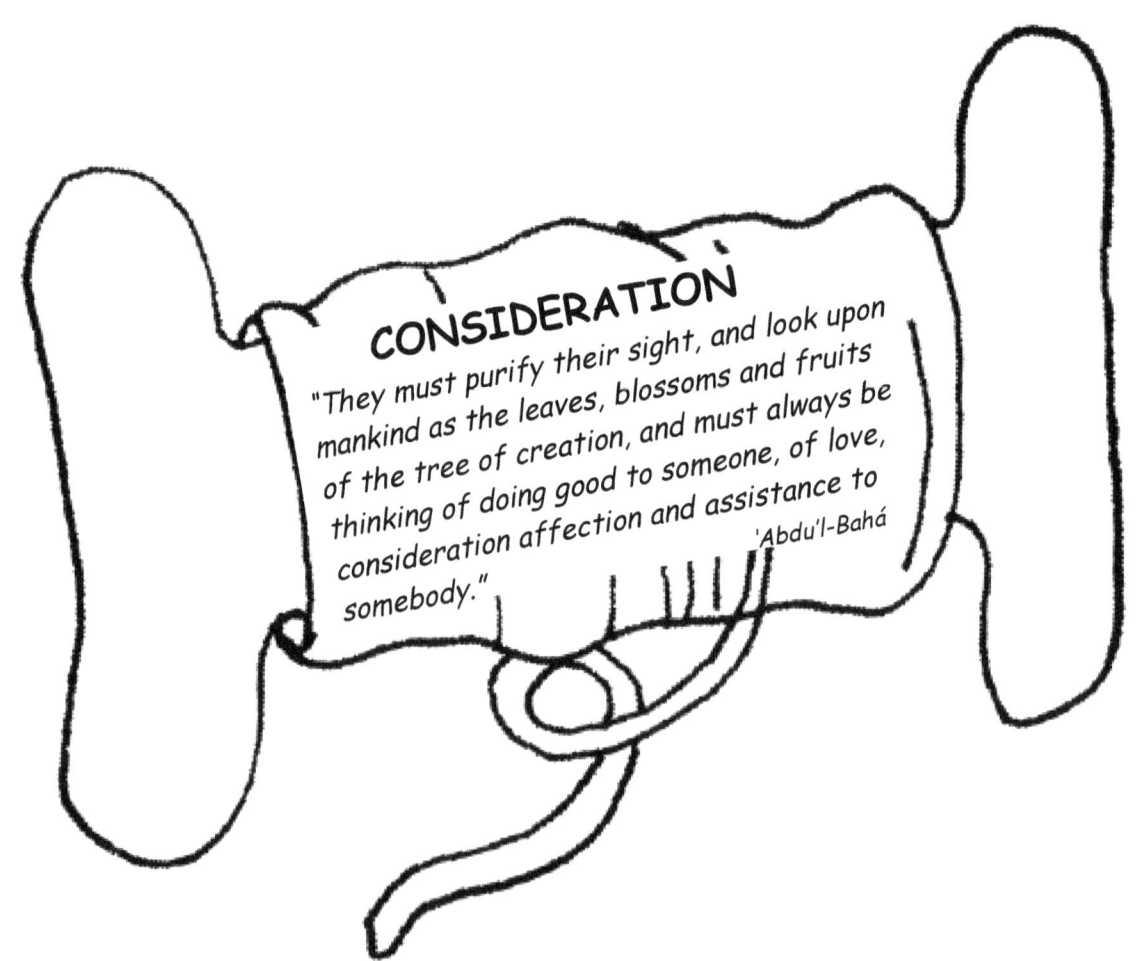

CONSIDERATION
"They must purify their sight, and look upon mankind as the leaves, blossoms and fruits of the tree of creation, and must always be thinking of doing good to someone, of love, consideration affection and assistance to somebody."
'Abdu'l-Bahá

CONSIDERATION
TREE OF CREATION

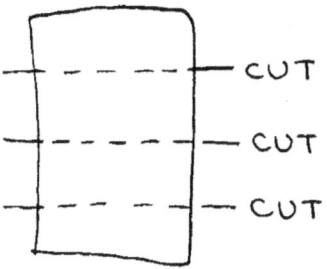

STEP 1
• Cut an A4 page into four strips.
• Give one to each child.

STEP 2
• Fold the strip into 8 parts.
• Cut out the template and place on top of the folded strip.
• Trace around template and cut out.

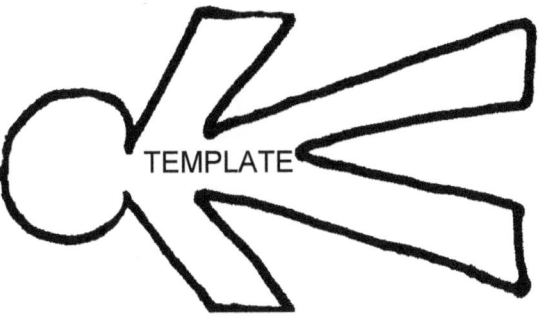

STEP 3
• Cut out the branch.
• Tape the people around the branch like leaves.

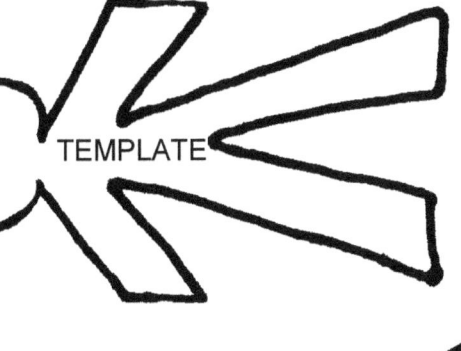

"They must purify their sight, and look upon mankind as the leaves, blossoms and fruits of the tree of creation, and must always be thinking of doing good to someone, of love, consideration, affection and assistance to somebody." 'Abdu'l-Bahá

EACH CHILD WILL NEED:
• A strip from a piece of green A4 paper.
• A copy of a branch and template on brown paper.
• Sticky tape / scissors.
• Coloured pencils.

"They must purify their sight, and look upon mankind as the leaves, blossoms and fruits of the tree of creation, and must always be thinking of doing good to someone, of love, consideration, affection and assistance to somebody." 'Abdu'l-Bahá

Quote Visualization

CONSIDERATION

CONSIDERATION

"They must purify their sight, and look upon mankind as the leaves, blossoms and fruits of the tree of creation, and must always be thinking of doing good to someone, of love, consideration, affection and assistance to somebody."

'Abdu'l-Bahá

Quotation activity worksheet

CONSIDERATION

CONSIDERATION

"They must purify their sight, and look upon mankind as the leaves, blossoms and fruits of the tree of creation, and must always be thinking of doing good to someone, of love, consideration, affection and assistance to somebody."

'Abdu'l-Bahá

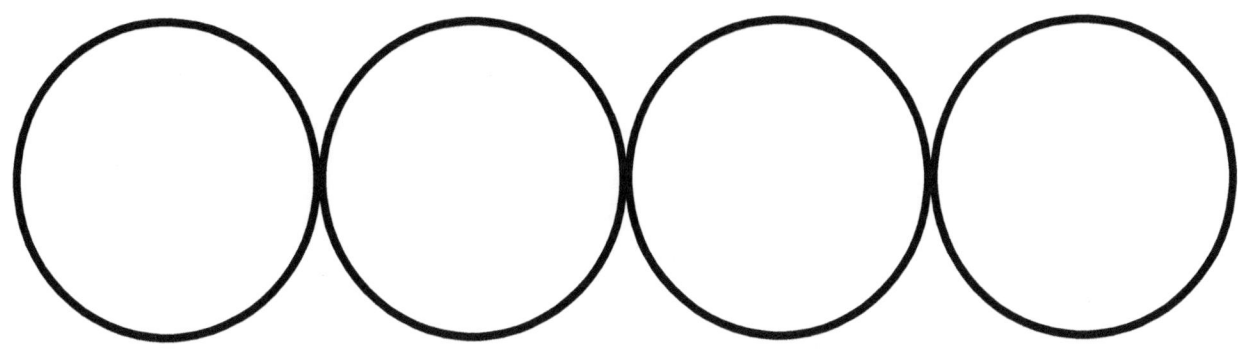

I need to be Considerate when ....
....

CONSIDERATION

"They must purify their sight, and look upon mankind as the leaves, blossoms and fruits of the tree of creation, and must always be thinking of doing good to someone, of love, consideration, affection and assistance to somebody."

'Abdu'l-Bahá

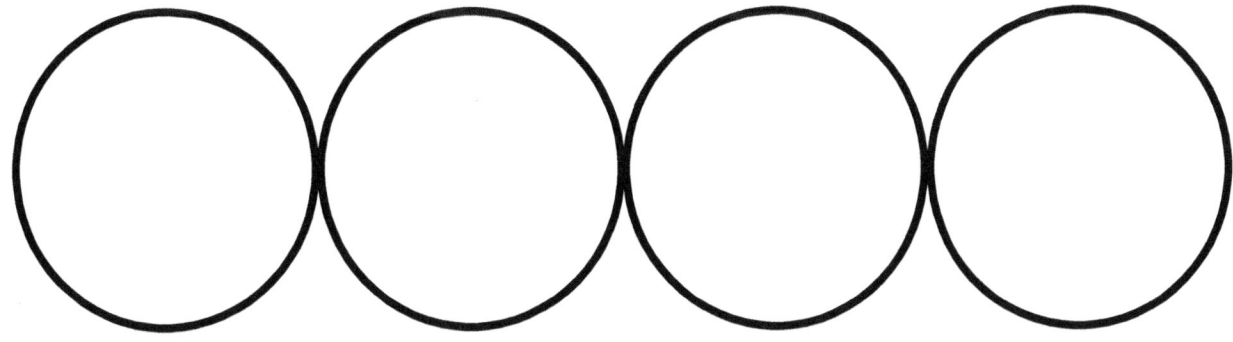

I need to be Considerate when ....
....

CONSIDERATION

Quotation activity worksheet

CONSIDERATION

Game

Bingo boards – copy and cut out one for each child.

CONSIDERATION

Game

BINGO QUESTIONS

HOW CAN YOU SHOW CONSIDERATION WHEN...

- **someone comes to your house to play on a very hot day?**
  Offer them a drink of water.
- **someone is finding it difficult to put their shoes on?**
  Help them to put their shoes on.
- **someone is trying to lift something very heavy?**
  You could help them lift it.
- **the teacher is talking?**
  Listen quietly.
- **your friend is crying?**
  Put your arm around them and ask them what is wrong.
- **your dad is telling you a story?**
  Listen quietly.
- **someone is very tired and is trying to have a sleep?**
  Play quietly while they are sleeping or play in another room.
- **A friend is very sad because they have lost a special toy?**
  Help them find it or give them one of your toys.
- **A friend forgot to bring their coloured pencils to school?**
  Share your coloured pencils with them.
- **your mum is talking on the telephone?**
  Play quietly and say "excuse me" if you need to speak to her.
- **you are playing with some blocks and someone else wants to play too?**
  Ask them to join in.
- **your mum is doing the shopping?**
  Don't wander off, help her put things in the shopping trolley
- **someone is eating their lunch all alone?**
  Ask them if they would like to sit and eat with you.
- **someone is standing in the doorway and you want to get through?**
  Say "excuse me" and wait for them to move.
- **you have two friends who have come to play but there is only one piece of cake left?**
  Cut the cake into three or leave it till after they have gone.

SITTING ALONE

CONSIDERATION
STORY

Jasmine enjoyed colouring and it was while they were colouring in at school that a new girl arrived into the class. The new girl's name was Tana and she was asked to sit in the spare seat next to Jasmine. The class settled down and the children continued colouring. Jasmine suddenly realized that Tana only had a black pencil to colour with so she kindly moved all her coloured pencils into the middle of the desk and asked if she would like to use them too. Tana smiled and thanked her.

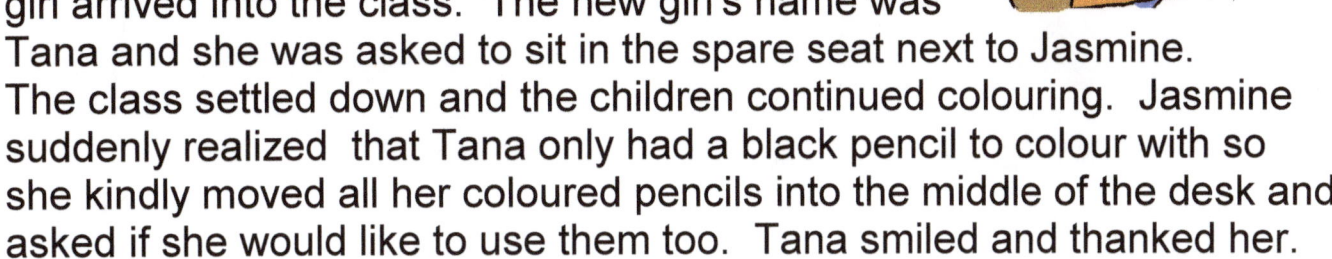

Later at lunch time, Jasmine noticed that Tana was sitting eating by herself. She looked very lonely, so Jasmine went and asked Tana to come and sit with her and her friends. They all ate lunch and chatted and played until it was time to go inside again.

When they got inside the teacher asked them to get into pairs and practice reading books to each other. Again Tana was left sitting alone so Jasmine went and joined her with her book to practice reading.

By this time the two girls were starting to become real friends. The class went out to play sport on the oval and this time Tana and Jasmine walked together. Jasmine was not very good at sport. She kept dropping the ball and throwing it too high or too low and so this time Jasmine was left standing alone because no-one wanted to play sport with someone who couldn't throw or catch. Jasmine was just starting to feel left out when Tana came and joined her. Tana threw the ball gently to help Jasmine catch it and because Tana was good at sports she always managed to catch the ball even when Jasmine threw it too high or too low.

The girls said goodbye to each other that day like two old friends who had known each other for years even though it had only been a day. Each day after that they always made sure they looked after each other so that neither ever felt left out or alone.

MORAL – We can show consideration by thinking about how others are feeling and helping them feel included.

SELFLESSNESS

LESSON PLAN

SESSION 1

PRAYER: Sing prayers that have been learnt and any others that the children know. Ask them to be reverent because they are talking to God.

SCENARIO:
Read out the scenario on the next page to the children.

Use the Happy / Sad Face (as described in the beginning of the book) to discuss what could turn the situation around from a sad one to a happy one. Let the child who comes up with the solution first turn the mouth from a gloomy face to a smiling one.

Bring out the toolbox (as described in the beginning of the book) and let the children guess which tool (virtue) they could use to fix the situation. Remind the children that these are the tools God gives us to help us in everything we do each day. Choose one child to take out the tool. Read out the virtue and the quotation. Ask the children to say the quotation with you a couple of times. Discuss what the quotation means

"Man is he who forgets his own interests for the sake of others. His own comfort he forfeits for the well-being of all."
    'Abdu'l-Bahá

Discussion Thoughts - Think of others before yourself and see every person you meet as important and special.

SONG: "Think of Others" - sing with actions.

ACTIVITY: Putting Others Before Yourself – Use activity sheet provided.
Purpose – to reflect on the meaning of the quotation and to visualize what it means to be selfless.

SESSION 2

PRAYER: Sing prayers that have been learnt and any others that the children know. Ask them to be reverent because they are talking to God.

DISCUSSION REVIEW: What does selflessness mean?
Optional - Use discussion prompts sheet from the beginning of the book to help with the discussion.

SONG: "Think of Others" - sing with actions.

STORY: "Sharing With Friends Tastes Better"

GAME: Ask the children to sit in a circle on the floor. Place a bowl of special stones or something similar. Ask each person to choose one that they think is the most beautiful. Once they all have taken one ask them to now give it to the person on their right. Explain that when we are selfless we sometimes need to make sacrifices or give up something special to us in order to make others happier.
Purpose – To reflect on what it means to be selfless.

ACTIVITY:
"Man is he who forgets his own interests for the sake of others. His own comfort he forfeits for the well-being of all."
    'Abdu'l-Bahá
Use the quote visualization page to review the meaning of the quotation.
Say the quotation with the children a few times. Older children may be able to memorize it.
Give each child a copy of the quotation activity provided. Cut and glue in each part of the quotation in the correct order, colour in and assist the child to write in something that they can do to practice selflessness.

SELFLESSNESS

SCENARIO

Scenario:
Has any one ever felt really, really cold?
What do you do if you are feeling really cold?
One day some children went camping. It was a very hot day so hardly anyone brought anything warm like jumpers or blankets. At night though, when the sun went down, it started to get very cold. Leslie was the only one who had thought to bring a blanket and so she pulled it out and wrapped it around herself tightly. The other children sat shivering and rubbing their hands together. What could Leslie do to help the other children feel warm again?

Possible solution:
She could ask everyone to sit close together and wrap her blanket around everyone so that they can all be warm.

The tool to fix the problem is: **Selflessness**

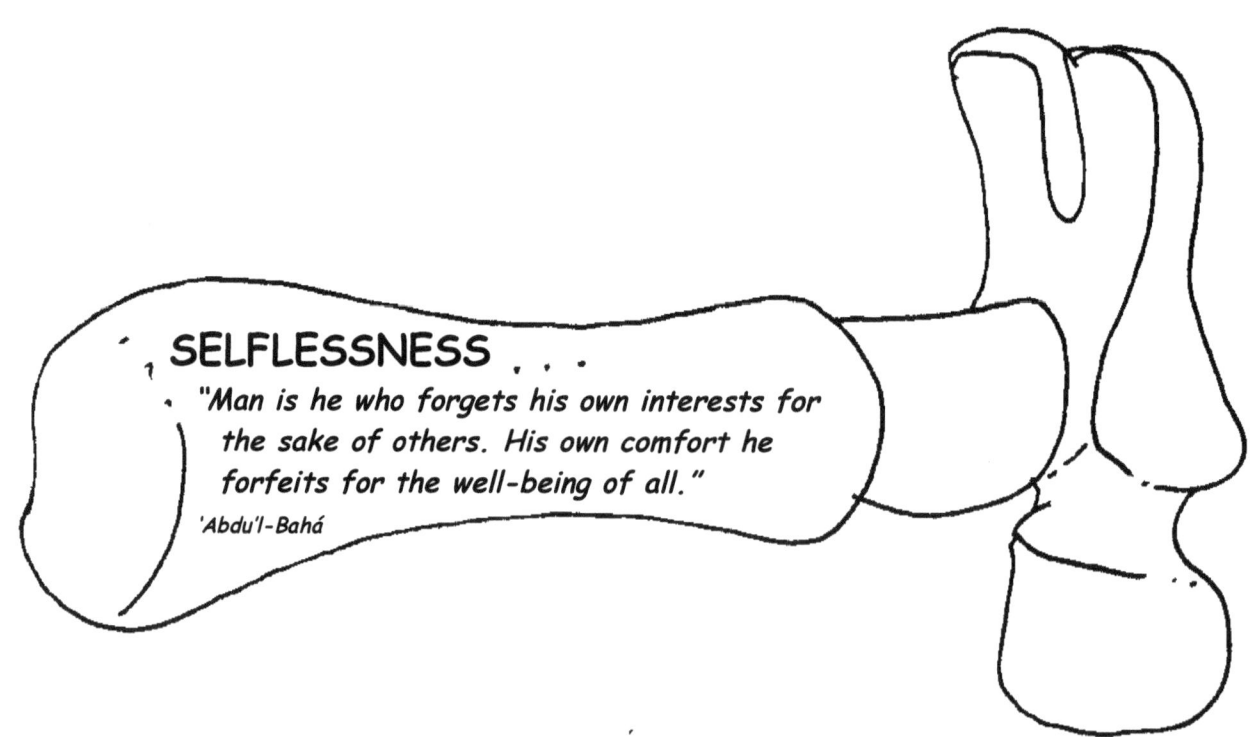

SELFLESSNESS...
"Man is he who forgets his own interests for the sake of others. His own comfort he forfeits for the well-being of all."
'Abdu'l-Bahá

SELFLESSNESS
PUTTING OTHERS BEFORE YOURSELF

INSTRUCTIONS:
- Photocopy this page on to white paper.
- Cut out.
- Draw a picture of yourself into the spot behind all the other people. (putting others before yourself)
- Colour in.

EACH CHILD WILL NEED:
- Scissors
- A copy of the activity
- Crayons / Pencils

"Man is he who forgets his own interests for the sake of others. His own comfort he forfeits for the well-being of all."   'Abdu'l-Bahá

"Man is he who forgets his own interests for the sake of others. His own comfort he forfeits for the well-being of all."   'Abdu'l-Bahá

Quote Visualization

SELFLESSNESS

"Man is he who forgets his own interests for the sake of others. His own comfort he forfeits for the well-being of all."

'Abdu'l-Bahá

Quote Visualization — SELFLESSNESS

SELFLESSNESS
"Man is he who forgets his own interests for the sake of others. His own comfort he forfeits for the well-being of all."
'Abdu'l-Bahá

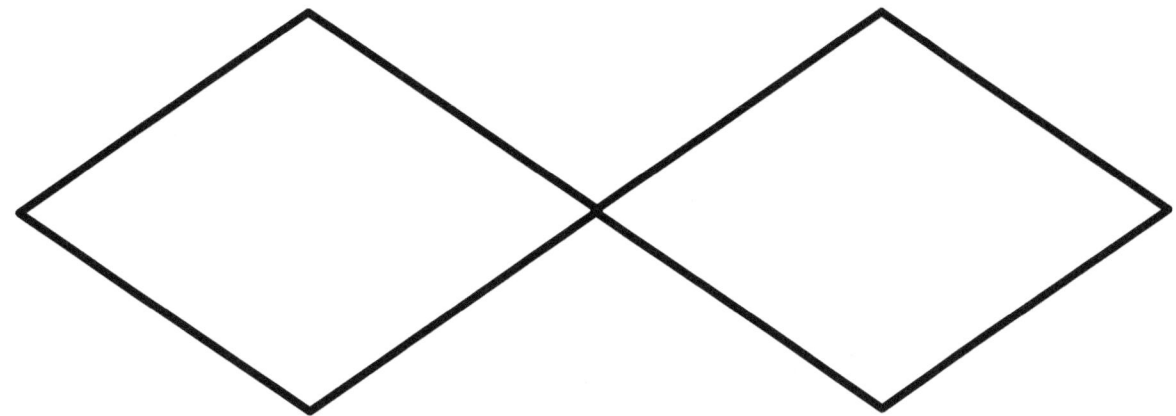

I am being selfless when I..........................
....

SELFLESSNESS
"Man is he who forgets his own interests for the sake of others. His own comfort he forfeits for the well-being of all."
'Abdu'l-Bahá

I am being selfless when I..........................
....

Quote Visualization

SELFLESSNESS

SHARING WITH FRIENDS TASTES BETTER

SELFLESSNESS STORY

Joan was feeling very happy as she skipped along to school. She had had her birthday on the weekend and was given five dollars to spend any way she wanted. As she skipped along she thought of all the wonderful things she could buy from the canteen at school. They were selling extra big chocolate icecreams at lunch time and she felt like she could already taste the cold icecream in her mouth.

She tried to concentrate on her work in the classroom but it was very hard because she kept thinking about that delicious extra big chocolate icecream she was going to buy at lunch time. Finally the time came and she ran out with her friends very excitedly. They ran towards the canteen and then all her friends suddenly stopped. She looked back and asked "What's the matter, aren't you coming."
"We don't have any money," they replied, "We'll wait for you here."

Joan lined up with the other children while she waited her turn to be served. She kept thinking of her friends who were waiting patiently for her to come back with her extra big chocolate icecream. It was soon her turn to buy something, but when she opened her mouth, instead of asking for an extra big chocolate icecream which would have cost her all her money, she asked for five icy poles which didn't cost very much and would mean she could buy enough for herself and each of her friends. She walked back to where her friends were waiting. She felt very happy when she saw the smiles on her friends' faces as they were each given an icy pole. All thoughts of the extra big chocolate ice cream had disappeared. Everything tastes much better when you share them with your friends.

MORAL – Selflessness is thinking about others first before you think about yourself.

UNDERSTANDING

LESSON PLAN

SESSION 1

PRAYER: Sing prayers that have been learnt and any others that the children know. Ask them to be reverent because they are talking to God.

SCENARIO:
Read out the scenario on the next page to the children.

Use the Happy / Sad Face (as described in the beginning of the book) to discuss what could turn the situation around from a sad one to a happy one. Let the child who comes up with the solution first turn the mouth from a gloomy face to a smiling one.

Bring out the toolbox (as described in the beginning of the book) and let the children guess which tool (virtue) they could use to fix the situation. Remind the children that these are the tools God gives us to help us in everything we do each day. Choose one child to take out the tool. Read out the virtue and the quotation. Ask the children to say the quotation with you a couple of times. Discuss what the quotation means

"....each must... investigate independently in order that he may find the truth."
    'Abdu'l-Bahá

Discussion Thoughts - We should not be satisfied with what someone else tells us is the truth and we should not make assumptions about things. We should continue to search, understand and find out for ourselves the truth of every situation.

SONG: "Search Till You Find" - sing with actions.

ACTIVITY: Friends – Use activity sheet provided.
Purpose – to reflect on the quotation and practice being friendly.

SESSION 2

PRAYER: Sing prayers that have been learnt and any others that the children know. Ask them to be reverent because they are talking to God.

DISCUSSION REVIEW: What does it mean to be understanding?
Optional - Use discussion prompts sheet from the beginning of the book to help with the discussion.

SONG: "Search Till You Find" - sing with actions.

STORY: "The Scary Creature"

GAME: Put some miscellaneous objects in a bag. Give each child a chance of closing their eyes (or you could put a blindfold on them) and taking something from the bag. The child guesses what the object is just by feeling before taking, opening their eyes and seeing if they were correct. Explain to the children that we should never make assumptions about things but find out for ourselves. If we only search with our hands we might make a mistake but if we use our eyes and ears and smell and ask questions etc... we can find out the truth.
Purpose – To reflect on what it means to seek understanding.

ACTIVITY:
"....each must... investigate independently in order that he may find the truth."
    'Abdu'l-Bahá
Use the quote visualization page to review the meaning of the quotation.
Say the quotation with the children a few times. Older children may be able to memorize it.
Give each child a copy of the quotation activity provided. Cut and glue in each part of the quotation in the correct order, colour in and assist the child to write in something that they can do to practice understanding.

UNDERSTANDING

SCENARIO

Scenario:

Do you like discovering new things?

If we see something strange or interesting how can we find out what it is? Some children were once playing at school when a new boy came and sat nearby them. He got out a book and started reading to himself. He was wearing something funny on his face. It had two round circles and long sticks on each side that curled around his ears. "He must be an alien," said one child. Another said, "Maybe he lives under the ground and those things on his face stop the dirt going into his eyes." A third child said, "Maybe they were stuck to his face when he was born."

What do you think the boy has on his face and how do you think these children could find out the truth?

Possible solution:

The boy is wearing glasses to help him read because his eyes can't focus properly on the words. The children could go and say hello to the boy, make friends with him and ask him about his glasses.

The tool to fix the problem is: **Understanding**

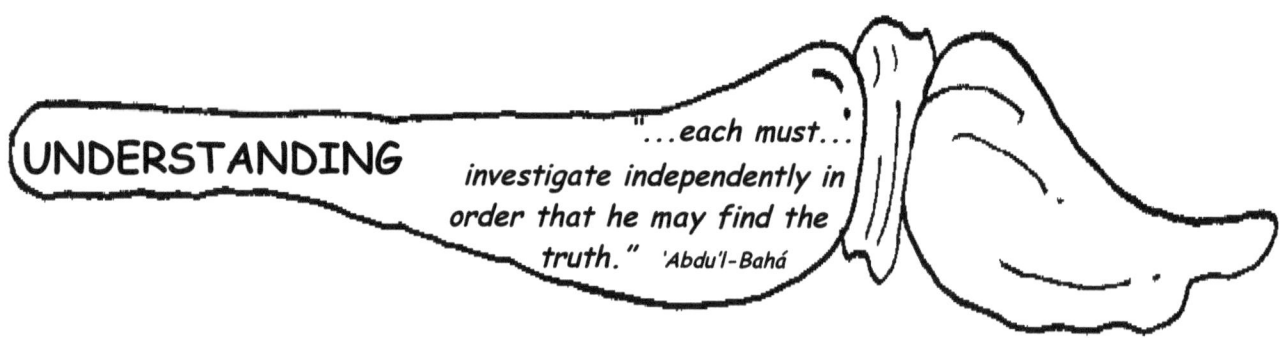

UNDERSTANDING — "...each must... investigate independently in order that he may find the truth." 'Abdu'l-Bahá

UNDERSTANDING
MAGNIFYING GLASS

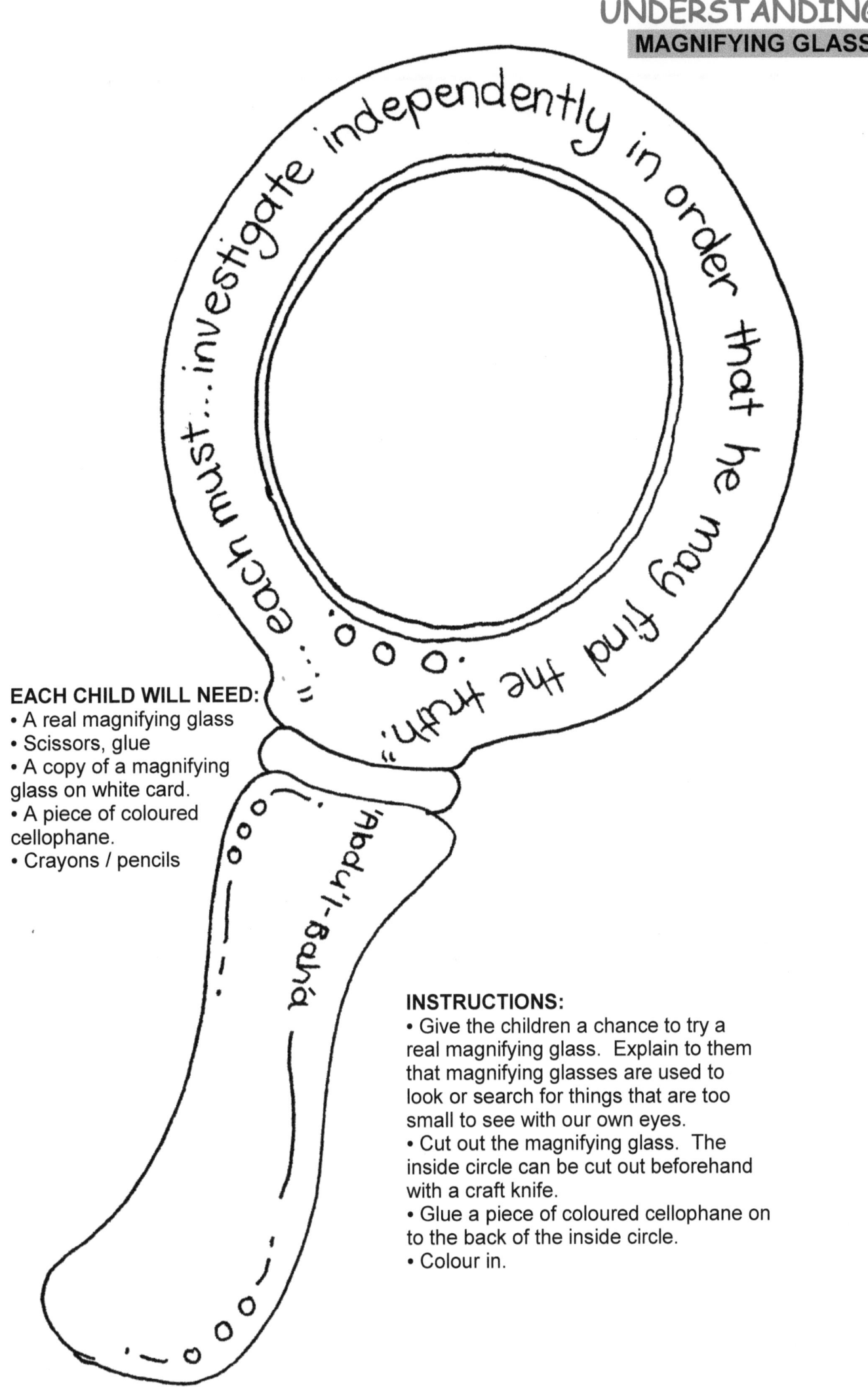

"...each must...investigate independently in order that he may find the truth." 'Abdu'l-Bahá

EACH CHILD WILL NEED:
• A real magnifying glass
• Scissors, glue
• A copy of a magnifying glass on white card.
• A piece of coloured cellophane.
• Crayons / pencils

INSTRUCTIONS:
• Give the children a chance to try a real magnifying glass. Explain to them that magnifying glasses are used to look or search for things that are too small to see with our own eyes.
• Cut out the magnifying glass. The inside circle can be cut out beforehand with a craft knife.
• Glue a piece of coloured cellophane on to the back of the inside circle.
• Colour in.

UNDERSTANDING

Quote Visualization

UNDERSTANDING

"....each must... investigate independently in order that he may find the truth."

'Abdu'l-Bahá

Quotation activity worksheet — UNDERSTANDING

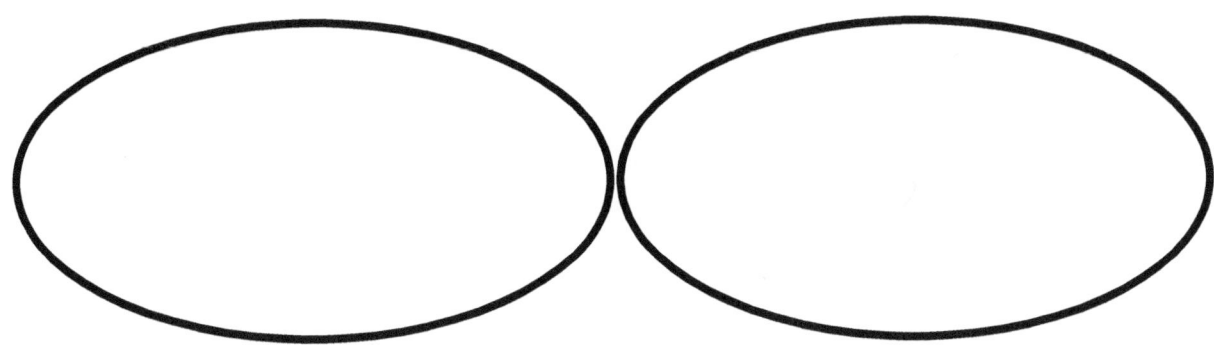

I can show understanding when ....
....

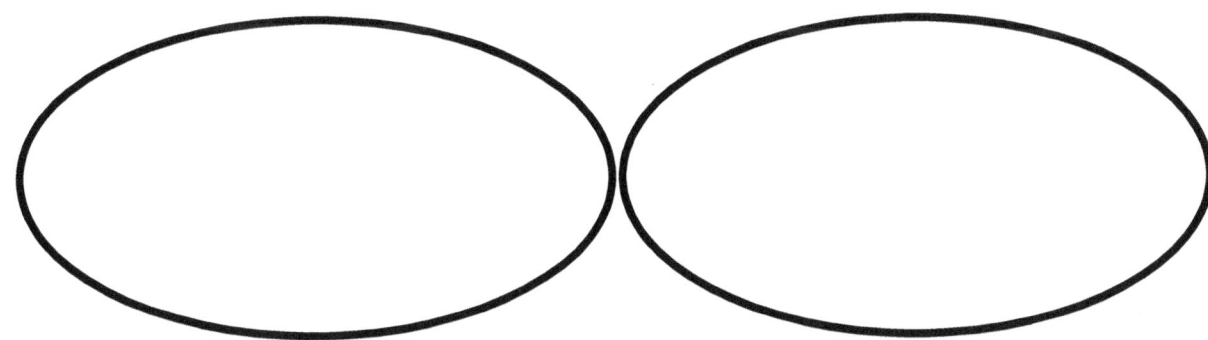

I can show understanding when ....
....

UNDERSTANDING

Quotation activity worksheet

THE SCARY CREATURE

UNDERSTANDING STORY

Carl was a Private Investigator. Private Investigators get called when strange things happen that people want answers to. One day Carl was presented with some extra large footprints. The people in the town thought it might be a monster or a giant or some kind of dangerous creature. The people were very scared and wanted to know what it really was.

Carl examined the footprints carefully. They were definitely very big and each one had three marks where three big toes had been. Carl followed the prints around a tree and next to a pond. He noticed that the ducks didn't seem to have been scared at all. "Interesting," he thought to himself.

Next he tracked the prints into a tunnel and out the other side. The tunnel had no light in it so Carl concluded that the creature must not be afraid of the dark. He was starting to feel a bit worried. What was this strange creature and where did it come from?

The prints continued across to the playground. Carl noticed they went up and down and all around the play equipment as if the creature had been enjoying itself. "What would a scary creature want to play in a playground for?" thought Carl. It didn't seem a very scary thing to do. Now Carl was feeling confused.

He then followed the prints to a fence and suddenly looked up and saw it. It was big and green and Carl stood still in fright. Then the creature slowly turned around and what Carl saw was the bright smiling face of little Johnny from the village. He was just playing dress-ups and was pretending to be a big green creature. Carl laughed out loud and thought how surprised all the people would be when they found out who their scary creature really was. Carl and Johnny walked back together with big smiles on their faces to tell everyone.

MORAL – Always seek to understand the truth and don't be satisfied with anything else.

CO-OPERATION

LESSON PLAN

SESSION 1

PRAYER: Sing prayers that have been learnt and any others that the children know. Ask them to be reverent because they are talking to God.

SCENARIO:
Read out the scenario on the next page to the children.

Use the Happy / Sad Face (as described in the beginning of the book) to discuss what could turn the situation around from a sad one to a happy one. Let the child who comes up with the solution first turn the mouth from a gloomy face to a smiling one.

Bring out the toolbox (as described in the beginning of the book) and let the children guess which tool (virtue) they could use to fix the situation. Remind the children that these are the tools God gives us to help us in everything we do each day. Choose one child to take out the tool. Read out the virtue and the quotation. Ask the children to say the quotation with you a couple of times. Discuss what the quotation means

"...co-operation and mutual understanding are seen to produce the greatest welfare of mankind."
    'Abdu'l-Bahá

Discussion Thoughts - Working together co-operatively allows us to achieve things that we cannot do if we fight and argue with each other.

SONG: "Together" - sing with actions.

ACTIVITY: Co-operative jigsaws – Copy the picture provided on to A3 paper or card. Cut into random pieces so that each child can have one. Ask the children to collage or colour their piece. Place them all together and take a picture. Give each child a picture of the whole jigsaw and the piece that they decorated to take home. If copying on to A3 is difficult you can take a large sheet of white card, draw your own picture and cut it up in the same way.
Purpose – to reflect how co-operation allows us to accomplish things together that we could not do or would not be as good on our own.

SESSION 2

PRAYER: Sing prayers that have been learnt and any others that the children know. Ask them to be reverent because they are talking to God.

DISCUSSION REVIEW: What does co-operation mean?
    Optional - Use discussions prompts sheet from the beginning of the book to help with the discussion.

SONG: "Together" - sing with actions.

STORY: "Together"

GAME: Give the children some blocks (Divide the class into small groups if necessary). Ask them to build a tower together using co-operation. The aim is to see how high they can build it before it falls down.
Purpose – To practice being co-operative.

ACTIVITY:
"...co-operation and mutual understanding are seen to produce the greatest welfare of mankind."
    'Abdu'l-Bahá
Use the quote visualization page to review the meaning of the quotation.
Say the quotation with the children a few times. Older children may be able to memorize it.
Give each child a copy of the quotation activity provided. Cut and glue in each part of the quotation in the correct order, colour in and assist the child to write in something that they can do to practice co-operation.

CO-OPERATION

SCENARIO

Scenario:
Who likes painting?
Do you like finger painting or painting with brushes?
There was once two children who also liked painting so they decided to paint their cubby house. The first child wanted to paint it red and the second wanted to paint it yellow. They argued for a long time about which colour they should use but neither wanted to give in to the other one. In the end they both walked away unhappily. What could these two children do in order that they can both paint the cubby house happily together?

Possible solutions:
The two children could decide that some walls get painted yellow and some get painted red.
They could paint the inside one colour and the outside another colour.
Or they could mix the two colours together to make orange and then paint the cubby together.

The tool to fix the problem is: **Co-operation**

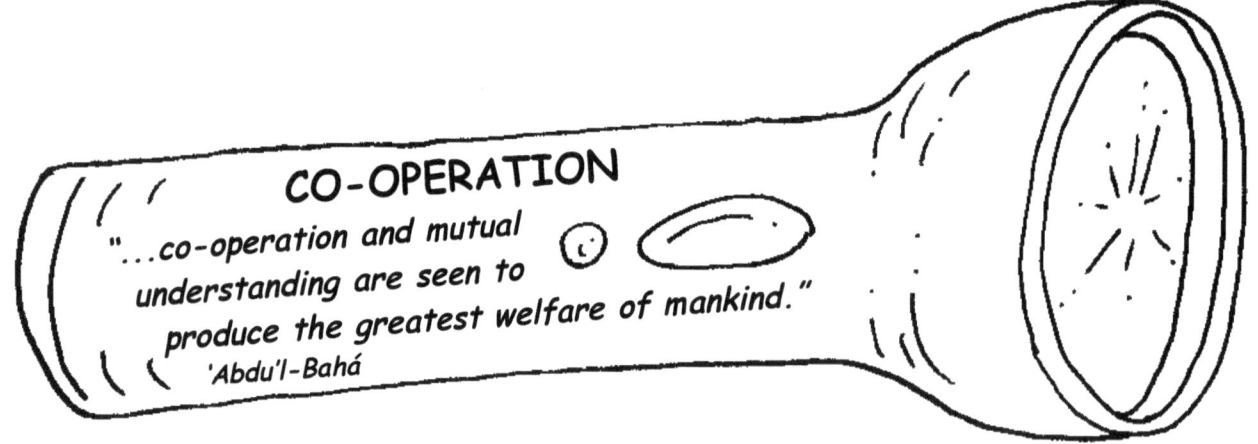

CO-OPERATION
"...co-operation and mutual understanding are seen to produce the greatest welfare of mankind."
'Abdu'l-Bahá

CO-OPERATION
CO-OPERATIVE JIGSAW

"...co-operation and mutual understanding are seen to produce the greatest welfare of mankind." — 'Abdu'l-Bahá

CO-OPERATION

Quote Visualization

CO-OPERATION
"...co-operation and mutual understanding are seen to produce the greatest welfare of mankind."
'Abdu'l-Bahá

Quotation activity worksheet

CO-OPERATION

CO-OPERATION
"...co-operation and mutual understanding are seen to produce the greatest welfare of mankind."
'Abdu'l-Bahá

I am being co-operative when I ....
....

CO-OPERATION
"...co-operation and mutual understanding are seen to produce the greatest welfare of mankind."
'Abdu'l-Bahá

I am being co-operative when I ....
....

CO-OPERATION

Quotation activity worksheet

TOGETHER

CO-OPERATION
STORY

The whole town was talking about the prize that was going to be given to the winner of the end of year talent show. Lana, Billy and Greg were very excited because the prize was a big basket of all different kinds of chocolate.

"I am such a good dancer," boasted Lana. "No-one can dance better than me."

"I am sure to win because of my fantastic singing voice," stated Billy excitedly.

Greg smiled eagerly, "When people hear my guitar playing they will just sit and listen for ages."

"Well we can't all win," exclaimed Lana.

"Yes we could and I know how," said Greg brightly. "If we all use our talents to make one really good performance then we could all share the prize."

"That's a great idea," Billy said excitedly.

That afternoon they all practiced together. Lana danced, Billy sang and Greg played his guitar. They practiced all the next day and the day after that. In fact they practiced every day until the day of the talent show arrived.

Lots of people performed. Someone played the piano, someone did a tap dance, someone else read a funny story and someone even did a magic trick, but only Billy, Lana and Greg did a performance together. When it was finished everyone clapped very loudly. With Lana dancing, Billy singing and Greg playing it made a truly wonderful show. Everyone agreed that they were the best but the three friends new that they were only the best because they had co-operated and worked together.

MORAL – Co-peration means working together to do things that we could not have done as well by ourself.

MODERATION

LESSON PLAN

SESSION 1

PRAYER: Sing prayers that have been learnt and any others that the children know. Ask them to be reverent because they are talking to God.

SCENARIO:
Read out the scenario on the next page to the children.

Use the Happy / Sad Face (as described in the beginning of the book) to discuss what could turn the situation around from a sad one to a happy one. Let the child who comes up with the solution first turn the mouth from a gloomy face to a smiling one.

Bring out the toolbox (as described in the beginning of the book) and let the children guess which tool (virtue) they could use to fix the situation. Remind the children that these are the tools God gives us to help us in everything we do each day. Choose one child to take out the tool. Read out the virtue and the quotation. Ask the children to say the quotation with you a couple of times.
Discuss what the quotation means

"Whatsoever passeth beyond the limits of moderation will cease to exert a beneficial influence."
  Bahá'u'lláh

Discussion Thoughts - Most things have a purpose or a benefit but if we have too much of anything then it no longer helps us and often can hurt us in some way. One lolly is nice, too many lollies make us sick. Running makes us fit and healthy but if we don't rest then we will always be very tired.

SONG: "This and That" - sing with actions.

ACTIVITY: Circle of Moderation – Use activity sheet provided.
Purpose – to reflect on the quotation and understand what it means to practice moderation.

SESSION 2

PRAYER: Sing prayers that have been learnt and any others that the children know. Ask them to be reverent because they are talking to God.

DISCUSSION REVIEW: What does moderation mean?
Optional - Use discussion prompts sheet from the beginning of the book to help with the discussion.

SONG: "This and That" - sing with actions.

STORY: "Strawberries"

GAME: Provide the children with a whole selection of clothing. Example; three hats, gloves, a scarf, two jumpers, a jacket and some big shoes. Ask one child to volunteer to get dressed in all the clothes. The other children can help them. When they have all the clothes on talk about how heavy and hot it would be to walk around with so much on all day. Discuss how having no clothes on would make us cold and that moderation in this situation would be having just enough clothes to be comfortable and warm.
Purpose – To visually demonstrate what it means to be in moderation.

ACTIVITY:
"Whatsoever passeth beyond the limits of moderation will cease to exert a beneficial influence."
  Bahá'u'lláh
Use the quote visualization page to review the meaning of the quotation.
Say the quotation with the children a few times. Older children may be able to memorize it. Give each child a copy of the quotation activity provided. Cut and glue in each part of the quotation in the correct order, colour in and assist the child to write in something that they can do to practice moderation.

SCENARIO

Scenario:
Does anyone like to run?
Sometimes do you like to run as fast as you can just to see how fast you can go? Graham was a boy who liked running. He was determined to be the fittest, strongest and fastest boy in his class at school. He would run everywhere. The teacher couldn't even get him to sit still in the classroom and he would move his feet up and down when he was sitting in the car. Graham was very fast but he was also always very tired. What could Graham do to stay good at running but not be so tired all the time?

Possible solution:
He could run just some of the day and also have some rest and do other things.

The tool to fix the problem is: **Moderation**

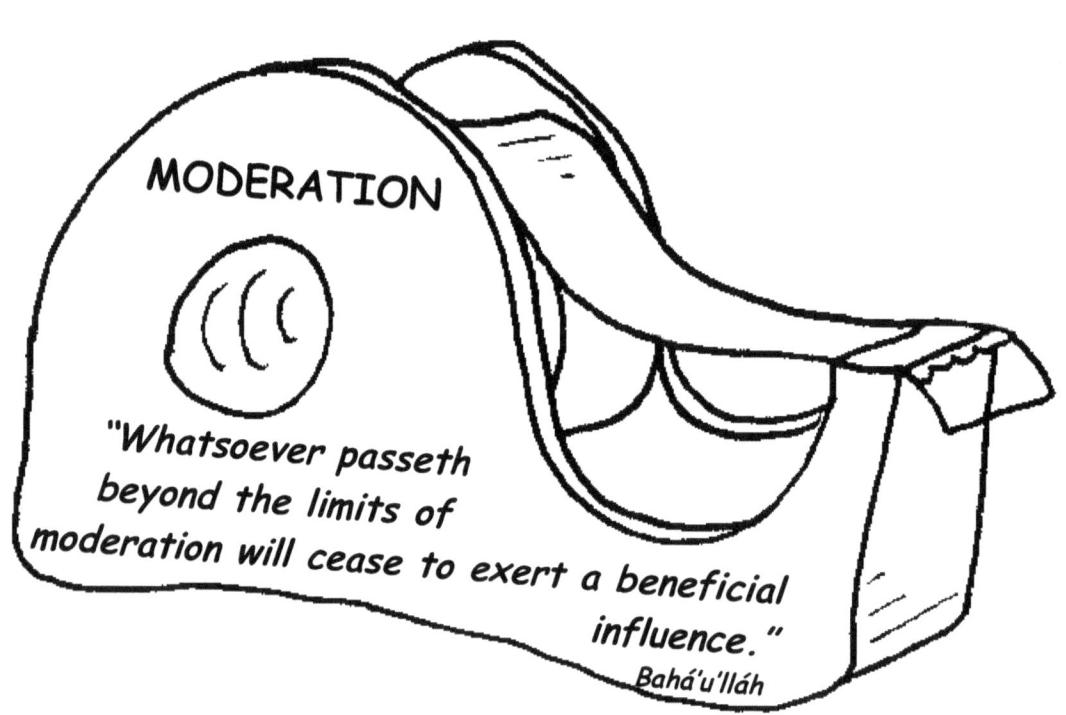

MODERATION

"Whatsoever passeth beyond the limits of moderation will cease to exert a beneficial influence."
— Bahá'u'lláh

MODERATION
CIRCLE OF MODERATION

INSTRUCTIONS:
- Photocopy this page on to white card
- Give each child a copy of a circle and a quotation. Cut out both shapes.
- Place the quotation on top of the circle and join together using a paper fastener so that the top spins around the bottom.
- Fill in the missing gaps on the circle with the things we need to have in moderation.
- Colour in.

EACH CHILD WILL NEED:
- Scissors, a paper fastener
- A copy of this page
- Crayons / pencils

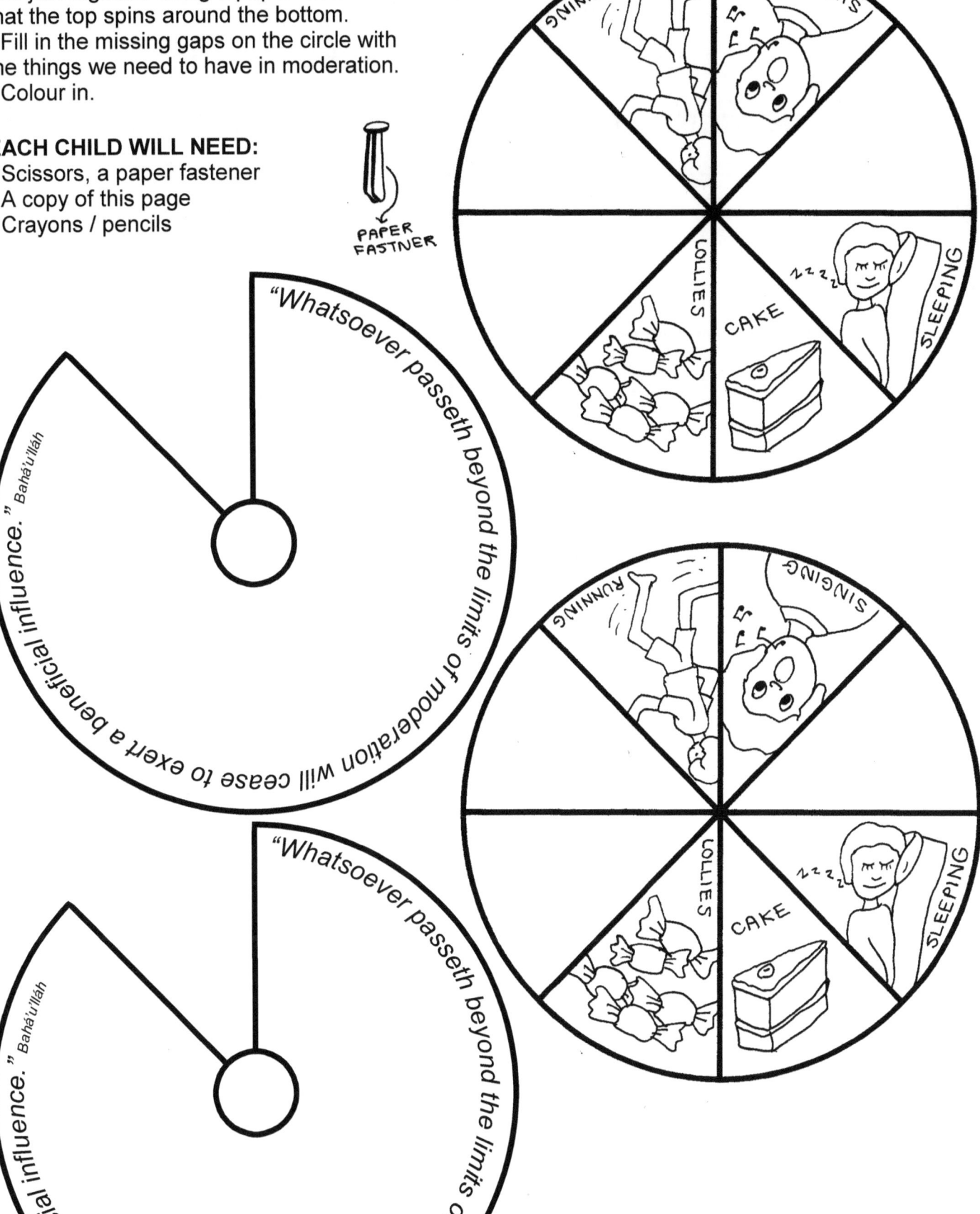

189

MODERATION

"Whatsoever passeth beyond the limits of moderation will cease to exert a beneficial influence."

Bahá'u'lláh

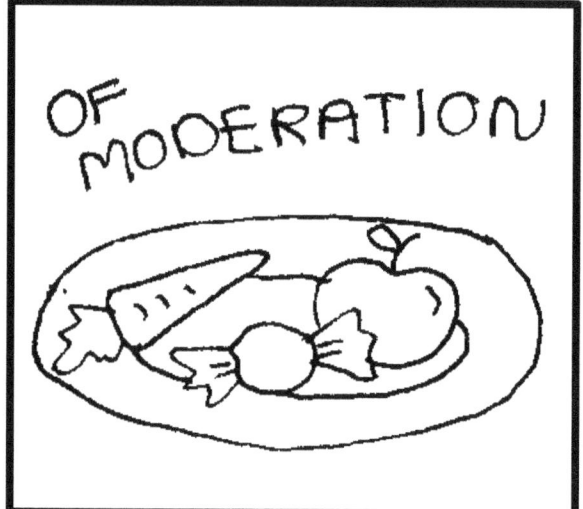

Quotation activity worksheet

MODERATION

MODERATION
"Whatsoever passeth beyond the limits of moderation will cease to exert a beneficial influence."
Bahá'u'lláh

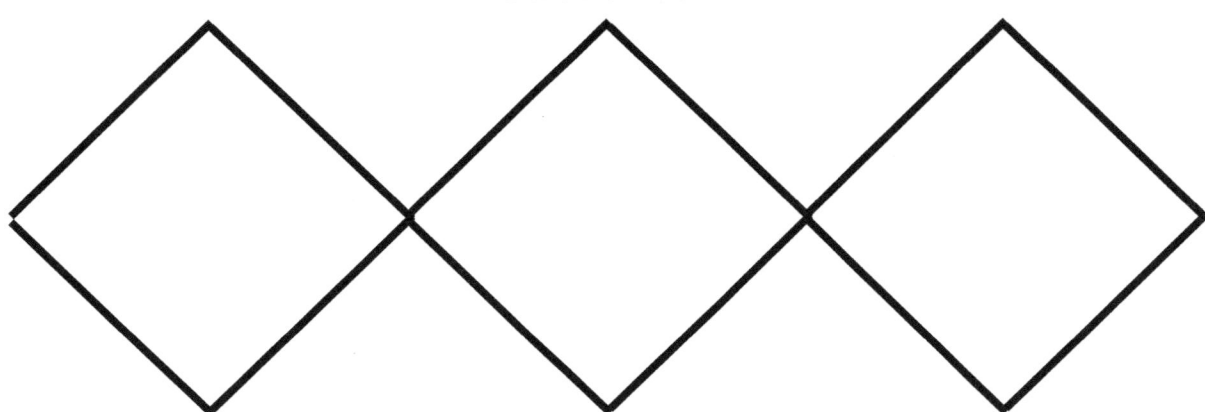

Moderation is when I ....
....

MODERATION
"Whatsoever passeth beyond the limits of moderation will cease to exert a beneficial influence."
Bahá'u'lláh

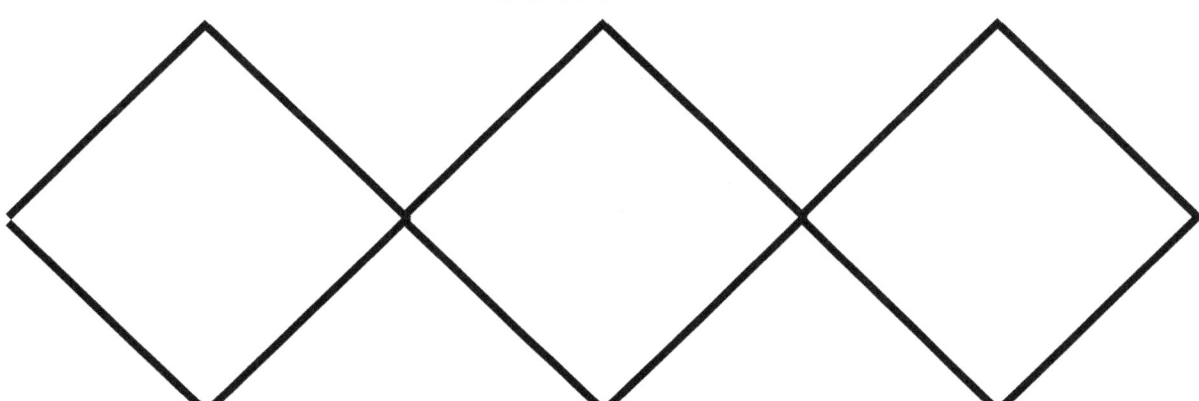

Moderation is when I ....
....

MODERATION

Quotation activity worksheet

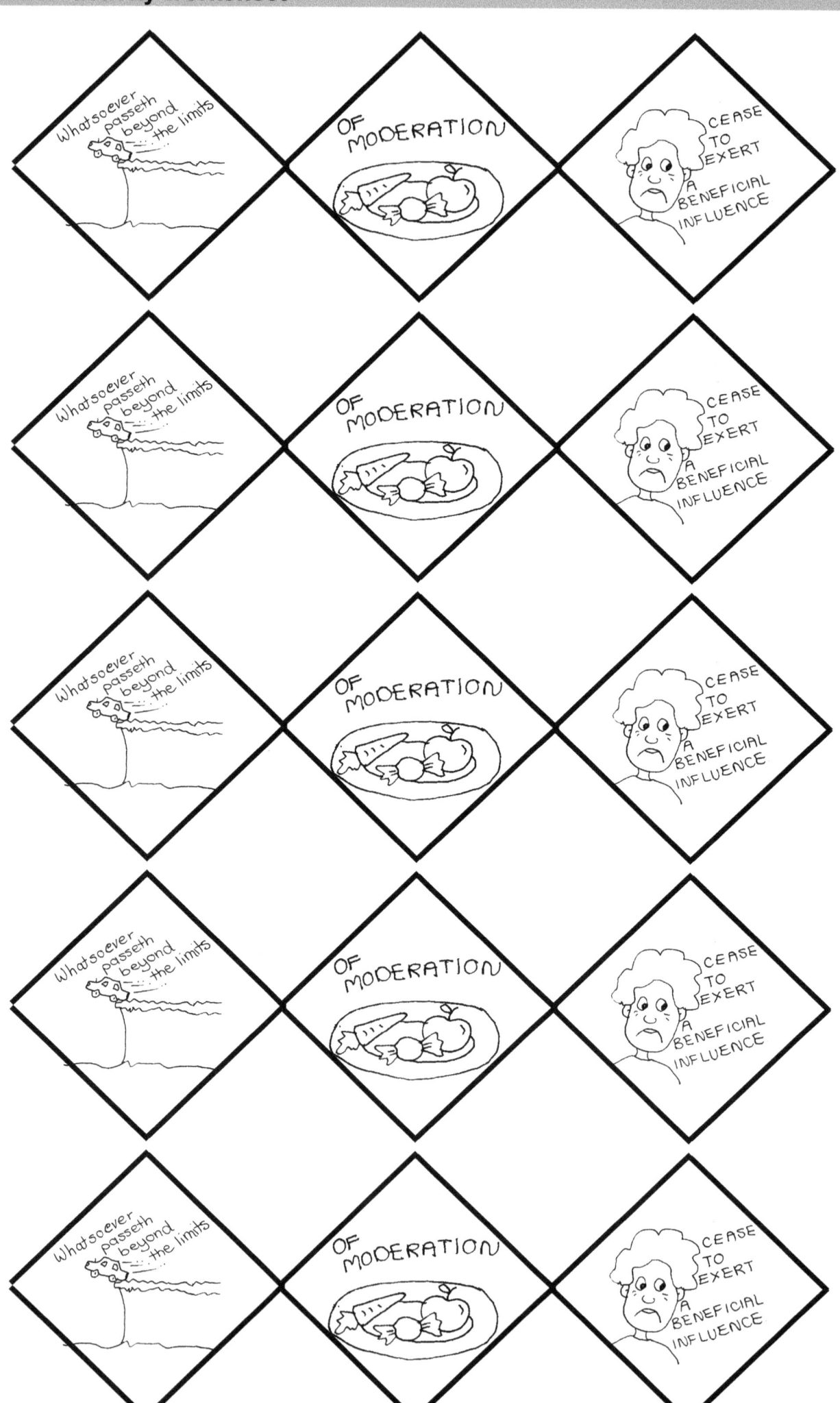

STRAWBERRIES

MODERATION STORY

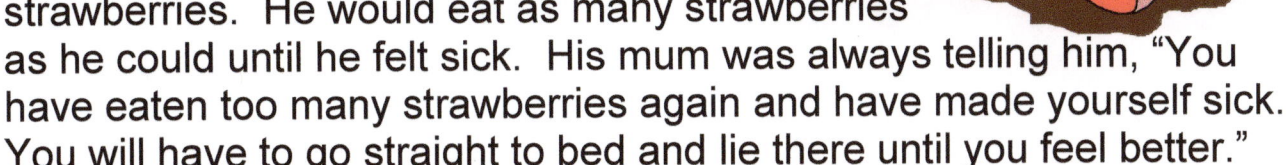

Ralph was a rabbit who lived next to a little garden. In the garden were fruit trees and a vegetable patch so Ralph always had plenty to eat. However, there was one problem. Ralph loved strawberries. He would eat as many strawberries as he could until he felt sick. His mum was always telling him, "You have eaten too many strawberries again and have made yourself sick. You will have to go straight to bed and lie there until you feel better."

Ralph loved strawberries but he hated staying in bed. While he was lying there feeling sorry for himself he could hear the other rabbits playing games, munching on fruit and vegetables and laughing out loud at something they found funny. Why am I always the one who ends up in bed he moaned. The other rabbits are never sick. I am tired of being sent to bed and he curled up under the blankets so that he couldn't hear the laughing rabbits any more.

The next day he was feeling a bit better so he went and sat out near where the other rabbits were playing. He watched them carefully and saw that they too ate lots of strawberries. "It can't be the strawberries that make me sick if the other rabbits eat them too," he thought to himself. He watched a bit more carefully and saw that although they all ate a lot of strawberries they also ate carrots, lettuce, apples and other fruit and vegetables. He thought about this for the rest of the day.

When the next morning came he was feeling full of energy again and raced out to eat more strawberries. He had eaten five and was about to have another when he stopped and instead dug up a big juicy carrot. That day he had lots of strawberries but he also had lots of other things to eat and that night when he came home he did not feel sick at all.
"Did you have a good day?" his mother asked him as he came home. "Yes," Ralph replied, "I had a very good day and tomorrow I am going to have another good day filled with lots of strawberries and carrots and lettuce." Then he wandered off to bed to have a good night's sleep so that he would be full of energy and ready for another good day.

MORAL – Moderation is enjoying everything without having too much at one time.

CARING

LESSON PLAN

SESSION 1

PRAYER: Sing prayers that have been learnt and any others that the children know. Ask them to be reverent because they are talking to God.

SCENARIO:
Read out the scenario on the next page to the children.

Use the Happy / Sad Face (as described in the beginning of the book) to discuss what could turn the situation around from a sad one to a happy one. Let the child who comes up with the solution first turn the mouth from a gloomy face to a smiling one.

Bring out the toolbox (as described in the beginning of the book) and let the children guess which tool (virtue) they could use to fix the situation. Remind the children that these are the tools God gives us to help us in everything we do each day. Choose one child to take out the tool. Read out the virtue and the quotation. Ask the children to say the quotation with you a couple of times. Discuss what the quotation means

"You must love and be kind to everybody, care for the poor, protect the weak, heal the sick, teach and educate the ignorant."
    'Abdu'l-Bahá

Discussion Thoughts - When we care for people we think about the needs of others and help people to feel better. Caring is knowing that each person is important and always looking for ways to assist others.

SONG: "Care" - sing with actions.

ACTIVITY: Friendship Bracelets – Use activity sheet on the next page.
    Purpose – to reflect on the quotation and practice being friendly.

SESSION 2

PRAYER: Sing prayers that have been learnt and any others that the children know. Ask them to be reverent because they are talking to God.

DISCUSSION REVIEW: What does it mean to be Caring?
    Optional - Use discussion prompts sheet from the beginning of the book to help with the discussion.

SONG: "Care" - sing with actions.

STORY: "The Magic Medicine Bag"

GAME: Divide the class into pairs. Give each pair a bandage or strip of material. Each child then has a turn at bandaging up the other child's leg or arm. Ask them to do this gently and pretend that the child has a sore leg/arm.
    Purpose – To practice being caring.

ACTIVITY:
"You must love and be kind to everybody, care for the poor, protect the weak, heal the sick, teach and educate the ignorant."
    'Abdu'l-Bahá
Use the quote visualization page to review the meaning of the quotation.
Say the quotation with the children a few times. Older children may be able to memorize it.
Give each child a copy of the quotation activity provided. Cut and glue in each part of the quotation in the correct order, colour in and assist the child to write in something that they can do to practice being caring.

SCENARIO

Scenario:

Has anyone been very sick before?

Has anyone ever been to the doctor or the hospital?

Ken was walking home from school one day when he noticed a younger child sitting crying on the edge of the road. She was holding her leg which was bleeding. What could Ken do to help this girl?

Possible solution:

He could help her to walk home or get an adult to come and help her.

The tool to fix the problem is: **Caring**

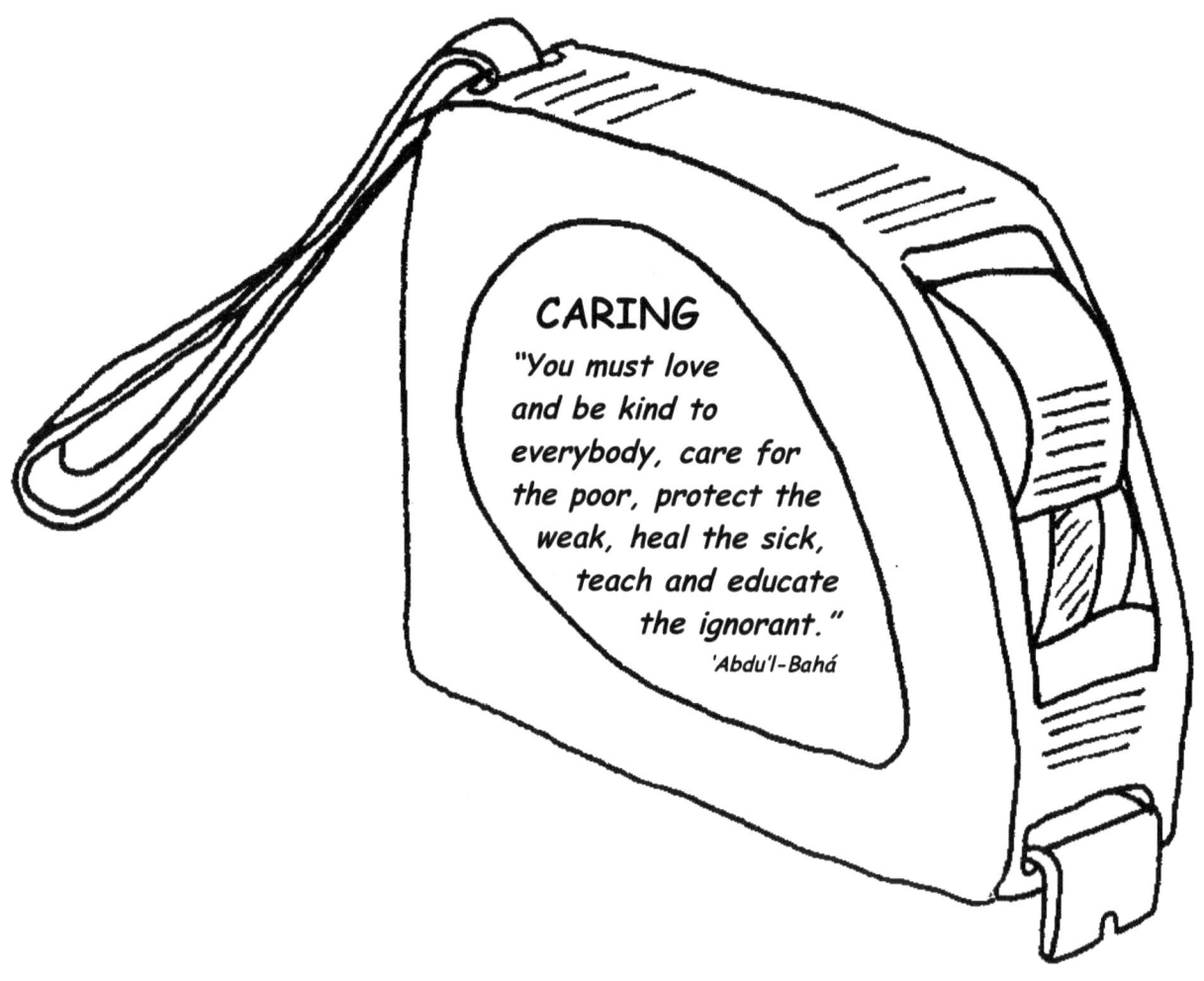

CARING

"You must love and be kind to everybody, care for the poor, protect the weak, heal the sick, teach and educate the ignorant."

'Abdu'l-Bahá

CARING
MEDICINE BAG

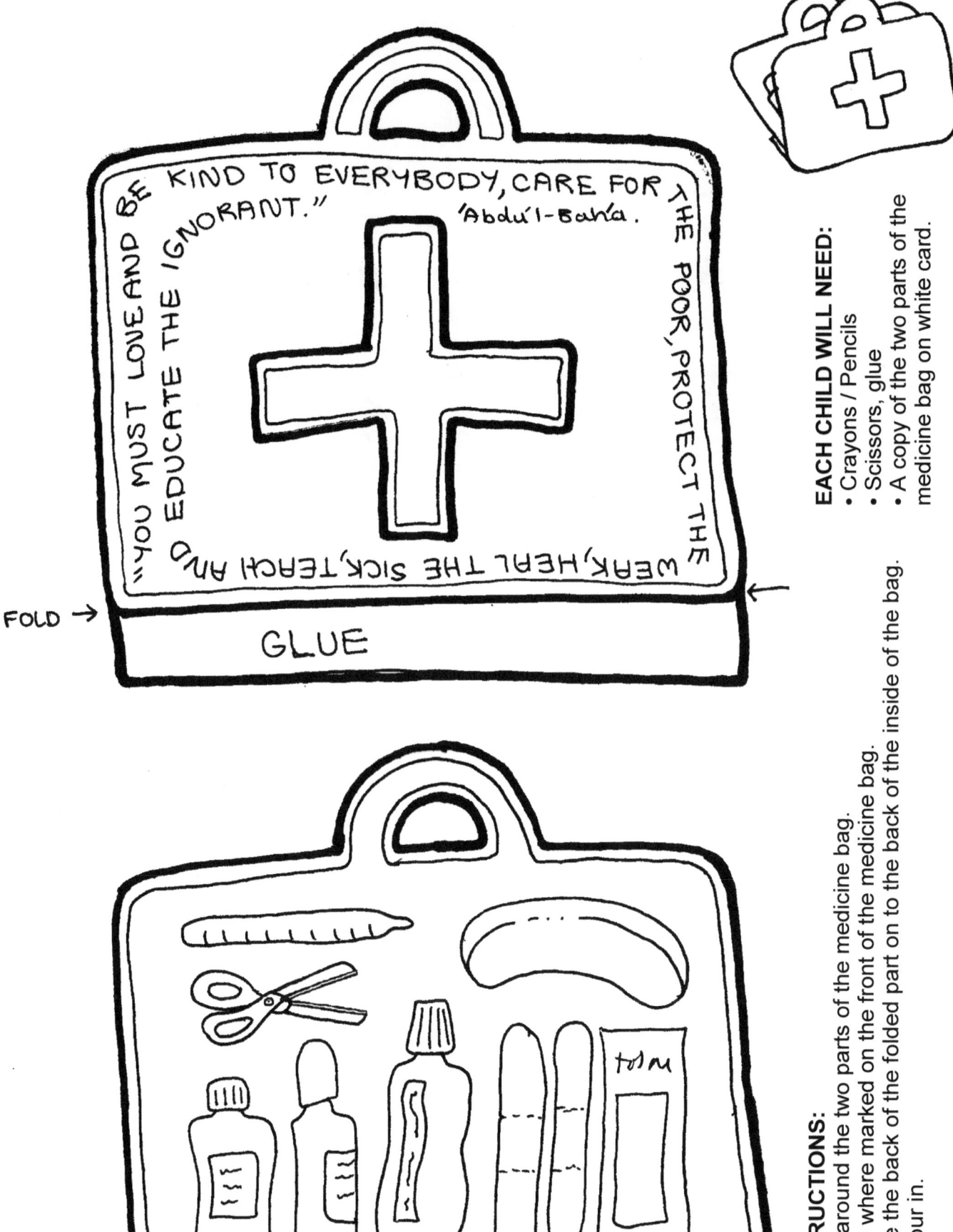

"YOU MUST LOVE AND BE KIND TO EVERYBODY, CARE FOR THE POOR, PROTECT THE WEAK, HEAL THE SICK, TEACH AND EDUCATE THE IGNORANT." 'Abdu'l-Bahá.

FOLD →
GLUE

EACH CHILD WILL NEED:
- Crayons / Pencils
- Scissors, glue
- A copy of the two parts of the medicine bag on white card.

INSTRUCTIONS:
- Cut around the two parts of the medicine bag.
- Fold where marked on the front of the medicine bag.
- Glue the back of the folded part on to the back of the inside of the bag.
- Colour in.

Quote Visualization

CARING

CARING
"You must love and be kind to everybody,
care for the poor, protect the weak,
heal the sick, teach and educate the ignorant."

'Abdu'l-Bahá

Quotation activity worksheet

CARING

CARING
"You must love and be kind to everybody, care for the poor, protect the weak, heal the sick, teach and educate the ignorant."
'Abdu'l-Bahá

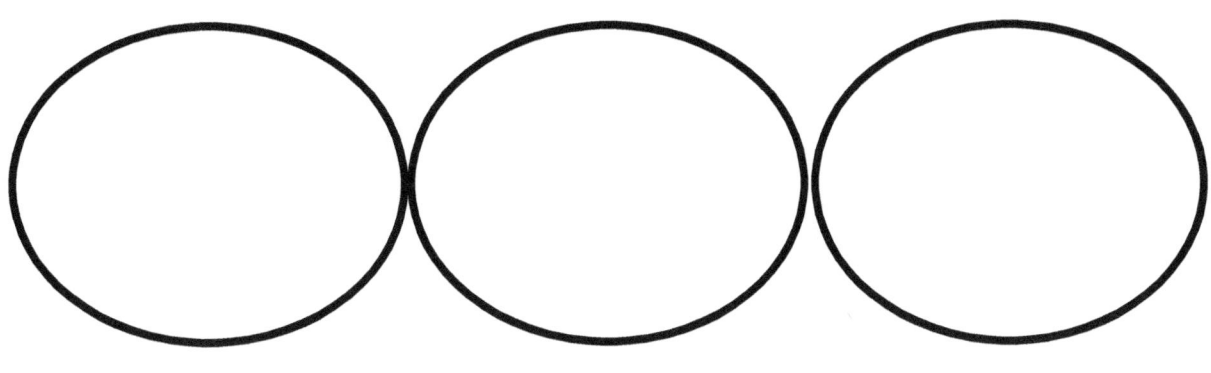

I can show caring by ....
....

CARING
"You must love and be kind to everybody, care for the poor, protect the weak, heal the sick, teach and educate the ignorant."
'Abdu'l-Bahá

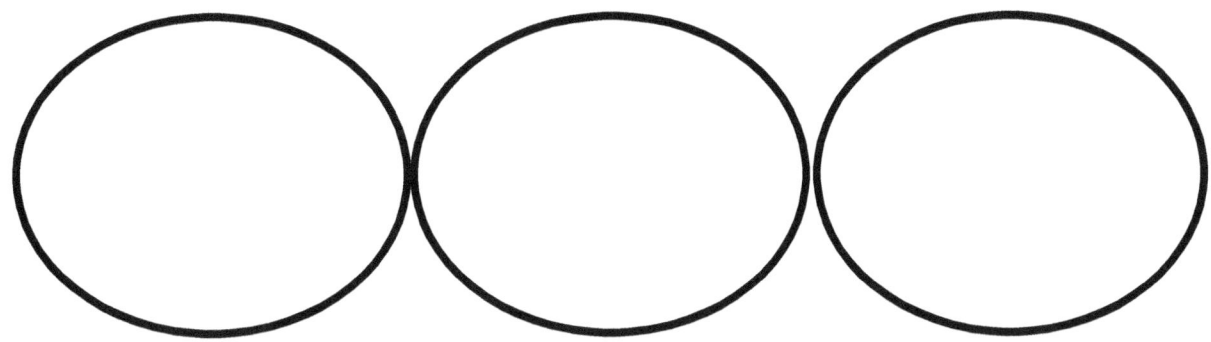

I can show caring by ....
....

CARING

Quotation activity worksheet

THE MAGIC MEDICINE BAG

CARING STORY

The was once a magic medicine bag that would spend its days helping people. It would wander from place to place and person to person caring for people who needed help. The magic medicine bag was magic because the thing people needed most would magically appear inside it. If people needed a bandaid to protect a sore then a bandaid would appear inside it. If someone was hungry then a lovely meal would appear inside it. If a child was cold then the bag would produce a nice warm blanket.

The magic medicine bag belonged to a little girl called Samantha who loved the bag very much. She would take it everywhere with her and help people every day to feel better. One day Samantha was feeling sad because she had to go to school and her mum said that she would not be allowed to take the medicine bag. Instead, she was to take a school bag. Samantha cried and sulked for a long time until the medicine bag finally said, "What is wrong Samantha?"
"I am going to school," she said, "and you must stay at home. How am I going to be able to help people without you. You can do so much and I can't do anything special."
"You can help people in ways that I could never care for them," explained the medicine bag.
"How can that be?" asked Samantha, "I can't make all the things you can."
"You can give hugs and love and help people get up when they fall down. You can play with someone who feels lonely and tell a story to someone to make them laugh. I can't do any of those things."
Samantha thought about this for a long time and when it was time to go to school she was feeling happy again. Samantha loved her medicine bag and all the wonderful magic it could do but now realized that she had a special kind of magic too and it's secret lay in her heart. She had the ability to care for and love everyone she met.

MORAL – When we care for someone it is like a magic gift that not only helps them on the outside but also makes them feel good on the inside and makes our own hearts happy too.

COMPASSION

LESSON PLAN

SESSION 1

PRAYER: Sing prayers that have been learnt and any others that the children know. Ask them to be reverent because they are talking to God.

SCENARIO:
Read out the scenario on the next page to the children.

Use the Happy / Sad Face (as described in the beginning of the book) to discuss what could turn the situation around from a sad one to a happy one. Let the child who comes up with the solution first turn the mouth from a gloomy face to a smiling one.

Bring out the toolbox (as described in the beginning of the book) and let the children guess which tool (virtue) they could use to fix the situation. Remind the children that these are the tools God gives us to help us in everything we do each day. Choose one child to take out the tool. Read out the virtue and the quotation. Ask the children to say the quotation with you a couple of times. Discuss what the quotation means

"...show forth love and affection, wisdom and compassion, faithfulness and unity towards all, without any discrimination."
    'Abdu'l-Bahá

Discussion Thoughts - When we see that someone needs help in some way, we don't just walk away. Even if someone is dirty or doesn't speak the same language as us or is not always kind to us we should still be compassionate, loving and kind towards them.

SONG: "Be a Friend" - sing with actions.

ACTIVITY: Compassionate Person – Use activity sheet provided.
Purpose – to visualize the quotation.

SESSION 2

PRAYER: Sing prayers that have been learnt and any others that the children know. Ask them to be reverent because they are talking to God.

DISCUSSION REVIEW: What does compassion mean?
Optional - Use discussion prompts sheet from the beginning of the book to help with the discussion.

SONG: "Be a Friend" - sing with actions.

STORY: "The Sun and the Rain"

GAME: Ask for one volunteer at a time to demonstrate the virtue of compassion through some role plays. Ask the first volunteer to pretend to have been hurt from falling off their bike. Ask the second volunteer to pretend to be very sorry for breaking their friend's special toy. Ask the third volunteer to pretend to be a new person at school sitting by themselves because they don't know any of the other children. After each role play ask other children in the class to show how they could be compassionate in that situation.
Purpose – To reflect on what it means to be compassionate.

ACTIVITY:
"...show forth love and affection, wisdom and compassion, faithfulness and unity towards all, without any discrimination."
    'Abdu'l-Bahá
Use the quote visualization page to review the meaning of the quotation.
Say the quotation with the children a few times. Older children may be able to memorize it.
Give each child a copy of the quotation activity provided. Cut and glue in each part of the quotation in the correct order, colour in and assist the child to write in something that they can do to practice compassion.

COMPASSION

SCENARIO

Scenario:
Do you get really hungry sometimes?
What do you like to eat when you are really hungry?
Tilly was a little girl who loved eating ham and cheese sandwiches. She would take them to school with her each day and always look forward to lunch time so she could eat them all up. One day she was just sitting down and getting ready to eat when her friend came over to join her. She was just about to sit down when her friend tripped and her lunch fell on to the ground. Her friend tried to pick up the food but it was covered in too much dirt so she had to throw it away. Her friend sat down next to her sadly, she had nothing left to eat. What could Tilly do to help her friend feel better?

Possible solution:
Tilly could share her lunch with her friend.

The tool to fix the problem is: **Compassion**

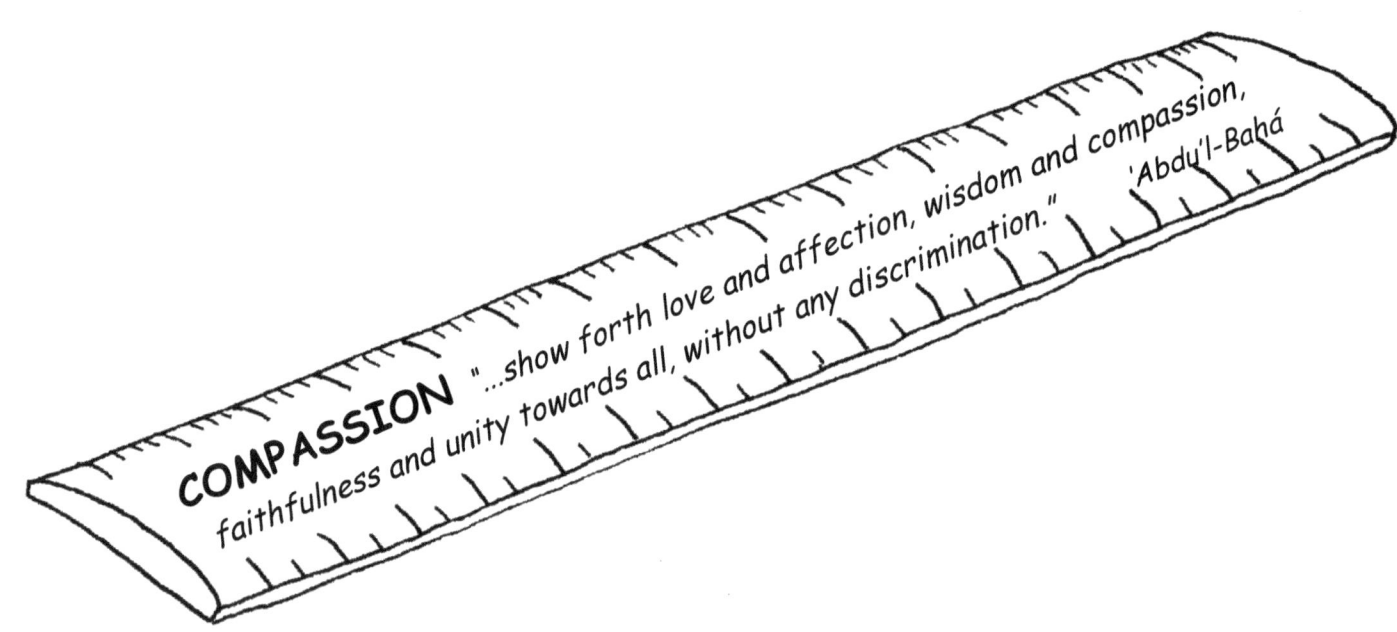
COMPASSION "...show forth love and affection, wisdom and compassion, faithfulness and unity towards all, without any discrimination." 'Abdu'l-Bahá

COMPASSION
COMPASSIONATE PERSON

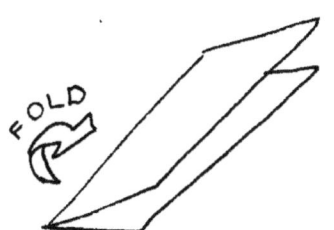
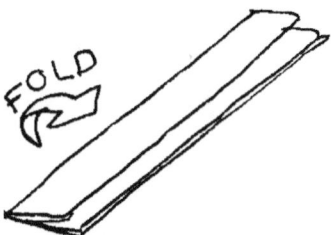
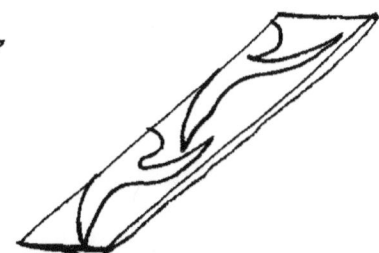

STEP 1
Fold an A4 page in half length wise.

STEP 2
Fold lengthwise again.

STEP 3
Give each child a copy of a template. Trace twice onto the folded paper with marked edge against the fold. Cut out. You should have four folded people.

STEP 4
Tie the people together with a piece of string along the fold. Allow for some extra at the top for hanging.

EACH CHILD WILL NEED:
- Scissors
- A piece of string
- A template
- An A4 piece of paper.
- Crayons / pencils

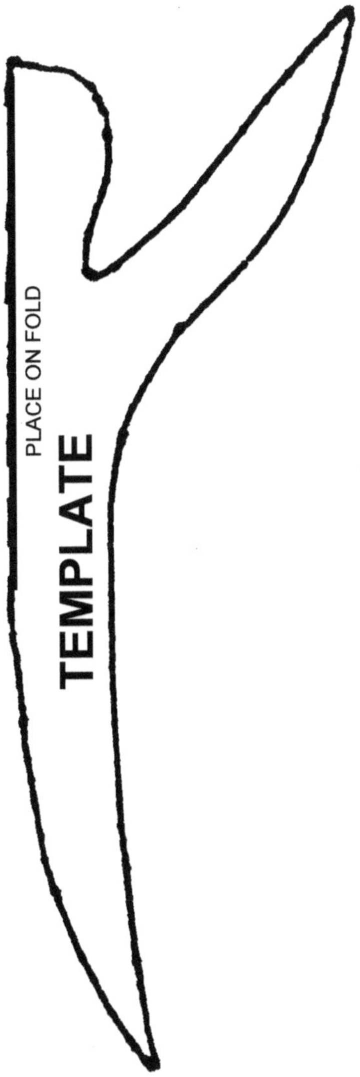

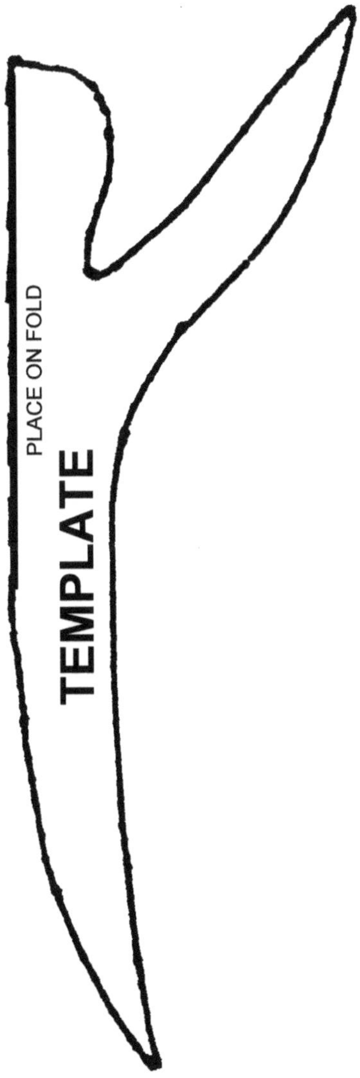

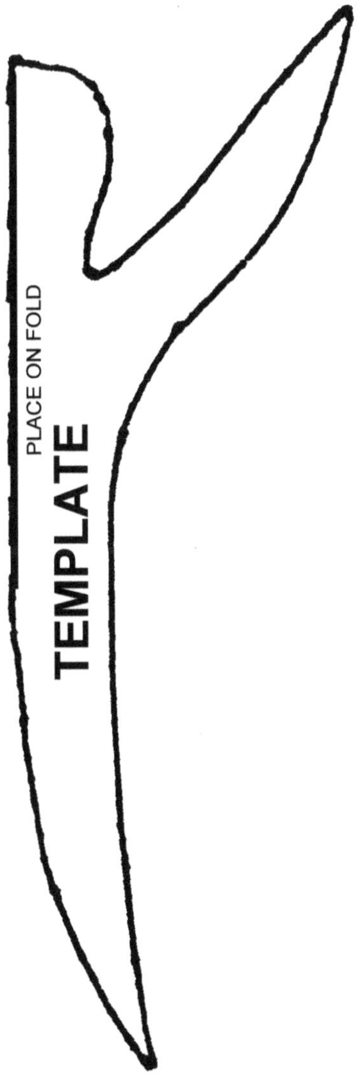

TEMPLATE — PLACE ON FOLD

COMPASSION

Quote Visualization

COMPASSION
*"...show forth love and affection,
wisdom and compassion,
faithfulness and unity towards all,
without any discrimination."*
'Abdu'l-Bahá

Quotation activity worksheet

COMPASSION

COMPASSION
"...show forth love and affection, wisdom and compassion, faithfulness and unity towards all, without any discrimination."
'Abdu'l-Bahá

I am being compassionate when I ....
....

COMPASSION
"...show forth love and affection, wisdom and compassion, faithfulness and unity towards all, without any discrimination."
'Abdu'l-Bahá

I am being compassionate when I ....
....

COMPASSION

Quotation activity worksheet

   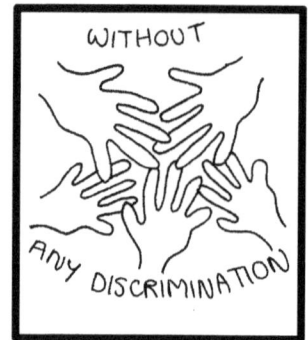

   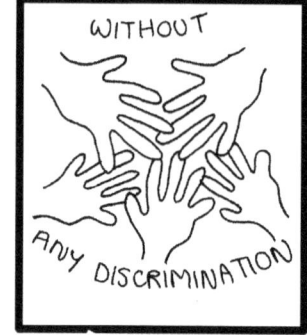

   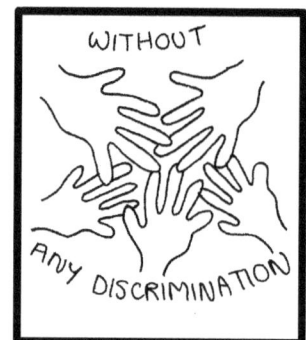

   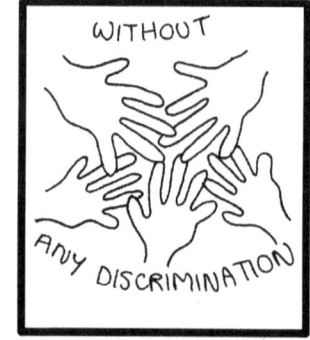

THE SUN AND THE RAIN

COMPASSION STORY

The sun shone on all the plants and all the people all day. It made the shadows disappear and the plants grow strong. The sun shone on everything. The rain however would hold on to its thousands of drops until they were too heavy to hold and then drop them all at one time causing big puddles and muddy roads in some places and leaving other places completely dry and thirsty.

"Why don't you spread your drops of water around," said the sun one day. "You could make things grow so beautifully."
"Why should I do that? They never thank me or remember me that way, but when I make big puddles then everyone talks about me." said the rain as he puffed himself out.
"See that garden over there on the edge of town," said the sun ignoring what the rain had said. "The lady who lives in that house cannot afford to have water brought to her house and so the garden is dying. Why don't you sprinkle just a little of your water over it and see what happens." The sun moved off to another part of the sky and left the rain to himself.

Now the rain happened to be having a very boring day and the people on the ground were particularly grumpy about the large puddles he had created that morning. People pointed up at him and shouted angrily. Their gardens were flooded and the plants couldn't grow. Children couldn't play outside and the ladies got their feet muddy on the way to the shops. Men had to wear big boots to get to work and the animals had to stay hidden in the trees.

COMPASSION
STORY

The rain looked over to where the sun had showed him the little garden on the edge of town. He moved over and slowly let down a little rain over the thirsty plants. Nothing seemed to happen so he moved off into the sky feeling even more grumpy. The next day however he happened to pass over the garden and noticed that new green leaves were beginning to grow there. The rain was now beginning to feel rather interested so he let down a little more rain before continuing off into the sky.

The next day he again passed by the garden and actually began to feel quite happy when he noticed some flowers opening on the bushes. Each day as he passed he let down a little rain and each day the garden grew more beautiful. One day the sun met him there and together they looked down on the garden that was growing so beautifully. After a little while the sun said,

"If you gave just a little water to each garden in the town like you did to this one it would become very beautiful instead of muddy and dirty like it is now."

And so that is what the rain did and it wasn't long before the town was green again and filled with beautiful flowers. Sometimes the people would smile at him but mostly they were just busy doing other things and hardly seemed to notice him at all. He didn't mind though because he was proud of the wonderful gardens. The children played, the ladies chatted on the way to the shops, the men whistled as they walked to work, the animals came out to look for food, the plants grew and together the sun and the rain silently cared for them day after day.

MORAL – Being compassionate is caring about everyone and everything and not expecting anything back in return.

EXTRAS

WORDS FOR SONGS AND BADGES

SONGS

OUR PURPOSE
A BETTER WAY

CHORUS
We're searching for a better way
to make our dreams come true.
We're searching for the things
to make this old world new.
We need tools, we need ways,
we need means and it pays
to find a better way
to make our dreams come true.

We talk amongst ourselves,
consult with all our friends.
We can serve each other and
learn to make amends.
CHORUS
We can strive for what is true,
have faith in our belief.
Pray with our whole heart,
cause joy instead of grief.
CHORUS

PRAYER
CONNECTED

Do you feel lonely,
do you feel left out,
do you feel unhappy,
then say a prayer and shout,

I am connected
and know it won't be ended,
through prayer I am united,
with God again.

Do you feel lonely,
do you feel left out,
do you feel unhappy,
"No" I say then shout,

I am connected
and know it won't be ended,
through prayer I am united,
with God again.

THE SPIRIT WITHIN
OUR LITTLE MIRROR

We all have a mirror
inside our little hearts
and if we clean it up a bit
guess what shines right out.

CHORUS
Qualities of kindness
and feelings of love.
Generous behaviour
and all that kind of stuff.

So give your little mirror
a rub now and then
to keep it clean and shiny
and ready to reflect.

CHORUS

DEEDS NOT WORDS
WITH ACTIONS

We talk about everything,
discuss what we can do,
but all of it is meaningless
unless we make it true,

with actions,
with actions,
that's how we make it true.

We say we will do something
and make a promise too,
but all of it is meaningless
unless we make it true,

with actions,
with actions,
that's how we make it true.

213

SONGS

CREATIVITY

MANY WAYS

Unlock your creativity
and you will see,
with your own eyes
your own eyes
you will see.

There are many ways
to do things
and many ways to be.

MODERATION

THIS AND THAT

A little bit of this,
a little bit of that,
keep the balance,
with this and that.

Everything in moderation,
helps the growth of all creation.

Too much of this,
or too much of that,
and out goes the balance,
bam, boom, splat.

Everything in moderation,
helps the growth of all creation.

A little bit of this,
a little bit of that,
keep the balance,
with this and that.

GENEROSITY

GIVE IT AWAY

Give it away,
share it around,
and it comes back,
I have found.

Every time
you give or share
a friend you'll find
standing there.

REVERENCE

REVERENCE MAKES ME STRONGER

When I have God in me,
then I am strong inside,
I can take on anything
and travel far and wide.

Cause reverence makes me stronger
and makes God a part of me.
Reverence makes me stronger
and lets my inner strength free.

SONGS

HELPFULNESS

HELPFULNESS

We can't do without each other,
we need each other for support.
If God meant us to be loners
we'd be on a planet by ourself.

Cause we were created
      to help each other
in any way we can.
And its helping that makes
      the whole place better,
for child, woman and man.

GENTLENESS

GENTLE HANDS

When my hurtful hands
come creeping up on me,
I will change my hurtful hands
and make them play gently.

Come and see my gentle hands,
I use them when I play
and now I have my gentle hands,
they are here to stay.

FRIENDLINESS

TRUE FRIENDS

I can be a true friend,
a loving friend a trusted friend.
I can be a true friend,
so come and play with me.

We will be together,
happily,
cause true friends
are good friends,
its the way to be.

Can you be a true friend,
a loving friend a trusted friend.
Can you be a true friend,
when you play with me.

We will be together,
happily,
cause true friends
are good friends,
its the way to be.

CONSIDERATION

BROTHERS AND SISTERS

Just think of doing good
to everyone you meet.
Consideration helps you find
a friend on every street.

I consider you my brother
perhaps you need a hand.
I consider you my sister,
I will always understand.

SONGS

FORGIVENESS

I FORGIVE YOU

You're sorry,
I forgive you,
I leave the past behind.
So together,
for forever,
you'll be a friend of mine.

I forgive you,
You didn't mean to,
things will work out fine.
Cause together,
for forever,
you'll be a friend of mine.

THANKFULNESS

THANK YOU

Thank you mum, thank you dad,
thank you God for all I have.
I feel lucky just to be,
here with you and
you with me.

Thank you friends for all you share,
and for the way you always care.
I feel lucky just to be,
here with you and
you with me.

ASSERTIVENESS

STAND UP

Stand up, stand up,
don't sit down,
don't let bullies,
mess you around.

Cause bullies only grow,
when we don't say,
stop this now,
I don't like it that way.

EXCELLENCE

STRIVE AND TRY

Strive and try
and do your best,
don't give up
and leave the rest.

Finish things off,
I know you can,
you can't get better
unless you...

Strive and try
and face each test
with nothing but
your very best.

SONGS

PEACEFULNESS

NICE AND SLOW

When I feel frizzled
and frazzled,
and think I might blow,
I take a breath,
in and out,
nice and slow.

Dizzle, dazzle,
frizzle, frazzle,
out you go,
cause I am breathing,
in and out,
nice and slow.

UNDERSTANDING

SEARCH TILL YOU FIND

Search till you find
what you're looking for.
Search till you find
don't give up before,

you find out
all the truth
discover what is real

Don't be satisfied
with only just a guess.
Don't be satisfied
with anything less,

than to find out
all the truth
discover what is real.

CO-OPERATION

TOGETHER

Let's work together,
and produce the very best,
let's work together,
you, me and all the rest.

We are strong, we are together,
and we'll make it last forever.
So, let's work together
and be our best.

ENTHUSIASM

BE FREE

Have enthusiasm,
let your heart be free.
Have enthusiasm,
jump for joy with me.

Be happy, be joyous,
live enthusiastically.

Be happy, be joyous,
let your heart be free.

SELFLESSNESS

THINK OF OTHERS

Stand if it means others can sit,
listen to what friends have to say,
share so people can all join in,
think of others when you play.

Think of others,
think of others,
think of others every day.

Help a friend when they fall down,
give a drink on a hot thirsty day,
be a friend when someone's alone,
think of others when you play.

Think of others,
think of others,
think of others every day.

CARING

CARE

We all have our down days
and need some tender care,
we all have sad days
and need a friend right there.

To care for us,
and share with us,
and make us feel o.k

Then there are other days,
when we can be the one,
to make a friend's sad day,
one of joy and fun.

We can care for them,
and share with them,
and make them feel o.k.

COMPASSION

BE A FRIEND

If your friend is feeling sad,
If your friend is feeling bad,
don't just stand and stare at them
help them up and be a friend.

If your friend has fallen down,
If your friend has one big frown,
don't just let them cry their tears
help them up and shed their fears.

SONGS

TOLERANCE

WORDS WITHOUT SOUND

When a lamp is burning brightly,
it shines all around.
When a person shares a smile,
it is words without sound,
that say:
I see you,
can you see me,
won't you come and play.

When a star comes out at night,
it twinkles all around,
sharing light with everyone
like words without sound,
that say:
I see you,
can you see me,
I will light your way.

When a rose blooms in a garden
and shares its beauty round,
we know it has an inner smile
like words without sound,
that say:
I see you,
can you see me,
let's share this lovely day.

A light doesn't shine one way
or leave someone in the dark.
A person shouldn't share one smile
and leave the others out.

We should smile on everyone
and let it go around.
When we share in this way,
it is words without sound,
that say:
I see you,
can you see me,
won't you come and play.

BADGES

IDENTIFICATION BADGES

INSTRUCTIONS:
- Copy this sheet on to a coloured piece of card.
- Laminate
- Cut out stars.
- Tape a safety pin on to the back of each star.
- Write in name of teacher or assistant.

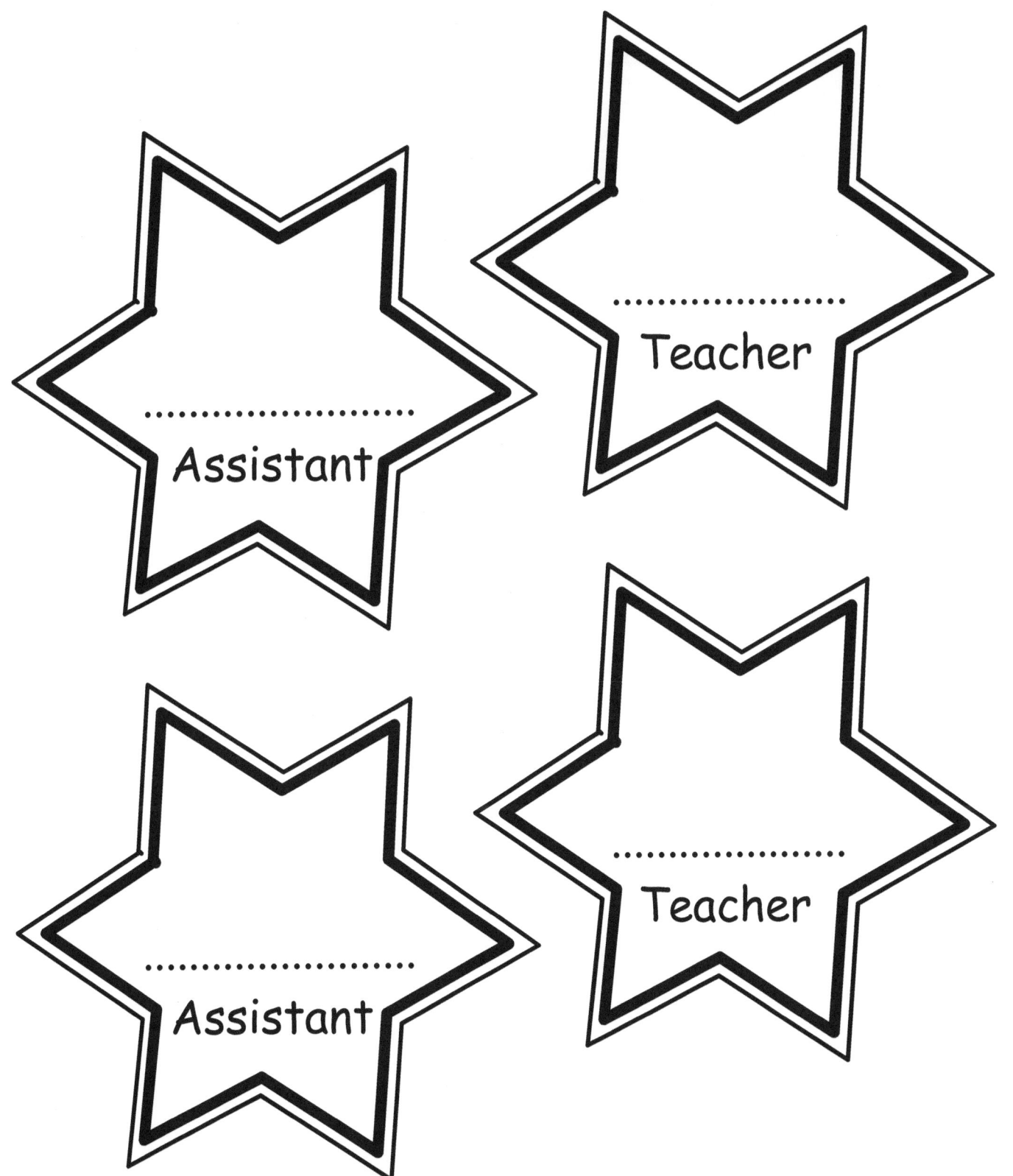

www.ingramcontent.com/pod-product-compliance
Lightning Source LLC
Chambersburg PA
CBHW040316240426
43664CB00028B/2939